Rich in America

Rich in America

Secrets to Creating and Preserving Wealth

Jeffrey S. Maurer
for U.S. Trust

John Wiley & Sons, Inc.

Published by John Wiley & Sons, Inc., Hoboken, New Jersey.
Published simultaneously in Canada.

For general information on our other products and services, or technical support, please contact our Customer Care Department within the United States at 800-762-2974, outside the United States at 317-572-3993 or fax 317-572-4002.

Wiley also publishes its books in a variety of electronic formats. Some content that appears in print may not be available in electronic books.

For additional information about Wiley products, visit our web site at www.wiley.com.

Library of Congress Cataloging-in-Publication Data:

Maurer, Jeffrey S.
  Rich in America : secrets to creating and preserving wealth / Jeffrey S. Maurer.
      p. cm.
Published simultaneously in Canada.
  ISBN: 0-471-44548-7 (cloth)
  1. Finance, Personal—United States. 2. Investments. 3. United States Trust Company of New York. I. Title.
  HG179.M354 2003
  332.024'01—dc21

                                                                    2003011339

Printed in the United States of America

10 9 8 7 6 5 4 3 2 1

To my wife Wendy,
for her love, support, and
encouragement—and for sharing me with
U.S. Trust, its staff, and its clients for 33 years.

Contents

ACKNOWLEDGMENTS ix

PREFACE xi

INTRODUCTION 1

CHAPTER 1 19
  Financial Planning

CHAPTER 2 43
  Investments

CHAPTER 3 103
  Taxes

CHAPTER 4 139
  Insurance

CHAPTER 5 161
  Retirement

CHAPTER 6 187
  Estate Planning

CHAPTER 7 217
  How to Choose a Financial Advisor

CONCLUSION 239

APPENDIX 247
  Examples of Financial Planning Schedules

INDEX 259

Acknowledgments

Writing a book may sound like a solitary occupation, but the truth is that without the help of countless people, this book could never have been finished.

Most of all, I would like to thank the current and former staff of U.S. Trust for their remarkable professionalism and talent. Without them, there wouldn't be a U.S. Trust, nor a book.

There are a few people who deserve special mention for their superb support and guidance: John Apruzzese, Drew Bender, Matt Canner, Leslie Draper, Mitchell Drossman, Linda Franciscovich, Nancy Gabel, Daina Hill, Stephen Kao, Steve Lavner, Lynn Lederman, Geraldine McNamara, Lee Paula Miller, Teresa Periera, Ralph Rittenour, Donna Romer, Ray Russolillo, Kathy Segal, Fraser Seitel, Fred Taylor, and Chris Zander. I am very grateful to each and everyone of the above. Thank you.

Also helpful were: Gene Bernstein, Gerald Calder, Kevin Casey, Gavin Cuneo, Marti Dinerstein, Kathleen Donohue, Tom Evnin, Dick Foley, Gary Gildersleeve, John Gregg, Kathy Kamerer, Lori Jackson, Robert MacDonnell, Lisa Marcus, Paul Napoli, Robin Petty, Susan Porter, Paul Sawina, Carol Strickland, Bob Stolar, Bruce Tavel, Barry Waldorf, and Sean White.

I would also like to thank Jeanne Glasser, my editor at John Wiley, for her steadfast commitment to the project, as well as my agent, Andrew Wylie. In addition, I am grateful to Gene Stone, who was able to grasp the complexities of wealth management at U.S. Trust and turn my experiences, ideas and advice into enlightening and entertaining prose.

Finally, I must give a special thank you to Allison Kellogg. Allison was there at the beginning of this project, she was there whenever extra work needed to be done, and she was there to make sure the project came to a successful conclusion. I can't thank her enough, nor the supportive and skillful people on her staff, including Kathleen McGraw, Heather Fontaine and Bill Rigler.

Preface

For 150 years, U.S. Trust has been one of the world's leading experts on the affluent and their money. I am proud to have worked at this organization—now the world's oldest trust company—for more than 30 years, and to have absorbed a great deal of the knowledge such a venerable institution can impart.

U.S. Trust was founded in 1853 by a group of financial pioneers who raised $1 million to create an innovative financial institution chartered as the United States Trust Company of New York. It was established to serve as manager, executor, and trustee of personal and corporate funds. At that time this was an original and innovative idea. Trust functions, if they existed at all, were performed by individuals, not by institutions. Among our founders were entrepreneurs and industrialists such as Peter Cooper, Erastus Corning, and Marshall Field. Our earliest clients were also entrepreneurs and industrialists—railroad barons, merchants, shipbuilders—and the large corporations that they created.

The firm's impressive history has meant that many of the most prominent and wealthy businessmen of their times served on our board and often became clients. The roster of these board members included three generations of Astors (John Jacob, Vincent, and William Waldorf),

William Dodge, John Phelps, William Rockefeller, and John Hay Whitney and Payne Whitney. However, it took time for the idea behind U.S. Trust to catch on. In the mid- to late 1800s, most affluent Americans held their assets in local real estate or business ventures. Cash holdings were not abundant, and there was little opportunity to invest in stocks, because few business were publicly held. But U.S. Trust managed to flourish by offering personal banking, including commercial and personal loans, and by purchasing mortgages and other investments.

At the turn of the twentieth century, given the rise of large corporations, the transfer of wealth to a new generation, industrialization, and the establishment of the income tax, the economic climate U.S. Trust had envisioned 50 years earlier became a reality, and it was well situated to handle the country's changing economic needs. By 1928, U.S. Trust's seventy-fifth anniversary, our trusteed assets totaled over $1 billion, far exceeding those of any other trust institution.

Eventually, the company expanded from its New York roots to open offices in 12 states and the District of Columbia. We acquired other companies and added new services, and divested parts of the business to continue our focus on wealth management. Today, U.S. Trust holds managed investment assets of more than $75 billion, while its total assets under management top $90 billion. Including personal custody assets and clients' deposits, the firm's total client assets amount to almost $125 billion.

U.S. Trust has continuously prospered despite the various upturns and downturns in the nation's fortunes. In fact, the year I arrived at the company, 1970, was one of the most difficult this country has ever faced. In the spring of that year, Richard Nixon, recently sworn in as the nation's thirty-seventh president, was overseeing the turmoil caused by the Vietnam war. Virtually every American college campus was rocked by student protest, and the nation's urban areas were seething with discontent. On May 4, 1970, shortly after Nixon had ordered the invasion of Cambodia, the Ohio National Guard fired on protesters marching across the Kent State University campus, killing four students and wounding nine.

I had just graduated from Alfred University and was attending my second semester of an MBA program at New York University. Almost 500 colleges closed down or went on strike in sympathy, NYU among them. I spent several weeks as an organizer for a group called Business Students for Peace. We marched in protest up and down Wall Street, where the business school campus was located.

A few weeks later, as the climate of social unrest simmered down, I began marching up and down Wall Street once again, but this time I was looking for a job. Despite my moments as an activist, my primary goal was to establish a career in business that would lead to job satisfaction, financial security, and if I was lucky, maybe even affluence. Why not? I was young and ambitious, and the world was there to conquer.

One of my visits was to 45 Wall Street, then the home of U.S. Trust. It was a fortuitous stop. Still, at that time I didn't know from wealthy. Although I grew up in a comfortable, middle-class environment, I was in debt with college loans and felt as if I barely had the proverbial two nickels to rub together. Still, I liked the company and was delighted when I was offered a job as an assistant trust administrator. I started at The Trust Company, as it is known among its aficionados, on June 8, 1970, and began a career that lasted for almost 33 years; when I left the firm I had risen to chairman and chief executive officer.

My task throughout my career was to help people manage their wealth, as well as to take care of their families and their favorite charities. Along the way, I attended school at night, finishing my MBA degree and a law degree as well. But my best training was on the job, collaborating with experts in all aspects of wealth management, including my co-workers, such as Henry Heil, the senior vice president who trained me and who was devoted to U.S. Trust, its clients, and its culture of trust and respect. Henry taught me early on that if you do what is right for the client, good things will always follow.

I also learned from our clients, who represented a broad panoply of the affluent, as well as from our clients' advisors, who were some of the most talented lawyers and accountants in the nation. I worked with those who inherited their money and those who earned it, dealt with the superwealthy and those who were merely affluent, and learned something from every client experience.

My very first assignment at U.S. Trust opened my eyes to the world of the truly affluent. I served as assistant to the senior vice president assigned to settle the estate of Harold Sterling Vanderbilt, who died on July 4, 1970 (Let me say right here that this isn't a tell-all book; instead, virtually every story and example I share with you will be thoroughly disguised to protect the confidentiality of U.S. Trust clients. However, information about certain public figures is already in the public domain. Such is the case with Mr. Vanderbilt, the railroad financier and yachtsman.) Harold Vanderbilt was the great-grandson of Commodore Cornelius Vanderbilt, the financier who founded the New York Central Railroad in the mid-nineteenth century, and later Vanderbilt University. Harold was born on July 6, 1884, the youngest of the three children of William Kissam Vanderbilt who, when he died in 1920, left his heirs an estate appraised at $54 million.

Harold graduated from Harvard College and Harvard Law School, and joined the family business: the New York Central. He proceeded to use his wealth as a successful platform to excel in business, yachting, and philanthropy. He also is considered the father of contract bridge—he first established the idea of a scoring system based only on tricks that a player had bid (or contracted), as well as the idea of vulnerability and large bonuses for slam contracts bid and made. Harold was survived by his wife of 37 years (they had no children) with whom he'd clearly lived a life of affluence. At the time of his death, he owned residences in Rhode Island, Florida, New York, and

Virginia. (Most of the Vanderbilt wealth eventually went to Vanderbilt University in Nashville, where Harold had served as president of the board of trustees.)

I had a difficult time grasping the enormity of the Vanderbilt wealth. At the time I calculated that the income from the Vanderbilt municipal bond portfolio alone produced more income on a daily basis than I was likely to make in the entire year. The company flew me down to his home in Manalapan, Florida, south of Palm Beach. I had never seen anything like it before, except for historical homes and museums.

It's worth bearing in mind that Harold was the beneficiary of a family fortune built before the income or estate tax. It seemed unlikely to me that such fortunes could be built again. But I am happy to report that, during the rest of my career at U.S. Trust, I witnessed time and time again the ability of the capitalist system to produce fortunes, usually created by hard-working entrepreneurs, executives, and professionals.

What does it take to be affluent in today's world? U.S. Trust feels that being in the top 1 percent, or the top 1 million households, in terms of income and net worth, sufficiently distinguishes one from the population at large and would qualify as affluence. Specifically, this richest 1 percent consists of individuals and families having a net worth greater than $3.75 million, or adjusted gross income greater than $300,000.

This book shares with you some of the core advice that U.S. Trust gives to these well-off people. Moreover, you will learn what the affluent are like and how they manage their wealth, information culled from 10 years of U.S. Trust surveys that investigated their attitudes on a wide range of subjects, from how they became affluent to how they stay that way. You'll see what they invest in, what they worry about, and how they bring up their children. By the end of the book, you'll possess enough knowledge about wealth and the wealthy that even if you don't have $3.75 million (yet), you can handle your money as though you do.

Introduction

Not long ago, several members of a well-known American dynasty came into the offices of U.S. Trust. The patriarch of this family, once a penniless immigrant, had made a great deal of money in the early 1900s. He had been very generous to his children—none of them had had to work a day in their lives. In fact, over the next two generations, not a single member of this family ever held a job. Instead, they developed into a highly dysfunctional group, riddled with problems such as drug abuse, alcoholism, and broken marriages, along with the sense that the world owed them a living because of their heritage. The grandfather told us that he was becoming very concerned about his family—there were now so many descendants dividing up the money that they had reached the point where, he muttered unhappily, "One of them might just have to get a job."

That same week, another family came in to see us. Their progenitor had worked equally hard and had also created a well-known business. But this man had required his children to find jobs (and keep them), and he treated them as would the father of any ordinary child. Today the man's six grandchildren are well-adjusted and hardworking. One is training to become a social worker, but also wants to live in a nice neighborhood, and the family has agreed to help him as long as he holds his job. Two others work for charities but draw no salary; they both put in more hours than anyone else in their organizations. The parents support them because they admire their children's willingness to commit so much time and energy to their beliefs.

These two family situations represent extremes. More often, U.S. Trust sees a combination of these situations. In the same family the firm may see children who react well or respond poorly to their affluent upbringing. It's hard to predict how people will react to money, whether they've earned it or inherited it. In fact, it's hard to make any generalizations about the wealthy in America—unless you have worked with them and their advisors over several generations. U.S. Trust has done exactly that. No one knows money like U.S. Trust, and no one knows so much about the people who have it. For 150 years we have served as one of the foremost financial advisors to the nation's wealthiest families.

U.S. Trust Surveys of Affluent Americans

Much of our knowledge comes from working directly with affluent individuals. But we have amassed other important information from a series of surveys that U.S. Trust has commissioned over the past decade.

We first began conducting the surveys in 1993, when we hired an independent market research firm to question the wealthiest 1 percent of America's citizens—currently defined as those with an adjusted annual gross income of more than $300,000 or a net worth greater than $3.75 million. These surveys have provided us with a treasure trove of information about the affluent—how they got their money and how they keep it, their favorite and least favorite investments, and their families and their lifestyles.

One of the most startling findings, backed up by our own anecdotal evidence at U.S. Trust, is that the wealthy are much more mainstream than the image presented in the media. Compared to the viewpoint generally shown on televisions programs highlighting wealthy celebrities, these people's concerns are relatively conventional. For the most part, the affluent do not spend their time skiing in Aspen, buying diamonds in fancy jewelry stores, or sitting around heart-shaped pools eating caviar and drinking champagne. Instead, a very large percentage of the people surveyed are working hard, if not harder, than most other Americans—and have no intention of stopping just because they have already earned a great deal of money. Certainly, they enjoy some luxuries, and they give a considerable portion of their money to charity. But like most of us, their major concerns are their jobs, their families, and their children, not the size of their houses or cars.

In fact, nearly 60 percent of affluent households are two-income families, often with both spouses working to reach the affluent income criteria. In major urban settings, such as New York City, an adjusted gross income of $300,000 can sometimes seem inadequate to cover the costs of housing, food, childcare, and private education, let alone life's luxuries.

According to the U.S. Trust Survey of Affluent Americans, the average affluent person spends 24 percent of his or her after-tax money on housing, utilities, and maintenance, followed by 23 percent on savings and investments, 15 percent on children, 13 percent on food and clothing, 9 percent on health care and insurance, 8 percent on vacations and travel, and 8 percent on charitable contributions. Only 39 percent of respondents said that they often dine in fine restaurants, and more than half never or rarely purchase fine jewelry. Sixty-seven percent never or rarely purchase fine arts. Similarly, only a quarter ever travel internationally. Sixty-three percent of respondents own only one home, and a little more than half of them say it is worth less than half a million dollars. Similarly, the same number of car owners said the average value of their car is less than $30,000. Some 21 percent employ full-time domestic help, but 87 percent of those employ only one person.

Another surprise: Very few of the affluent attained their wealth through inheritance. In fact, 69 percent of our survey respondents reported that their childhood was either poor, lower class, or middle class. Only 4 percent said that they came from a wealthy upbringing. Sometimes their sources of wealth can be unusual. For instance, one of our clients, a couple, became wealthy through travel. For years the husband and wife spent their summer vacation in Asia, where they had purchased a small condominium to save hotel costs. While there, the couple would spend days wandering through the local markets; both were serious shoppers with an excellent eye for unusual items. Eventually, they began a business importing some of the small gadgets they discovered, one of which became so popular in the United States that the income they received from selling it provided this couple with so much money they were able to retire permanently at the age of 50. They haven't given up shopping, though: They now live full time in their Asian condo and are diligently seeking another product to push them into the financial stratosphere.

Indirectly, another couple became affluent because of a poor educational system. Because the public school system in their small Northwestern community wasn't very good, they hoped to eventually put their children in private schools. Their combined income was a healthy $100,000, but once they understood how much the schooling would cost, they realized they couldn't afford it. Undeterred, this entrepreneurial couple sat down and came up with a plan for a small business. It took a long time, and a lot of effort, but it worked—the couple is now worth well over $75 million (and their kids went to private schools after all).

These two couples illustrate an important survey finding: In order to become affluent, hard work was necessary, as well as a great deal of time. The average respondent put in an average of 21 years before attaining his or her present financial status, and currently works a 48-hour week. A quarter of the affluent surveyed have worked more than 30 years to attain their present status, and 60 percent have worked more than 20 years (seven percent have been lucky—they've worked 10 years or fewer). Even today, although affluent, the respondents work an ample number of hours per week. Twenty-nine percent said they work up to 40 hours, 40 percent work between 41 and 50 hours, and 31 percent work more than 50 hours per week. The characteristics of high-net-worth households shown in Table I.1 reflect these facts.

What is the source of their current wealth? For most, it's from their job. Forty-one percent say that their money represents their earnings from corporate employment, and 37 percent say their wealth springs from their earnings from a private business (see Table I.2). Contrary to popular belief, by far the least important source of wealth was inheritance, which was cited by only 5 percent of those surveyed.

How do the affluent account for their success? When presented with a wide range of possible attributes, 89 percent claimed it comes from their willingness to work hard. More interesting is that the second most commonly picked trait is the ability to get along with others—selected by 71 percent of those surveyed. Another 69 percent said their money was due to their professional or technical skills, 64 percent credited their intelligence, and a similar percentage cited their

TABLE I.1   CHARACTERISTICS OF HIGH-NET-WORTH HOUSEHOLDS, 2001

	Net Worth $500K–$1M	Net Worth $1–5M	Net Worth >$5M	Family Income $200–500K	Family Income >$500K
Percent Aged 65+	32.7%	30.3%	25.4%	12.0%	11.7%
Percent Aged 45–64	44.6	50.3	59.8	47.5	55.3
Percent Aged <45	22.9	19.5	14.8	40.9	33.0
Percent with Wage and Salary Income	74.3	69.6	68.2	74.8	72.3
Percent Retired	20.9	16.4	17.3	13.5	12.6
Percent Married	83.3	83.3	88.7	89.6	90.1

SOURCE: Author's tabulations from Survey of Consumer Finances, 2001.

management ability. Sixty-three percent quoted their willingness to take a risk, and 62 percent endorsed support and encouragement of their spouse. Finally, 61 percent simply felt that they had chosen a good industry to enter, while 57 percent acknowledged their educational background.

Dedication obviously played an important role in becoming wealthy. Nearly all respondents felt that some sacrifices had to be made on the way up. Sixty-seven percent of those surveyed felt they

TABLE I.2   SOURCES OF FINANCIAL SUCCESS

One-third or more of the affluent surveyed state the following have been a very important source of their financial success:

- ◆ Earnings from corporate employment (41%)
- ◆ Earnings from a private business (37%)
- ◆- Earnings from a professional practice (36%)
- ◆ Securities (33%)

SOURCE: U.S. Trust Survey of Affluent Americans XXI, June 2002

had given up time to relax; the second most frequently cited sacrifice was vacations, at 58 percent. Fifty-six percent felt that they'd lost out on time to exercise or participate in sports, 52 percent wished they'd had more time for their hobbies, and the same percentage acknowledged they hadn't gotten as involved as they would have liked in civic, charitable, or other philanthropic work. Other areas suffered to a lesser degree: Forty-one percent felt they didn't have time for a good relationship with friends, 37 percent felt they lacked time with their children, and a third felt they didn't spend enough time with their spouse.

The Importance of a Financial Plan

Perhaps the most important lesson from our survey data is that hard work makes you affluent. But that's not enough to stay affluent. Having a financial blueprint that matches your goals and career aspirations and suits your family life is the best way to help you preserve and enhance your wealth as efficiently as possible.

As reflected in the survey, you have to create your own wealth. All but a few of the affluent have done so, with roughly a third doing it through their own businesses, a third doing it through corporations, and the other third doing it through professional services. When you create your own wealth you either do it through an event, such as selling your own business, or by saving or both. When you save you make a conscious decision that you will devote a portion of your after-tax income to saving for the future. You also need a plan on how to invest your savings to preserve their purchasing power. Saving and the power of compounding your returns through an investment plan helps you become wealthy. So you can forget the notion that investing alone will make you a fortune. Although some people are able to do this, few do it well, and even fewer have become rich from it. The real purpose of investing is to help you protect yourself and your wealth against inflation, and to take the assets you possess and preserve them.

All those books that say you can make millions in real estate or the stock market overnight are not accurate, but you probably knew that already. You'd have to devote all your energies and resources to mastering the subject, and still there's no guarantee. Such books won't give you the investment blueprint you need. And as our survey shows, you can't go it completely alone. Those who are successful are too busy working hard while fighting to devote a little extra time to friends and family. They don't have time to do their own financial planning. That's why dispassionate financial advisors serve such a great purpose, especially in today's tough times.

Being wealthy isn't easy. Following the recent bear market led by the bursting of the technology, telecom, and Internet bubble, people are scared. Many have turned fiscally conservative and are letting their money sit on the sidelines, and this means it's earning money market rates. That's not enough: Today money markets earn less than 2 percent, which is less than 1 percent after taxes and less than the rate of inflation. So by not subscribing to a plan, such people are actually losing ground.

A plan is necessary. One thing investors have learned over the last few years is that nothing lasts forever. The pace of the market has quickened immeasurably, and cycles that used to last years now appear to come and go in a relatively short time. The reliable and tax-efficient buy-and-hold strategy employed by many, including U.S. Trust, must now be augmented with a more active asset allocation. (*Buy and hold* means that you buy a stock, hold onto it for years, and sell it at a much higher price. By buying and holding, you enjoy the increase in value and in dividends undiminished by capital gains taxes and transaction costs. While the buy-and-hold style of investment management has proven itself, many feel that it doesn't do enough to protect against valuation excesses, such as the recent run-up in technology stocks. As respected economist Peter Bernstein has pointed out, market timing has become key, as he wrote in a recent issue of his *Economics and Portfolio Strategy* newsletter, in which he stressed the change from a long-run framework to a much shorter-run strategy and said, "That dirty word, market timing, assumes new respectability under those kinds of conditions.")

Like Bernstein, we believe that today's environment calls for a more flexible approach to portfolio management. This involves evaluating asset class projected returns more frequently and employing different strategies to augment buy-and-hold equity management in order to enhance returns. One such strategy is the use of so-called *alternative investment asset classes*, like hedge fund management. Many institutional investors who do not have to deal with the tax inefficiencies of hedge funds have dramatically increased their exposure to this asset class, replacing their traditional equity managers in the process. Although hedge funds are not as tax-efficient as buy-and-hold equity investing because they tend to produce short-term capital gains (taxed as ordinary income) rather than long-term capital gains, they benefit from a higher risk-adjusted rate-of-return than equities. This trade-off seems to make sense in the environment in which we now find ourselves. This is one of many new approaches that require someone with a great deal of time and knowledge to make them work.

Decisions seem ever more complex today. Perhaps every generation says something similar, but they all may be correct. Life does grow increasingly complicated; certainly, financial decisions do. Capitalism is wonderful, but it continually creates new financial products to fill whatever gaps exist. There was a time when it was easy enough to do your own income taxes; that has changed. Insurance was once a simple decision; now there are so many choices that only an expert really can decide what is best for you. How much do you need? Who should own it? Is there a way of combining your life insurance issues with financing college? And speaking of college, it could cost as much as

$400,000 in the year 2022: Do you know all the ways you can save for it? What about retirement? Should you start an IRA or a Keogh? What about a Roth? How should that money be invested?

Should you buy a house, or should you rent? If you do buy a house, what kind of mortgage should you take—short-term, long-term, fixed or variable? Are you aware that the location of your residence can be a major financial planning issue? Where you declare your domicile for tax purposes has estate planning, income tax, and gift tax consequences. For instance, we had a client who owned homes in New York City and in Connecticut. Before we advised him otherwise, he spent most of his time in the former, but refused to pay New York City taxes, thinking he could get away with claiming his suburban home as his primary residence. New York State and New York City taxes are expensive, but they are also a tax trap for the uneducated. The city (as well as the state) is notorious for tracking down people who claim the city is not their domicile; they'll check everything from telephone bills to dry-cleaning services to see where you've spent most of your time. If they catch you, not only will you owe the tax (and the interest), but you will have to pay penalties, too. (In case you were wondering, the law says that if you own or rent a residence in New York City, you must remain outside the city for more than 183 days to avoid being classified as a resident and therefore liable for the taxes.)

Having more than one home is just one complication. Now that life isn't as linear as it once was, people seldom have just one employer throughout their career. Instead, they move from job to job, raising all kinds of issues regarding retirement, 401(k) plans, and insurance needs. You must consider how these shifts may impact your planning.

Also, keep in mind that the older you get, the more potentially catastrophic a mistake will be. You can recover easily from a financial glitch when you're 30, and you'll have to work harder at recovering when you're 40. But when you make a mistake at 55, you may have just changed your life forever. This point has been driven home over the last couple of years as a large number of people got caught up in the 1990s boom and put too many eggs in one or two proverbial baskets, which then broke. Now, instead of being able to retire comfortably, they're having to downsize their lifestyle (see Figure I.1).

The enormous range of financial products available can seem overwhelming. Then you must consider all the more personal issues that arise as you begin to make more money, especially if you have a family. Most people don't create a will until they have children. This step is often the first time I see an otherwise contented couple fight

You must also address questions such as who should be the guardian of your property and children, and should your kids inherit property. As you age, your ideas may change. When you're 30, you may begin planning for your newborn child. At that age, you may think 30 is a mature age, and perhaps you choose to hold whatever money you intend to pass along in a trust until then. But when you're 40, 30 can seem much too young for such a responsibility. Then when you're 50, even 40 can seem too young, and 30 seems like a baby. Such questions don't fade with age. In fact, some people start thinking about exerting a certain amount of control even from the grave, and these are among the most fascinating decisions I've seen.

As should now be clear, few people can answer all these questions and make all these decisions alone. It isn't that they aren't smart enough, but that the time required to be an expert in all the relevant fields of financial planning is a full-time job. For example, one of U.S. Trust's most senior executives and one of the smartest people in the business, has been advising clients for several decades now. Her husband is a lawyer with several degrees and is probably as smart as she is. He can tell you the difference between a tort and a trover, but he doesn't know the difference between a dividend and a derivative. For years she had told him that he had to sign up for his firm's 401(k) plan. Each year he would respond, "Don't worry, it's under control." And each year he would forget.

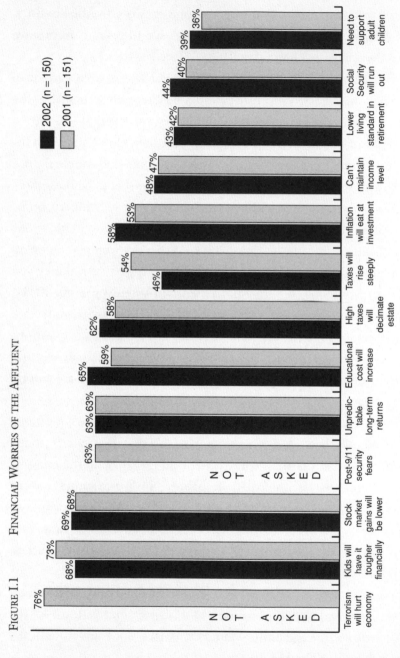

FIGURE I.1   FINANCIAL WORRIES OF THE AFFLUENT

NOTE: Percent responding 4–10 on a 1–10 scale, where 10 means "very worried."
SOURCE: U.S. Trust Survey of Affluent Americans XXI, June 2002

Finally, after many years of being pressured to enroll in the program, he absolutely promised to call his human resources office. And he did. But later that afternoon he called his wife, very upset. Confused, she asked him what happened.

"Well," he said, "I did what you told me to do, and I asked about their K-9 plan. They said that they didn't offer medical insurance for pets. Why did you tell me to ask for this?"

"It's called a 401(k)," she explained.

"Oh," he said.

In other words, there are few people who can prosper without good financial planning.

Historical Wealth Trends in the U.S.

Although an economic boom in the 1920s served to bolster temporarily the position of the top 1 percent, the Great Depression and World War II produced what economists have called the "great compression" of wages and incomes. Both wealthy and average households saw a huge decline in income during the depression. However, although incomes later recovered, the share of total assets held by the richest 1 percent declined considerably, from 18 percent in 1903 to 10 percent in 1953. Incomes were also more equal even before taxes.

The year 1953 represents the peak of equalization. This compression in incomes coincided with a compression in the distribution of wealth. This development has usually been attributed to a slowing of population growth, the rise of unions, and an increase in the growth of skills and education, which increased the relative incomes of people at the lower end of the income distribution.

After the great compression, income disparities began to widen again, beginning sometime between 1974 and 1980 and reaching a new extreme at the end of the twentieth century, similar to their zenith at its beginning. The top 5 percent of households gained in income,

What Does It Mean to Be Rich in America?

In its early days, America was a relatively egalitarian society. Compared to the situation in other countries, wealth was more equally distributed and wage gaps between different groups were smaller. However, beginning in the nineteenth century, wealth and income inequality began to rise; from 1774 to 1860, the share of total assets held by the richest 1 percent rose from approximately 13 percent to 30 percent.

Between the Civil War and World War I, the wealth gaps remained wide and, in fact, may have increased further as the population swelled. Nevertheless, the income of the richest 1 percent and the average income of the general population both increased substantially between 1853 and 1903 (see Table I.3). At the same time, the cost-of-living increased dramatically for the affluent (see Table I.4).

TABLE I.3   HISTORICAL ANALYSIS OF WEALTH (1853–1998)

Year	Average Income of Top 1% in 1998 Dollars	Percentage of Household Income Earned by Top 1%	Average Household Income in 1998 Dollars	Consumer Price Index; 1998 = 100	Consumer Price Index; 1913 = 100
1853	$150,000	15%	$ 9,000	4.4	78.2
1903	$211,471	18%	$11,431	5.6	100.0
1953	$221,498	10%	$22,280	16.4	294.0
1998	$790,558	19%	$41,810	100.0	1792.1

TABLE I.4   HOW PRICES HAVE CHANGED (1853–2003)

	1853 Prices	1853 (2003 Prices)	1903 Prices	1903 (2003 Prices)	1953 Prices	1953 (2003 Prices)	2003 Prices
Consumer Price Index; 2003 = 100	4.0		5.1		14.9		100.0
Female domestic, per year	$336	$8,064	$576	$10,718	$2,160	$12,312	$21,850
New York brownstone	$20,000–$30,000	$480,000–$720,000	$50,000–$60,000	$950,000–$1,140,000	$50,000–$100,000	$285,000–$570,000	$3,000,000–$5,000,000
New York to London roundtrip fare by ship	$240	$5,820	$240	$4,464	$1,000	$5,700	
New York to London roundtrip fare by plane					$1,000	$8,500	$5,831
Metropolitan Opera orchestra ticket	$1	$24	$2.50	$42.14	$20	$114	$160

15

while the bottom 60 percent lost in relative shares of total assets, with the biggest gains accruing to the richest 1 percent. Consequently, the most affluent Americans regained their relative position of influence, and their absolute level of income also rose to a new high. From $221,000 in 1953, the top 1 percent saw their average incomes soar to $791,000 by 1998. Furthermore, their share of the national income returned to what it had been, 18 percent, in 1903.

By any standard, wealthy Americans find themselves in an unusual position, having enjoyed one of the most prosperous 20-year periods in history. The fortunes of many families who were already rich have soared since 1980, but so did the ranks of the newly wealthy, with the number of households worth at least $1 million increasing to 7.1 million, or 6.6% of all U.S. households, by the turn of the century (see Table I.5). More than 2.7 million of the 130 million families filing tax returns in 2000 reported at least $200,000 in income, up from 1.3 families million in 1995 (see Table I.6).

Still, according to the U.S. Trust Survey of Affluent Americans, being in the upper 1 percent of incomes doesn't make everyone feel as though they are rich. Although 38 percent of those surveyed believe that they are wealthy, a majority of the affluent (56 percent) consider themselves only upper middle class. You can certainly understand this

TABLE I.5   DISTRIBUTION OF U.S. HOUSEHOLDS
                 BY NET WORTH, 2001

Household Net Worth ($000s)	Estimated Number of Households (millions)	Percentage of Households
<100	53.1	49.9%
100–500	32.0	30.1
500–1,000	7.7	7.3
1,000–5,000	5.9	5.5
>5,000	1.2	1.1

SOURCE: Author's tabulations based on the 2001 Survey of Consumer Finances.

TABLE I.6   DISTRIBUTION OF TAX RETURNS BY AGI, 2000

2000 AGI ($000s)	Tax Returns (000s)	Tax Returns (%)
< 20	50,522	39.1%
20–30	18,362	14.2
30–50	23,960	18.5
50–100	25,673	19.8
100–200	8,083	6.3
200–500	2,135	1.7
500 1,000	396	0.3
>1,000	240	0.2
Total	129,373	100.0

SOURCE: David Campbell and Michael Parisi, "Individual Income Tax Returns, 2000," *Statistics of Income Bulletin* 22 (Fall 2002), pp. 7–44.

if you live in New York, Chicago, or Los Angeles and earn around $300,000 a year—you don't feel rich. And 5 percent still think of themselves as middle class.

By the beginning of this century, even the super affluent have suffered a reversal of fortune as shown by the drop in the aggregate new worth of the *Forbes* 400 (see Figure I.2).

FIGURE I.2   CHANGES IN AGGREGATE NET WORTH OF *FORBES* 400
                    (1982–2002)

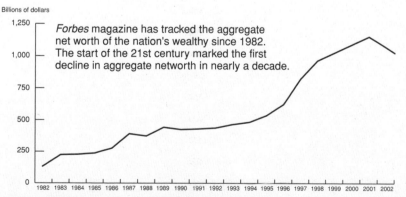

Billions of dollars

Forbes magazine has tracked the aggregate net worth of the nation's wealthy since 1982. The start of the 21st century marked the first decline in aggregate networth in nearly a decade.

Reprinted by permission of *Forbes Magazine* © 2003 Forbes Inc.

CHAPTER 1

Financial Planning

Money is like a sixth sense without which you cannot make a complete use of the other five.

—W. Somerset Maugham,
British Novelist

The universal regard for money is the one hopeful fact in our civilization. Money is the most important thing in the world. It represents health, strength, honor, generosity and beauty . . . Not the least of its virtues is that it destroys base people as certainly as it fortifies and dignifies noble people.

—George Bernard Shaw,
Anglo-Irish playwright

Scenarios

Jim

Until Jim fell into a coma, he had worked for most of his life at a construction company, where he rose through the ranks to become a top executive. He was a client of ours for many years, and we had become close to his wife and two children. Jim, 53, was one of those unusually charismatic people who seemed to have it all, but he was so charming and good-natured that he didn't have an enemy in the world.

Then one day his company called us to tell us that this vibrant man had collapsed on the job. The medical situation did not look good, and over the next few days, as we scrambled to make sure that his affairs were in order, the company hit us with an interesting question: If Jim were to die, would his family be better off if he died as an employee, or as a retiree? The company needed to know this immediately, because Jim's doctor wasn't sure how long he would live; the company needed to take immediate action because they loved Jim and wanted the absolute best for his family.

Jim's company couldn't answer the question because they didn't know Jim's complete financial picture. His lawyer knew only Jim's will, and his accountant knew only his taxes; his family knew even less. Luckily, because we had worked so closely with Jim over the years and had a current financial plan in place, we were able to do the math vis-à-vis his pensions and other employee benefit options. We discovered that he would do better as an employee, and advised the family and Jim's boss to keep him employed. Jim remained in the coma for two months before he died. In the meantime, we worked closely with his company and his wife to make sure that all his affairs were in order.

If tragedy befalls you, are your affairs in order? Is all of your important legal and financial information easily accessible so that others can make critical and timely decisions on your behalf? To whom would your spouse or children turn in a severe financial crisis?

Hillary and Jason

Hillary and Jason were prospective clients because Hillary's parents had worked with us for many years. But the couple postponed the decision to see us because they didn't feel their assets were sufficient enough, nor did they feel they needed financial planning because they were only in their late twenties. Hillary had married Jason when they were just out of college, and the couple settled in the Midwest, where Jason worked as a lawyer and Hillary was a teacher. However, Jason didn't like his job and soon switched careers. The couple moved around for a while, trying to figure out what to do with their lives, before both husband and wife settled on new positions that brought them to New York.

Things were going well—they had a child and enjoyed their work. Then disaster struck on September 11, 2001, when Jason died in the terrorist attacks. Based on New York state law, Hillary would have simply inherited all of Jason's assets. However, they still owned property in the Midwest, and it was there that the couple's wills had been executed. According to local state law, Jason's sister might also stand to inherit some of his property. The issue was which state controlled the will: New York, where they now lived, or the state where the will was executed. Not only was it questionable whether Jason would have wanted his sister to inherit anything at all—they had fought frequently—but confusing tax issues arose as well. This unfortunate situation would never have come up if the couple had planned properly for the unforeseen.

The fact was brought home when Hillary came in to see us, bringing with her an old shopping bag. She sat down, put it on a desk, and said, "I was told I could come to you for help. My life, or what's left of it, is in this bag. I also was told I could ask you any question I want, but I don't even know what the questions are."

What would it be like for your loved ones and heirs if you died suddenly?

Eloise

Eloise is a lovely woman. Single since her husband died many years ago, she has one adult daughter and two Pekinese dogs; these three are the loves of her life. Eloise started working with us a few years ago because, although she wasn't worried about money, she began to realize that each year she had less and less of it. This made little sense to her because her husband had left her a large sum. Nonetheless, every year she checked her balance sheet and saw a smaller number than the year before. She even began to wonder if her broker was cheating her somehow—could he have been embezzling from her account?

When we sat down with Eloise for a financial planning session, we began to wonder about the accuracy of the figures she'd given us. She told us that she spent $15,000 a month, which appeared to be more than adequate because there was no mortgage on her co-op apartment and she didn't have very many other necessary expenses. But since her assets could well generate $180,000 a year after taxes and still provide protection against inflation, Eloise wasn't going to lose money through spending, only through bad investments.

The more closely we worked with her, the more we realized something was amiss. Finally, we asked Eloise to write down everything she spent for one month. For a while she simply couldn't do it because she was forgetful, or perhaps she didn't want to know. But eventually, when it appeared that her money was slipping away, she complied. The figure she gave us was probably still short of the truth, but even so, it was $30,000. Eloise was spending at least twice as much as she'd originally thought. "Where in the world does it all go?" she wondered, but one look at her clothes closets and jewelry collection made the answer obvious.

If Eloise couldn't curtail her spending (especially considering that the actual tally was probably closer to $40,000 a month), she would have blown through what was left of her inheritance in a little more than 10 years. Luckily, we were able to coax her into understanding what was going to happen if she couldn't follow a budget.

Do you know how much you actually spend—and more importantly, what you can afford to spend?

Why People Don't Plan

Few of us have qualms about going to a doctor, asking for advice, and then following it. We're reconciled to letting an accountant prepare our taxes. Certainly, when the drains are stopped up, we don't hesitate to call a plumber. A good financial planner can be just as important to your well-being as any of these professionals, yet many people still shy away from seeing one.

Part of the fear of dealing with a financial planner stems from distrust—many people don't like having anyone, even family members, know everything about their finances. We may live in an openly capitalist society, but taboos linger against talking openly about money, and some people extend this reticence to private situations. It helps to remember that any good advisor will be as trustworthy as your doctor, your psychiatrist, or your religious confidant,

Some people are afraid of talking about anything that implies mortality. They are willing to monitor their investments or even turn them over to an advisor. But they don't want to talk about estate planning, because they feel superstitious or afraid, or are uncomfortable with the subject. But as you will see, working on just one part of financial planning without working on the others is like trying to finish a jigsaw puzzle without knowing what the completed picture looks like. This tunnel vision may eventually create much more work for you and your financial planner, and perhaps even point you and your money off in an inappropriate direction.

At U.S. Trust we have occasionally completed a financial plan for clients only to discover later that they had withheld information—information revealed only after we had earned their trust. Although we appreciated gaining their confidence, it meant we had to go back over their plan and correct it in light of the new information. Sometimes this has meant redoing the entire plan from start to finish.

Many other people are lethargic. They know they should make a plan, they understand its importance, and they realize that without one, their financial situation will be unpredictable. However, they just don't get around to actually planning it. Life is so busy, they say, and there are so many other tasks to accomplish in the course of a day. We'll get around to it, they promise. Too often, they don't and when circumstances change, they're caught off guard.

Other people don't complete their financial planning because they simply don't think about it. The subject isn't something that comes up in the course of a normal day, and because no one ever mentions it, it becomes a nonsubject. Of course, not thinking about something doesn't make it go away.

Many businesspeople will spend Christmas eve in their offices, making sure their spreadsheets or their accounts are in good shape. But they'll postpone working on their personal finances because personal affairs seem less important than business. A telling anecdote: One of our senior executives used to work in the financial planning business, and as a corporate perk, the employees were given a choice of either car allowance or a financial planning allowance; nearly every single one of these employees chose the car money—and these were people who should have known the ultimate value of financial planning.

What Financial Planning Is

What does financial planning mean? It means analyzing your current financial situation to develop a plan to meet your short- and long-term financial and related objectives. An effective financial plan will smooth the eventual transfer of your assets to family members, friends, or charities while minimizing the impact of estate taxes. It can also help you strike a balance between your need for current income and long-term asset growth to support your future living requirements.

Because everyone's life story is unique, good financial planning must be personalized; it cannot be successfully accomplished merely by filling out a form, feeding the information into a computer, and then reviewing a large and often irrelevant report. Nor can intelligent financial decisions be made in a vacuum. If you are going to be a smart investor, you must have a handle on your tax situation. If you want to minimize taxes, you have to understand estate planning. If you hope to accumulate wealth, you'll need to have adequate insurance, and so on. Each of these areas is connected to the others. When you make decisions about one of them, you are in effect making decisions that alter your entire financial life.

For example, how do you know whom to name as the beneficiary of your 401(k) plan if you haven't done your retirement plan? The beneficiary designation itself is an estate planning item, but you must also examine your retirement plan to determine who that person should be. And both estate planning and retirement planning are in turn affected by your investment plan in light of your IRA or 401(k). Everything has to be viewed in totality to come up with the right answers. Here's an example: On an after-tax basis, 9 times out of 10 the income from a taxable bond (such as a Treasury bond) will not outperform a municipal bond. For the highest-bracket tax payers, municipals are almost always more sensible. But if you need to create income against which to take charitable contributions (because they would be limited otherwise), your money might well be better placed in a taxable bond. Then you may deduct your charitable contribution against the taxable income from that bond; the after-tax return in this case will be higher than the municipal bond income you would have earned.

Do you know whether to prepay your real estate taxes in the tax year before they are due or in the tax year afterwards? Do you want to consolidate your real estate and local income tax payments into a single year in order to maximize the value of the deductions? Are you even aware of the Alternative Minimum Tax, and why, if you're not careful, you may have to pay this hidden tax instead of your regular income tax? Good financial planning answers all of these questions and more. It is a form of what we call holistic wealth. Similar to the philosophy of holistic health, which holds that the health of one part of your body is inseparable from the health of the other parts, holistic wealth management is a system of examining all aspects of your financial self. It looks at not just your financial goals, but your personal goals as well.

Merely possessing a great deal of money isn't a primary objective for most of our clients. When we've asked, "What do you want to do with your wealth?," one client told us, "I want to spend a lot before I die." Another said, "I want to leave the maximum amount to my kids." Still another replied, "My goal is to leave nothing more than the maximum the law allows free of estate tax. After that, it goes into my foundation to fight leukemia."

To switch metaphors, try to conceive of your personal finances as you do a business plan. You need to view the issues you face in totality so that you always approach financial decisions in an integrative way. If you are the CEO of your own financial life, a good advisor is the equivalent of the CFO, someone who helps facilitate and implement the decisions you make as chief executive.

Setting Up Your Financial Plan

How do you begin? What is the process? Who is on your team? First, you will need to know the primary categories of financial planning:

Investment planning: What are your objectives and risk tolerance? What are the trade-offs between the two? How do you diversify out of concentrated stock positions (such as company stock)? Does your asset allocation reflect your actual needs and preferences? Let's say you decide you want a conservative portfolio, but it turns out that your advisor has been investing heavily in the volatile technology sector. First, you'll need to find this out, and second, correct it.

Tax planning: What is your current income tax situation? Are you saving for retirement, or for your children's educational needs, in a tax-efficient manner? Is your income tax return prepared in a fashion that appropriately minimizes your taxes? What will your taxes look like over the next five years? How can you lower them? Are you selling assets, moving, getting a raise, or anticipating some other major life event? If so, make sure you are doing the right thing in terms of taxes. A fundamental goal is to minimize those taxes, so you must always be on the lookout for smart ways to do so.

Insurance planning: What are your objectives in minimizing financial risk? To meet them, should you have an umbrella excess liability policy? A personal corporate board liability policy? Does your company provide you with indemnity coverage? Is it enough? Do you have sufficient assets to protect your family if you were to die tomorrow? Should insurance vehicles play a role in your investment planning and retirement planning?

Retirement planning: When do you want to retire and how much income will you need to do so given your desired lifestyle? What vehicles are available to save for retirement? Once you are able to answer these questions, you must then detail your cash flow, which consists of your monthly expenses including your mortgage (or rent), automobile payments, food expenditures, insurance costs, and so on. Next, detail your income. Then place your lists side by side to see if money earned from stocks, bonds, mutual fund dividends, interest, and any other income (such as pensions or Social Security) will cover all those monthly expenses. It's important to remember that some of these costs are fixed, including basic necessities such as health insurance premiums and mortgage payments. No matter how frugal you want to be, you can't cut back on these expenses. But other expenses, such as food and entertainment, are variable, and if you wish to economize, don't dine in fancy restaurants every night or go to the theater twice a week.

Estate planning: How do you want your assets distributed? Should you leave all of them to your spouse and depend on him or her to take care of your children? Or should you use a specialized trust to ensure that your assets pass to your children upon your spouse's death? Should you use trusts? If so, what kind? A credit shelter trust? A charitable remainder trust? A generation skipping trust? Whom should you appoint as your executors, trustees, and guardians for your children?

During the process of developing these various and equally important aspects of a financial plan, there are seven steps to consider:

1. Creating a team

2. Gathering data

3. Identifying and prioritizing goals and objectives

4. Analyzing data

5. Reviewing potential strategies

6. Agreeing on strategies

7. Implementing your plan

Creating a Team

You must either commit to planning all of your own finances or hire a professional financial planner. As already mentioned, few people have the time, resources, or expertise to handle all these tasks themselves. Even financial planners don't do it all by themselves; they need to work with other advisors, including your lawyer, accountant, insurance broker, and investment counselor. I was trained in the financial planning disciplines and have stayed well-informed, but it was impossible for me to do my own financial planning, my job, and pay attention to the rest of my life. I needed the help of financial planners. I didn't abandon my responsibilities in the process; I just participated in a more disciplined process.

If you're married, it's also a good idea to ask your spouse to join the team. Planning is most often productive when it's done as a family. Although married couples don't necessarily share their financial secrets (even though it doesn't always seem this way, financial planners are not marriage counselors), the more each of you knows about the other's financial status, the better off you will be in an emergency. I am a true believer in complete disclosure between spouses, as well as arriving at mutually agreed upon goals and risk tolerances.

Gathering Data

Financial planning means stepping back and focusing on what you own. Where is your money? Do you even know? Do you have all of your account numbers handy? Is your money in your name, your spouse's, or in a joint account? What portions of your assets are liquid, deferred, or locked up in life insurance or real estate? Do you know what liquid assets are? If you had to, could you fill out a balance sheet for your assets? Do you understand your cash flow? Do you know how much money you spend each month? Do you remember who is the beneficiary of your accounts? Many people don't recall that they designated a beneficiary on their 401(k) a long time ago, and have never changed it. We've seen cases where someone has remarried, and only after his or her death did we discover that the former spouse was still listed as the beneficiary for the entire 401(k).

In other words, you must gather the data. To do this, you need to assemble such items as your current will, prior two years of Federal, state, and local income tax returns, current gift tax returns, all trust agreements in which you or your family have an interest, all other family agreements (e.g., family limited partnerships, separation or property settlement agreements), all insurance policies including property and liability policies and life, health, and disability policies, statements of company benefits, IRAs, Keogh plans, and so on. It can be quite formidable to gather all this data, and it's not unusual for clients to begin the financial planning process, realize how much work it entails, and then not return with their completed materials for over a year. By the way, once you gather your data, do your best to keep it current so you don't have to go through the exercise every few years.

Identifying and Prioritizing Goals and Objectives

Financial planning also means deciding what you want to do with your assets. What are your goals? Do you want to retire young, or do you plan to work for the rest of your life? Do you know how much money you'll need before you can retire? Are you one of those people who thinks a great deal about retirement, but hasn't written a will yet? Do you know what you want your will to accomplish? Do you know what you want for your children? Some people want to leave their children everything they have, while others feel that their children should make it on their own and leaving them anything would be a mistake. Maybe you understand your goals in one area of your life, but not in others. Good financial planning involves all areas of your financial life.

For some, this step can bring their values system to light. Perhaps you've spent your entire life making money, but now you want to give much of it away to a specific cause you admire. Or now that you've reached a certain income level, you're ready to try a new career—or no career at all.

Sometimes, when we talk to prospective clients, they'll explain that they are well acquainted with the idea of risk, and they understand that's it's an important element of investing. They tell us they want to take risks to earn a good return. Then, when we look over their financial information, we discover that they're almost entirely invested in low-risk, low-return bonds. Others may admit that they have a low tolerance for risk, and we discover that they've put all of their money into one stock because they trust that company and feel it is foolproof—as though any company, no matter how solid, can guarantee that it will never have a bad year. Investing in one stock, no matter how safe you think it is, is in fact a high-risk behavior.

As you can see, the process of clarifying your desires can reveal disconnects that planning can correct. I can't put it more strongly: You must identify and prioritize your goals and objectives so your finances can be structured to meet them.

Analyzing Data

Arraying the data in schedules allows you and your team to appropriately analyze data and identify trends and issues—see examples of schedules in the Appendix.

Reviewing Potential Strategies

Once the data analysis is completed, the task of reviewing the analysis against your desired goals and objectives becomes paramount. This process can be quite fluid; your goals and objectives may change as trade-offs are examined.

For example, we've had clients who, once their finances were organized, were able to make other major life decisions. One couple realized that they had enough money for one of them to quit his or her job and stay at home with their children. Another client who was single had always wanted to sail around the world but never had taken the time off from his busy job as an executive vice president at an insurance company to see whether he had enough to do so. Once we'd gone over his papers, he realized that he did have the money to quit his job and take a year off. (Unlike most people with dreams, this man actually quit his job and after buying a sailboat, traveled from California all the way to the east coast of Africa before deciding that sailing halfway around the world was good enough. He then returned to San Francisco and a new job.)

Agreeing on Strategies

The strategies you settled on need to be put in writing. Based on them, a plan has to be compiled for final review.

Implementing Your Plan

A detailed report of the steps you will take needs to be prepared, including due dates, and all responsibilities must be assigned to the appropriate members of your team. In addition, someone must take responsibility for follow-up. Your financial planner may assume this task, but sometimes you may wish to do it yourself. This final step is crucial. Failure to complete one part of the plan may well place your entire plan at risk. For example, suppose one of your plan's elements is moving assets into separate names to take advantage of opportunities to save on estate taxes. This may sound like a simple task, but the failure to complete it properly may not only eliminate the estate tax saving you desire, but in so doing leave insufficient assets to provide the survivorship income you had hoped for.

Creating and implementing your plan requires discipline and common sense. Your plan shouldn't be too cumbersome or difficult to accomplish. Deciding that you are going to save more each month toward retirement, and running your numbers based on that assumption, is a mistake if the required sacrifices cannot be made. A truly smart plan on paper may not be a smart plan in practice if it simply isn't practical.

What Happens Next?

Once a plan is in place, you will need to implement the action steps. However, you probably won't need to meet with your team again for at least a year to alter the plan unless there have been important changes in your circumstances (or changes in the world that would have an effect on the plan).

In-depth planning can take place every three to five years, again assuming that no great changes have taken place in your life. Your financial planner can turn the work over to a generalist wealth management professional or to an investment counselor. These days many financial planners are becoming wealth managers and are being paid to design, implement, and supervise.

Those with complicated and fluid finances might want to consider getting together with their advisor as often as two to four times a year. One of the aspects that can differentiate the affluent from the non-affluent is that the former tend to take their finances very seriously, and they realize the importance of organization.

However, it's not a good idea to look over your long-term finances more than four times a year. If you examine them too closely, you easily may lose perspective. It's like watching the stock market every hour—yes, your stocks may rise and fall in the space of a day, but because for the most part you're holding onto them for longer periods, what happens to them in shorter time periods is generally irrelevant (unless it is caused by a change in one of your key assumptions). Nor do you want to act upon these momentary shifts in stock values. The same goes for your entire plan. (Nonetheless, a sudden decrease in the values of certain assets could create opportunities for gift and tax planning.)

Your time horizon should be long because when doing intelligent financial planning, you are in fact setting up a long-term plan. Again, you may review it as often as four times a year if you wish, although for many people that's not necessary. And after you've been doing that for a few years, you may find you need to examine your plan less often. However, like the investment process, the world seems to be changing more rapidly these days, which can present opportunities that need to be addressed in short order.

15 Questions to Ask a Potential Financial Planner

1. Are you a Certified Financial Planner? If not, what professional qualifications do you hold (JD, MBA, CPA)?
2. How many years of financial planning experience do you have?
3. How many years of financial planning experience do you have at your current employer? Where were you previously employed?
4. Are you the only financial planner I will be working with? Or is it a team approach? If it is a team approach, how qualified are the other planners?
5. How many clients do you work with?
6. What is the profile of your typical financial planning client (net worth, occupation, objectives)?
7. Can I see a sample of a financial plan you have recently prepared?
8. How many times do we meet to discuss my financial plan?
9. Once we agree on the plan, do you help with the implementation of the recommendation?
10. Does your firm provide investment services? If we decide on investment changes, is it implied that I will use the investment services provided by your institution?
11. Do you sell life insurance? Are you a licensed insurance agent? Are you compensated for selling life insurance?
12. Once we finalize my plan and implement your recommendations, do you provide ongoing advice and regular revisions to the plan? If so, is there an additional fee?
13. Do you work with my other advisors (accountant, lawyer)?
14. How are you compensated? Is your fee based on the client's net worth? Is it a fixed-fee arrangement?
15. Will you provide me with a list of references whom I may contact?

Certain parts of your plan need less review than others. Although you want to keep abreast of your financial portfolio, you probably don't need to review your estate plan more than once every five years—unless your personal circumstances change or unless there is a change in the law or a dramatic move in interest rates. But if you don't do it at least every five years, you may risk having your assets distributed to people and places you didn't plan on. Life is complicated and hard to predict, and if you don't keep your estate plan up to date, things may go wrong after your death.

In the Appendix, we have provided examples of sample schedules from the financial planning process.

Private Banking

Many people hear the words "private banking" and think of secret vaults in Switzerland holding vast amounts of money. But private banking isn't just for the ultra-affluent. It's for any reasonably wealthy person who would prefer a personal relationship with a service-oriented banker over rote transactions with an impersonal institution.

With the average retail banking account, you enter a bank and whichever teller is available to attend to your needs is your banker of the moment (unless you use an ATM, in which case you have no human contact at all). If you want mortgage financing, you'll be ushered over to a stranger in the bank's mortgage area. If you want a loan, you'll likely be offered an installment loan with a regular payment that suits the bank's needs by someone you've just met. In other words, you'll receive the bank's product (instead of something tailored to your precise circumstances and preferences). And on any given day, if you don't have sufficient funds to cover a check, your retail bank will bounce your check.

When you have a private banking account, a specific individual is assigned to you. That banker is empowered with decision-making capabilities. He or she can structure your loans, advise and consult with you on your mortgage financing, and discuss your cash-flow needs. Your banker watches your account and won't routinely bounce a check, but instead will call you and ask if you need to transfer funds whenever your account appears to be overdrawn.

Private bankers are able to attend to your personal needs. They aren't distracted by commercial or corporate lending, nor are they encumbered by a large load of accounts. Retail bankers may have thousands of clients, whereas private bankers have a small number whom they can get to know very well.

With private banking, loans are structured to meet the needs of the client. Let's say you want to borrow money to buy an expensive car three months before your big bonus is due. Your retail bank wouldn't be interested in the details of your upcoming windfall—you'd have to take out a regular car loan and pay it out every month at a consumer rate of interest. But a private banker will help you out through a line of credit that will allow you to buy that car, knowing that you'll be able to pay it back when your bonus shows up at the end of the year. Because annual bonuses are so often a major aspect of the working affluent person's compensation, private bankers will help finance expensive purchases throughout the year, even when cash flow is poor, knowing that debts can be paid when that bonus comes in. In other words, private banking creates a relationship, not just a loan transaction; a good private banker will become one of your most trusted advisors.

Let's say your son wants to start a flower-arranging business. Among other things, he'll need to buy inventory, pay rent, meet payroll, and so on. You like his business plan and think it will work, but he isn't creditworthy and can't get a capital loan or a line of credit. You'd like to guarantee it for him, but no retail bank would go near this—venture capital is too risky. Here a private banker can help. If you don't want to give your son the money outright because you want him to get his feet wet in the business first, you and your private banker can work together to set up a capital loan with a repayment program and a line of credit, which you then back with your guarantee.

The best part of private banking is the personal touch. Recently, a client called her banker, a U.S. Trust managing director, to say that her daughter had just phoned from Paris. The girl's handbag had just been stolen, and she had no money, no friends, and was scared. Could they help? The banker discovered that the girl still had her passport, so she quickly arranged to wire her all the money she needed within an hour, and the crisis ended.

Another client came to us when all the partners in his firm were investing in a business venture that required a $100,000 outlay. But when we sat down with the man and went over his expenses and other obligations, we determined that the investment was beyond his means—he already had a high debt load and shouldn't be borrowing more money. We reviewed our reasoning with him, explaining that his liquidity and cash flow would be strained by the additional debt and might not be adequate to sustain his lifestyle if anything unexpected were to happen. The man realized we were correct and saw that he could use our meeting to turn down the offer without insulting his partners: He told them that although he liked their idea, his personal banker had strongly advised him against getting involved in it. This way, he was able to save face—and save himself from making an investment that would have stretched him too far.

Sometimes private bankers can come in handy in unusual ways. One of our clients was planning a surprise sixtieth birthday party for her husband and had to write checks to caterers, florists, and musicians. Because she knew that her husband regularly looked at their checkbook, her question was: Was there a way to keep him from seeing all these transactions? Our solution: We temporarily changed the account to reflect their summer residence address instead of their home address, and for a month, we had the statements sent there. The party was a complete surprise to the husband; for the life of him, he couldn't figure out how his wife had pulled it off.

Custody, Trading, and Record Keeping

If you want to manage your money yourself but like the idea of parking it in one centralized place, a custody account might be right for you. Unlike private banking, where you can handle all of your banking transactions, including check writing yourself, a custody account means that you create a custodian to keep your money—but the custodian doesn't act unless you want it to. And unlike the money in a regular bank or brokerage account, the assets in this account are not part of the bank's balance sheet. They sit off to the side, so if the bank (or brokerage house) were to fail, your money would still be available. In other words, the money in this account isn't being used by the institution for its own purposes. It's as though you still had it yourself.

The advantage of having a custodian is that you don't have to do your own bookkeeping, collect your own dividends, or perform any of the other arduous tasks attendant to managing money. For example, if you own 50 stocks, you'd probably receive dozens of dividend checks and have to walk or drive them over to the bank, fill out a deposit slip, and wait in line. But with a custody account, your dividends are credited automatically. A custodian also collects income and principal distributions in a timely fashion, especially the proceeds from called bonds and trade settlements, and provides tax-reporting services, including tax cost-lot accounting and performance measurement for your investment accounts.

The process of choosing a custodian often comes after you've arranged other investment management–related services. If your money is managed in a mutual fund, the safekeeping of the underlying assets is the responsibility of the mutual fund company, and the assets are generally kept by an institutional custodian such as a bank or trust company. If you choose to have a portion of your money managed by an investment management organization, they, too, may insist on keeping your assets at a particular broker or bank custodian. If you manage and trade all (or a portion) of your assets by yourself, you may choose to keep them at a broker or bank custodian. If you invest in government securities, they remain in book entry form at the Federal Reserve.

Your choice of custodian may center on the level of service you want. If you require a high level of access and involvement, consider a bank that will assign you a personal custody officer. If costs are a major issue, you might instead select a brokerage firm; the service can be excellent, but it may be online and through call centers. In general, banks will charge a fee for custody services based on the value of your accounts and/or on the number of transactions—these charges, depending on the size of the account, can run from 0.05 percent to 0.15 percent. Brokers do not charge for custody services, but they provide less service overall and require that you trade only through their own broker-dealer (or charge fees for trades executed elsewhere). Also many brokers are now charging minimum fees to customers who have few transactions.

Whether you work with a bank or with a broker, some costs may be hidden. For example, your custody institution or broker may limit the choice of money market funds available to your account—and that choice is often driven by the economics of your vendor rather than the best interests of the client. Therefore, you must become an informed consumer. This is especially true in regard to trade execution, where you must be concerned not only about the cost of a trade (which is a transparent figure) but also about the quality of execution (which may be a hidden cost).

Banks generally allow clients to execute trades through the broker-dealer of their choice and then settle the trades at the bank. Brokers expect that trades will settle within their own broker-dealer. When a broker or a bank trades through a captive broker-dealer and acts as a principal, you must pay attention to execution quality. The broker-dealer may be filling your order from inventory; this is especially troublesome and difficult to detect when trading municipal bonds. In other instances, it may be a perfectly reasonable process and allows the institution to increase margins with no disadvantage to the client.

The safety of your assets should be of paramount concern. Both bankers and brokers are well regulated, and you can probably feel quite safe if your assets are at well-capitalized firms. Banks maintain their client assets separately from their own, whereas brokers are permitted through their account agreements to use client assets to lend securities to others who "short" securities. Banks cannot pursue these activities without client authorization.

The distinction probably won't mean very much to you unless there is a problem. For example, if your bank becomes insolvent, the assets within the bank's custody department are more easily segregated and can be accessed by you, the client. Client assets parked with brokers are not as easily identified and must remain encumbered until any insolvency issues are resolved. To compensate, client assets at brokerages are generally insured up to $500,000 by the SIPC, and additional insurance may be available. Bank assets are generally not insured, because as noted, they are held separately from the bank's assets.

Ultimately, the custody of virtually all assets lies in the hands of a depository institution such as the Federal Reserve (for government securities) and the Depository Trust Company (for most other securities). The bank or broker is thus merely a record keeper, and your primary concern should be the quality of the firm's systems and controls. Whether the financial condition and controls of the institution are sound is more important than a minimal amount of insurance. Also, in today's electronic age and troublesome geopolitical climate, your custodian's contingency plans are very important. Do they have adequate back-up and is it in a different location and power grid? If you have concerns about your custodians in this regard, you should ask to see a copy of the most recent report from their external auditor on their controls and backup systems.

I have dealt with many clients who, for additional safety, choose to keep assets at more than one custodian. The events of September 11, 2001, which highlighted some shortcomings of the overall system, may have reinforced this preference. Multiple custodians probably are not necessary, but if such an arrangement enables you to sleep better at night, it might be worth the price in terms of extra expense and in having to provide consolidated record keeping.

Consolidated record keeping is another important consideration. If you end up with multiple custodians because you're invested in multiple investment management products, you'll need to consolidate your various reports for accounting and tax purposes. You either can do this yourself, or have your accountant and/or tax preparer do it. Bank trust departments provide this service and will be your master custodian. Several smaller wealth management firms are providing this service with new software that takes feeds from most of the larger financial services firms.

Almost all custodians and brokers allow you to retrieve account information online. Some custodians and brokers, along with certain Internet information companies, are trying to create systems under which you can aggregate information from other custodians on one site to provide a consolidated view of all of your accounts. To date, this process suffers from many flaws and a successful model has not yet emerged.

In addition, some clients insist on having an accounting firm audit their custodian. This, too, probably is not necessary, and is certainly expensive, but it does provide another safeguard for your money.

CHAPTER 2

Investments

*Money is a singular thing. It ranks with love as man's
greatest source of joy. And with death as his greatest
source of anxiety. Over all history it has oppressed nearly
all people in one of two ways: either it has been abundant and very unreliable, or reliable and very scarce.*

—John Kenneth Galbraith,
American economist

I sat over my keyboard and cried.
—Susan Traiman,
online trader, as quoted in *The Wall Street Journal*

Investment planning is a process through which you, the investor, study your financial condition and financial objectives in order to choose those asset classes most likely to produce the results you desire within your risk-tolerance level and thereby meet your goals. You should commit your investment plan to writing and review it every several years, or more often if your circumstances change.

U.S. Trust Survey of
Affluent Americans Results

For many years U.S. Trust has asked our survey respondents to pick the investment sectors they feel represent the best value. A close look at the results indicates that affluent investors are often momentum players; in other words, they buy stock in whichever industry or company seems to be doing well at the moment. Running with the herd is not something limited to amateurs. Many professional investors have fallen into a similar trap (or believed they could take advantage of the trends and make momentum their friend). This was the case with technology stocks, which were the leading pick through the 1990s; since 2000, that has changed radically.

Our surveys also reveal substantial swings in our respondents' attitudes toward asset allocation. Back in 1993, following a period of lackluster equity returns, investors felt that the best investment was municipal bonds, whereas their least favored investment was U.S. government securities. Unfortunately, respondents were also slightly negative about growth stocks, which would have proven to be been an excellent investment at the time. However, compared to the years that followed, their expectations were sensible—87 percent said they would be content if they could realize a 10 percent average return on their portfolio that year.

Respondents were also reasonably bullish—55 percent felt that the next two years would be favorable or very favorable to investors. Only 15 percent felt those years would be unfavorable. By 1995, investors had turned bearish, with only 31 percent expecting an increase in the U.S. stock market over the next year. Perhaps because the stock market indeed did advance, by 1996 investors had become more bullish—57 percent expected the U.S. stock market to increase in value over the next year. By 1998, investors were beginning to wonder how long the bull market would last. More than half the respondents (57 percent) felt it would end within two years (and they were right). Only 15 percent felt it would continue more than three years (and they were wrong).

Still, respondents remained bullish in 1998 about the U.S. stock market over the long term. Over the next 10 years, 25 percent of those surveyed expected to see annualized returns of 11 to 20 percent on their stock market investments. Another 20 percent expected returns greater than 20 percent. (The median response for anticipated returns was 12 percent.) It is clear that the market, currently mired at levels lower than in 1998, will have to do extraordinarily well for this prediction to come true. At U.S. Trust, we don't think it will.

By 2001, respondents were coming to terms with the stock market's reversal since mid-2000. Only 8 percent said that their investment portfolios had not declined in the last year—73 percent said theirs had declined a great deal or at least some, and 19 percent said slightly. Still, 57 percent said that they were not going to make any changes in their portfolio because of these declines. Only 2 percent had sold off all of their stocks or stock mutual funds and had moved their money to safer investments.

As of 2002, 78 percent of respondents felt that the top investment sectors were health care, pharmaceuticals, and biotechnology; the same proportion picked defense and aerospace. Right behind these sectors were real estate (chosen by 66 percent of respondents) and consumer products (63 percent). Another 55 percent also felt comfortable with energy and natural resources stocks.

We also asked respondents to tell us how they apportioned the assets in their portfolio. The breakdown appears in Figure 2.1. Table 2.1 provides an interesting comparison of investment portfolios based on household net worth. Fifty-seven percent of respondents said that the recent downturn in the stock market has not caused them to make any changes in their portfolio. Twenty-two percent saw the downturn as a buying opportunity, whereas 18 percent sold off some securities and moved their money into what they considered to be safer investments. Two percent of respondents simply sold everything in their portfolio. Of those who sold their stocks, 34 percent transferred their proceeds to cash, 22 percent invested them in bonds, 20 percent in real estate, 18 percent in private equity, and 6 percent in foreign stock.

Seventy percent of respondents said that the current volatility didn't prompt them to seek additional advice. But of the 30 percent who did seek such advice, 84 percent consulted a fee-based investment advisor, 73 percent went to a financial planner, 68 percent saw a stock-

FIGURE 2.1   AVERAGE PERCENTAGE OF PORTFOLIO HELD
                  IN VARIOUS INVESTMENT TYPES, 1996 & 2002

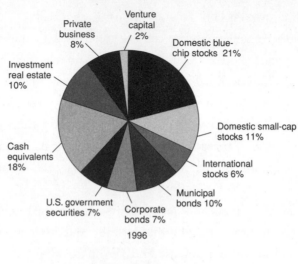

1996

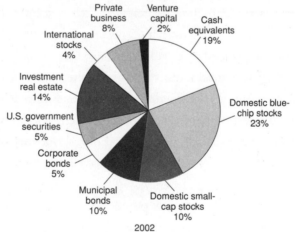

2002

SOURCE: U.S. Trust Survey of Affluent Americans X, XXI, 1996, 2002

broker, 38 percent chose a CPA, 32 percent went to a banker, 21 percent sought out an attorney, and 19 percent consulted with an insurance agent.

If the market continues its slump, 54 percent of respondents said they would postpone capital improvements to their home, 49 percent

TABLE 2.1   COMPOSITION OF FINANCIAL ASSET PORTFOLIOS
                   BY HOUSEHOLD NET WORTH

	Top 1% of Net Worth	95–99%	90–95%	80–90%	60–80%	0–60%
Taxable Equity	53.8%	38.7%	33.0%	26.2%	16.0%	11.6%
Taxable Bonds	4.8	4.2	2.9	2.6	3.0	1.7
Tax-Deferred Equity	7.1	22.5	25.1	28.4	27.1	24.8
Tax-Deferred Bonds	4.5	8.8	10.1	11.3	12.9	13.2
Tax-Exempt Bonds	9.2	5.9	3.8	2.1	1.9	1.0
Interest-Bearing Accounts	9.9	10.6	14.2	18.6	23.4	29.7
Other Financial Assets	10.7	9.3	11.0	10.8	15.9	17.4

SOURCE: Tabulations from 2001 Survey of Consumer Finances.

would cut back on any new big-ticket items (such as a new television), 43 percent would postpone the purchase of a new car or boat, 38 percent would eat out less often, 36 percent would postpone or reevaluate vacation plans, 34 percent would contribute less money to their favorite charities, and 26 percent would simply cut back on everyday expenses.

An Investment Scenario

Some years ago, one of our portfolio managers recommended that his clients buy stock in a large department store chain. This particular analyst had a contrarian philosophy—he tended to pick stocks that were out of favor rather than those that other analysts liked. This stock was especially unpopular at the time, but the analyst, who had spent many hours studying the company and its management, believed it had a strong blueprint for its future and expected the stock to make a dramatic comeback.

Among his clients was a widow named Muriel. Although dubious of his advice, she bought the stock. Contrarian picks don't necessarily move the day you buy them. They are bought for their future potential, not their immediate performance. Muriel said that she understood this concept, but she became impatient fairly quickly.

One day she called the analyst and said, "I just drove by the store and I saw only 60 cars in the parking lot. Is it time to sell?" The analyst explained that this wasn't the time to sell, and that while he appreciated her offbeat information-gathering techniques, she should hold on.

The next week he got another call. "I just drove by the parking lot," Muriel said, "and this time I only counted 50 cars. Should I sell?" The analyst again urged her to be patient. Sure enough, the next week she called again. "This time there are only about 35 cars. I really should sell, shouldn't I?"

From then on Muriel called every week with a report on how many cars were in the parking lot. She didn't sell the stock, although the week she saw only 10 cars she could barely restrain herself. Strangely enough, her research analysis bore fruit. A year later she was calling to say that there were now 100 cars in the lot, and within two years, as the number of cars increased, so did the company's stock price. What now decreased was the number of times Muriel called us. The stock went on to become a winner.

The rest of Muriel's family were equally idiosyncratic investors. Marvin, Muriel's husband, who had owned a successful business that he eventually sold when the couple reached their 60s, refused to buy any stocks at all, and put every penny he had into his business, claiming that the only investment he could count on was an investment he controlled. Luckily for him, the business flourished, although he died shortly after the sale. Both Marvin and Muriel had been shrewd about their estate, and had started giving money to their three sons in a tax-wise manner; eventually, after Muriel died, each of the sons received his full inheritance. And each of the sons handled his investments differently.

The eldest son couldn't find investments that made money fast enough. He didn't have a job, and his investment philosophy flew in the face of ours. Sober thoughts never entered his mind. When we told him honestly that we couldn't guarantee him the 20 percent return he demanded each year, he left us to invest on his own. Because he had started investing in the 1990s boom, he felt that double-digit returns were to be expected.

The middle son, however, was frugal to the point of exasperation—he inherited his parents' fear of risk, and he asked us to construct the most conservative portfolio possible. He decided that he preferred all his money in Treasury bills and bonds. Even when we showed him that his money, although safe, would lose its value because his return wouldn't be sufficient to compensate for inflation, he didn't care. "I can't sleep at night knowing that I could wake up with less money than I had the day before," he said.

The youngest son wasn't even slightly interested in his money or in investing. While the eldest son had tried his hand at the family business, but failed, and the middle son was still involved, this son decided never to enter the business, but to teach grade school instead. After obtaining his credentials, he moved to a town where few people knew his family, much less that he was very wealthy. He turned his portfolio over to us with complete discretion, and if we hadn't sent him regular statements, he might never have asked about his balances. He lived on his school salary, and that was enough for him.

Once a year the family meets to discuss their money, among other issues. Needless to say, these meetings are interesting: The youngest son acts as though he doesn't care, the middle son is afraid that he will lose everything he has by taking any investment risks, and the eldest son has lost a great deal in his eagerness to become as rich as possible as quickly as possible. He is still looking for that magic bullet.

Creating and Preserving Wealth by Investing

The art and science of investing are evolving—the conventional wisdom of the past decade is not necessarily wise today, but the lessons learned along the way must be added to our current store of wisdom. When I began my career at U.S. Trust, the firm was in the forefront of investing in the growth companies of the mid-twentieth century—firms including IBM, Xerox, General Electric, and Procter and Gamble. Identifying and investing in these excellent companies seemed easy, and betting on the performance of the Nifty 50, as the group was known, was a sure way to make money—until their values fell dramatically in the bear market of 1973 and 1974, and most of these stocks lost their popularity as well.

Still, many academic studies have shown that if investors had not sold when these stocks bottomed, but held on to them or their successor companies until the end of the twentieth century, they would still have made excellent returns of about 12 percent. The Nifty 50 were essentially good businesses whose valuations had become inflated because so many investors felt they were the only stocks to own (see Table 2.2). Yet holding on to them longer wasn't a mistake—some of these 50 faired well, and others failed, but the final outcome wasn't bad. The question remains: Could a more disciplined approach to valuation and asset allocation have permitted skilled investors to produce better results by rebalancing their portfolios prior to the market's precipitous decline? Unfortunately, many professional and private investors abandoned these stocks and invested in other asset classes that often didn't produce equivalent value.

The point is that investing requires discipline, a long-term time horizon, and the recognition that, given all the variables at work, markets are rarely predictable. The world is filled with uncertainties that make forecasts difficult. On any given day you are likely to find as many professionals on one side of a prediction as on the other.

TABLE 2.2   THE NIFTY FIFTY: 1972–DECEMBER 31, 2001

Company	Annualized Returns	1972 Actual P-E Ratio
Philip Morris Cos. Inc.	17.80%	24.0
Pfizer Inc.	17.39%	28.4
Bristol-Myers	15.60%	24.9
Pepsico Inc.	15.58%	27.6
General Electric Co.	15.44%	23.4
Merck & Co. Inc.	14.85%	43.0
Heublein Inc.	14.75%	29.4
Squibb Corp.	14.46%	30.1
Gillette Co.	14.07%	24.3
Anheuser-Busch Inc.	13.41%	31.5
Lilly Eli & Co.	13.38%	40.6
Johnson and Johnson	13.34%	57.1
Schering Plough Corp.	13.22%	48.1
First National City Corp.	13.20%	20.5
Coca-Cola Co.	13.18%	46.4
American Home Products Corp.	13.09%	36.7
American Hospital Supply Corp.	12.24%	48.1
Procter & Gamble Co.	11.89%	29.8
Texas Instruments Inc.	11.83%	39.5
AMP Inc.	11.19%	42.9
Dow Chemical Co.	11.19%	24.1
Chesebrough Ponds Inc.	10.95%	39.1
McDonald's Corp.	10.58%	71.0
Upjohn Co.	10.08%	38.8
American Express Co.	10.02%	37.7
Baxter Labs	9.97%	71.4
Schlumberger Ltd.	9.87%	45.6
Minnesota Mining & Manufacturing Co.	9.69%	39.0
International Business Machines	9.54%	35.5
Disney Walt Co.	8.92%	71.2
Int'l Telephone & Telegraph Corp.	8.74%	15.4
Lubrizol Corp.	7.29%	32.6
Sears Roebuck & Co.	6.79%	29.2
Schlitz Joe Brewing Co.	6.78%	39.6
Avon Products Inc.	6.15%	61.2
Int'l Flavors & Fragrances	5.77%	25.0
Halliburton Co.	4.97%	35.5
Revlon Inc.	4.77%	69.1
Louisiana Land & Exploration Co.	4.68%	26.6
Penney J.C. Inc.	4.62%	31.5
Black and Decker Corp.	2.38%	50.0
Simplicity Patterns	2.31%	43.5
Eastman Kodak Co.	1.82%	47.8

TABLE 2.2   (*Continued*)

Company	Annualized Returns	1972 Actual P-E Ratio
Digital Equipment Corp.	1.06%	56.2
Xerox Corp.	0.15%	45.8
Kresge (S.S.) Co.	−0.69%	49.5
Burroughs Co.	−1.82%	46.0
Emery Air Freight Corp.	−2.31%	55.3
M.G.I.C. Investment Corp.	−6.07%	68.5
Polaroid Corp.	−18.51%	94.8
Rebalanced Portfolio	11.76%	41.9
Equally Weighted	11.62%	41.9
S&P 500	12.14%	18.9

SOURCE: Adapted from *Forbes*, "The Nifty Fifty Revisited."

Like it or not, there is no magic when it comes to this kind of investing. Good investing consists of common sense, a great deal of hard work, and tremendous discipline. Although experts in the field have long known this, in the 1990s many individual investors lost track of these traits. Those years created a cluster of investors who felt that all they had to do was buy a stock—particularly if it was in the so-called TMT group (technology, media, telecommunications)—and it would rise. The only risk seemed to be that their stocks wouldn't rise as fast as everyone else's. These investors regularly watched CNBC, making them feel as though they were knowledgeable, and they never learned the lesson that markets are composed of risks as well as rewards.

Even many professional investors failed to stick to their discipline and suffered—or perhaps I should say, they and their clients suffered. Fred Taylor, U.S. Trust's vice chairman and chief investment officer during the last 22 years, warned clients in the spring of 1998 that many domestic equities were overvalued. Three years later he admitted that, although U.S. Trust emphasized a disciplined, long-term approach to investing throughout the cult-like market mania of the 1990s, like many investment organizations even we had not been immune to the irrational exuberance of the moment. Still, Fred says, "We welcome the return to reason."

What many people forgot, or didn't bother to learn, is that there is a difference between *creating* wealth and *investing* wealth. People began to believe that the quickest and easiest road to creating wealth was to speculate in the stock market and reap great rewards. Hundreds of books were written about how anyone could become a millionaire overnight by picking the right stocks, and the media were filled with stories of investors who made a fortune simply by investing in the right Internet stocks.

The problem is that this is not actually the way wealth is created. A handful of these investors did, indeed, make a great deal of money—but only if they got out of the markets early, which is the way all bubbles work. The other 99 percent did not get out early, and they lost money—sometimes a great deal of it. After all those breathtaking news stories of newly created millionaires during the 1990s, the early twenty-first century was filled with tragic tales of people who had lost their fortunes during the 2000s.

Risk

Creating wealth does involve risk—but not the kind of risk encountered when investing in the markets. For those who became affluent and stayed that way, risk may have meant starting a business with their entire life savings, or taking out a loan that they could ill afford to default on, or borrowing money from relatives who needed to be paid back. Perhaps they had an idea that needed a great deal of luck, timing, and hard work to carry off properly. Perhaps they worked at a large organization, but as they rose up the ladder took on risks that differentiated them from the others who were also fighting their way to the top. Muriel's husband Martin, who hated stock market risk, took another kind of risk as a young man when he walked away from a corporate career and founded his own business, with no guarantee that it would work.

Very few people created all their wealth through investments alone. Yes, there are always going to be a few stars, such as well-known investor Warren Buffett, who seems to be able to outsmart the market year after year. But the reason Mr. Buffett is famous is because he is such an exception. He wouldn't be so well known if there were tens of thousands of others just like him. Nonetheless, given the sizeable percentage of their net worth that is held in financial assets (see Table 2.3), investing wisely is of critical importance to the affluent.

For the most part, if you have money, you won't want to place it all in risky investments. You'll want the investing side of your life to be as intelligently managed as the rest of it, or perhaps more so. Risk is always a factor in investing, but taking undue risk should not be part of the equation. To help you preserve your money, maximize your potential returns, and manage the inherent risks, you should work with a good investment advisor or wealth management specialist. His or her (and your) concerns will be defining your investment objectives, ascertaining your risk tolerance, determining your time frame, and understanding your tax situation.

This process (see Figure 2.2) is called investment planning, and completing it will result in a personal policy that will be, in effect, a business plan for investing your assets. Your investment plan will help you develop a balanced portfolio of different asset classes. These asset classes, which will be discussed throughout the book, are common stocks (domestic and international), fixed-income investments (high-quality and high-yield bonds), alternative investments (private equity, real estate, hedge funds), and cash.

The return aspect of investing is straightforward. Return can be quantified. Each year, you know exactly how much return you have earned. Most people want the maximum possible.

The risk aspect of investing is much more difficult to quantify. It's even difficult to agree on its definition, as different schools of thought exist. The current wisdom is that risk equals volatility (also known as those gut-wrenching ups and downs for which the market is famous). The more volatility within an asset class, the higher the probability

TABLE 2.3　Composition of Asset Holdings by Net-Worth Ranking, 1995 and 2001

Net Worth Category	Financial Assets		Owner Occupied Housing		Other Property		Business Assets		Other Assets	
	1995	2001	1995	2001	1995	2001	1995	2001	1995	2001
Top 1%	39.3%	44.7%	7.7%	8.4%	12.5%	12.2%	37.1%	32.5%	3.5%	2.3%
Next 4%	42.6	47.0	22.0	18.1	16.3	14.5	12.8	17.9	6.0	2.6
Next 5%	40.1	50.5	32.3	28.2	14.4	8.8	7.5	9.3	5.8	3.3
Next 10%	32.7	41.0	45.0	37.9	9.4	8.3	4.7	8.2	8.2	4.6
Next 20%	26.3	33.0	55.3	49.9	5.8	6.1	2.9	4.1	9.7	6.9
Bottom 60%	17.2	21.1	61.3	59.8	3.2	2.9	1.5	1.5	16.7	14.6

SOURCE: Tabulations from 1995 and 2001 Survey of Consumer Finances.

FIGURE 2.2   INVESTMENT PLANNING PROCESS

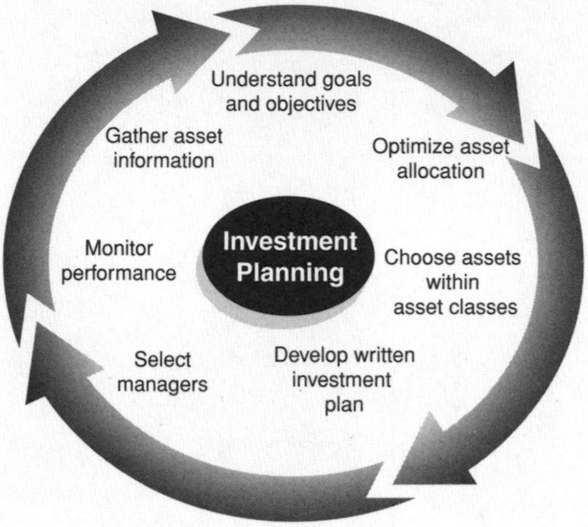

that you might sustain a permanent loss. After the TMT sector bubble burst, investors gained a much better understanding of risk. When your stock falls from $100 to $5 a share, you quickly come to understand that you have placed your money in a risky asset class.

Diversification

The accepted way to reduce risk is through diversification. The more diversified your portfolio, the more buffered you are against risk. However, diversification works only if the investments you are making have truly different risk characteristics. In other words, your portfolio should have many different types of investments—ones that have as little to do with each other as possible. If your investments are commonly affected by one factor, and that factor then drives them all down, you obviously weren't very well diversified. For example, U.S. Trust once had a client who had made a great deal of money as an oil executive. His idea of diversification was to own a basket of different stocks in the oil business. Although he owned equities, corporate bonds, and various other vehicles, almost every one of them was oil-related. When oil took a hit, his portfolio lost an unpleasantly large portion of its value.

Diversification should exist across asset classes—and within them. As noted, this means owning various kinds of investments, including bonds, real estate, stocks, private equities, and hedge funds. Within those vehicles, you need to be further diversified; within stocks, your portfolio could be divided into domestic and international stocks, as well as segregated by company size into what's known as large-, medium-, small-, and micro-cap stocks. *Cap* stands for capitalization. At this writing, the most heavily capitalized stock is Microsoft, at $280 billion; General Electric (GE) is second at $289 billion.

During the investment planning process, you can construct a number of diversified portfolios and measure their hypothetical risk and return characteristics. This process of examining possible port-folios is known as *optimization*, and the goal is to develop a portfolio with the highest likelihood of maximizing returns based on the level of risk you are willing to assume. A portfolio that satisfies your objectives is known as an *efficient* portfolio, and when you array a group of those portfolios based on different levels of return and risk, you have con-structed the *efficient frontier* of portfolio investing. The entire process is driven by making the appropriate assumptions based on both observ-ing past characteristics and predicting the future. Although not perfect, the process does allow the professional investor and the client a mech-anism for making important judgments.

To illustrate the benefits of diversification, we have included a chart showing the performance of different asset classes over the past decade (see Figure 2.3) and a chart that shows the relative correlation between various asset classes (see Table 2.4). We have also included a chart that forecasts the returns on asset classes, adjusted for risk, fees and taxes (see Table 2.5).

Some people don't like diversification, because it is an admission that you don't know what will happen in the future—no matter how much you study, you can't be certain about your investments. And yes,

FIGURE 2.3 LEADERSHIP OF MAJOR ASSET CLASSES (1991–2002)

Best → Worst	1991	1992	1993	1994	1995	1996	1997	1998	1999	2000	2001	2002	Annualized 5 Years	Annualized 10 Years
1	Emerging Markets 59.91%	Small Cap Value 29.14%	Emerging Markets 74.84%	Foreign Stocks 7.75%	Large Cap Value 38.35%	REITS 35.75%	Large Cap Value 35.18%	Large Cap Growth 38.71%	Emerging Markets 66.41%	REITS 25.88%	REITS 15.50%	Bonds 10.27%	HF Long/Short 11.87%	HF Long/Short 14.33%
2	Small Cap Growth 51.19%	Small Cap Stocks 18.41%	Foreign Stocks 32.67%	HF Absolute Return 2.97%	Large Cap Stocks 37.77%	Large Cap Growth 23.12%	Large Cap Stocks 32.85%	Large Cap Stocks 27.02%	HF Long/Short 44.22%	Small Cap Value 22.83%	Small Cap Value 14.03%	REITS 5.22%	HF Absolute Return 9.62%	HF Absolute Return 11.88%
3	Small Cap Stocks 46.05%	HF Long/Short 18.40%	HF Fund of Funds 26.32%	Large Cap Growth 2.66%	Large Cap Growth 37.19%	Large Cap Stocks 22.45%	Small Cap Value 31.78%	Foreign Stocks 20.09%	Small Cap Growth 43.09%	HF Absolute Return 15.31%	Bonds 8.42%	HF Absolute Return 4.43%	Bonds 7.54%	Small Cap Value 10.86%
4	Small Cap Value 41.70%	HF Absolute Return 15.42%	Small Cap Value 23.84%	REITS 0.81%	Small Cap Growth 31.04%	Large Cap Value 21.64%	Large Cap Growth 30.49%	HF Long/Short 15.98%	Large Cap Growth 33.16%	Bonds 11.63%	HF Absolute Return 8.35%	HF Fund of Funds 1.09%	HF Fund of Funds 5.35%	Large Cap Value 10.81%
5	Large Cap Growth 41.16%	Large Cap Value 13.81%	HF Long/Short 23.49%	Large Cap Stocks 0.38%	Small Cap Stocks 28.44%	Small Cap Value 21.37%	Small Cap Stocks 22.36%	Large Cap Value 15.63%	Foreign Stocks 26.72%	HF Long/Short 9.09%	HF Fund of Funds 2.80%	HF Long/Short -4.38%	REITS 3.04%	REITS 10.24%
6	REITS 35.68%	HF Fund of Funds 12.33%	HF Absolute Return 20.78%	Small Cap Value -1.55%	Small Cap Value 25.75%	HF Long/Short 21.32%	REITS 21.93%	Bonds 8.67%	HF Fund of Funds 26.47%	Large Cap Value 7.01%	Small Cap Stocks 2.49%	Emerging Markets -6.00%	Small Cap Value 2.71%	Large Cap Stocks 9.18%
7	Large Cap Stocks 33.03%	REITS 12.18%	Small Cap Stocks 18.91%	Small Cap Stocks -1.82%	HF Long/Short 23.47%	Small Cap Stocks 16.49%	HF Long/Short 18.87%	HF Absolute Return 5.94%	Small Cap Stocks 21.26%	HF Fund of Funds 4.07%	HF Long/Short 0.40%	Small Cap Value -11.43%	Large Cap Value 1.16%	HF Fund of Funds 8.86%
8	HF Long/Short 25.70%	Emerging Markets 11.40%	REITS 18.55%	Large Cap Value -1.99%	Bonds 18.48%	HF Absolute Return 15.22%	HF Fund of Funds 16.20%	Small Cap Growth 1.23%	Large Cap Stocks 20.91%	Small Cap Stocks -3.02%	Emerging Markets -2.37%	Large Cap Value -15.52%	Large Cap Stocks -0.58%	Bonds 7.51%
9	Large Cap Value 24.61%	Large Cap Stocks 9.04%	Large Cap Value 18.12%	Small Cap Growth -2.43%	REITS 18.31%	HF Fund of Funds 14.39%	HF Absolute Return 15.03%	Small Cap Stocks -2.55%	HF Absolute Return 14.52%	Large Cap Stocks -7.79%	Large Cap Value -5.59%	Foreign Stocks -15.94%	Small Cap Stocks -1.36%	Small Cap Stocks 7.16%
10	HF Absolute Return 16.57%	Small Cap Growth 7.77%	Small Cap Growth 13.36%	Bonds -2.92%	HF Absolute Return 17.78%	Small Cap Growth 11.26%	Small Cap Growth 12.95%	HF Fund of Funds -5.11%	Large Cap Value 7.35%	Foreign Stocks -14.17%	Small Cap Growth -9.23%	Small Cap Stocks -20.48%	Foreign Stocks -2.91%	Large Cap Growth 6.71%
11	Bonds 16.00%	Bonds 7.40%	Large Cap Stocks 10.15%	HF Long/Short -3.40%	Foreign Stocks 11.27%	Foreign Stocks 6.14%	Bonds 9.68%	Small Cap Value -6.45%	Bonds -0.83%	Large Cap Growth -22.42%	Large Cap Stocks -12.45%	Large Cap Stocks -21.65%	Large Cap Growth -3.84%	Foreign Stocks 3.99%
12	HF Fund of Funds 14.50%	Large Cap Growth 5.00%	Bonds 9.75%	HF Fund of Funds -3.48%	HF Fund of Funds 11.10%	Emerging Markets 6.03%	Foreign Stocks 1.55%	REITS -18.82%	Small Cap Value -1.49%	Small Cap Growth -22.43%	Large Cap Growth -20.42%	Large Cap Growth -27.89%	Emerging Markets -4.58%	Small Cap Growth 2.62%
13	Foreign Stocks 12.20%	Foreign Stocks -12.22%	Large Cap Growth 2.90%	Emerging Markets -7.32%	Emerging Markets -5.21%	Bonds 3.61%	Emerging Markets -11.59%	Emerging Markets -25.34%	REITS -6.48%	Emerging Markets -30.61%	Foreign Stocks -21.44%	Small Cap Growth -30.26%	Small Cap Growth -6.59%	Emerging Markets 1.31%

The benchmarks used for the following asset classes:

Bonds = Lehman Aggregate Bond Index

Emerging Markets = MSCI Emerging Markets (Free) Index

Foreign Stocks = MSCI EAFE Index (Net of Dividends)

Hedge Fund Absolute Return Strategies = 1/3 each of the following Hedge Fund Research Indices: Relative Value, Convertible Arbitrage and Merger Arbitrage

Hedge Fund of Funds = Hedge Fund Research Fund of Funds Index

Hedge Fund Long/Short Strategies = Hedge Fund Research Equity Hedge Index

REITS = NAREIT Index

Small Cap Stocks = Russell 2000 Index

Small Cap Growth = Russell 2000 Growth Index

Small Cap Value = Russell 2000 Value Index

Large Cap Stocks = Russell 1000 Index

Large Cap Growth = Russell 1000 Growth Index

Large Cap Value = Russell 1000 Value Index

SOURCE: CTC Consulting

TABLE 2.4   CORRELATIONS BETWEEN ASSET CLASSES

CORRELATION MATRIX 2003–2007

Asset Class	Asset Style	1	2	3	4	5	6	7	8	9	10	11	12	13	14	15
Cash	1 Short-Term Investments	1.00														
Fixed-Income	2 Municipal Bond Portfolio	0.82	1.00													
	3 Taxable Diversified Bond Portfolio	0.62	0.71	1.00												
Equity	4 Passive Large Cap Equity	0.11	0.13	0.18	1.00											
	5 Active Large Cap Equity	0.11	0.13	0.18	0.98	1.00										
	6 Passive Sm/Mid Cap Equity	0.06	0.10	0.06	0.76	0.76	1.00									
	7 Active Sm/Mid Cap Equity	0.06	0.10	0.06	0.76	0.76	0.98	1.00								
	8 Active International Equity	-0.04	0.10	0.08	0.64	0.64	0.60	0.60	1.00							
Alternative	9 Private Eq/LBO	0.08	0.12	0.11	0.85	0.85	0.93	0.93	0.60	1.00						
	10 Venture Capital	0.01	0.04	-0.01	0.68	0.68	0.96	0.96	0.56	0.83	1.00					
	11 Long/Short Equity Hedge	0.05	0.09	0.08	0.56	0.66	0.50	0.50	0.45	0.75	0.89	1.00				
	12 Low Volatility Strategies	0.15	0.20	0.25	0.17	0.17	0.29	0.29	0.12	0.28	0.24	0.37	1.00			
	13 Distressed Equity Hedge	0.27	0.20	0.34	-0.02	-0.02	-0.06	-0.06	-0.01	-0.05	-0.09	0.02	0.13	1.00		
Real Estate	14 REITs	0.13	0.19	0.13	0.28	0.28	0.43	0.43	0.21	0.40	0.31	0.30	0.29	0.04	1.00	
	15 Real Estate Partnerships	-0.25	-0.17	-0.12	-0.01	-0.01	-0.14	-0.14	-0.01	-0.09	-0.14	-0.11	-0.02	-0.24	-0.13	1.00

The correlation co-efficient between two asset classes measures the extent to which two assets are related.
It measures the sensitivity of returns for one asset class or portfolio to that of another.
All correlations are based on the historical (primarily monthly) returns of benchmark indices for the period Jan. 1990 to Dec. 2001.

TABLE 2.5   TEN-YEAR FORECASTED RISKS AND RETURNS

Federal Bond Income/Short-Term Gains Tax Rate: 35.00%
Federal Dividend/Long-Term Capital Gains Tax Rate: 15.00%

Asset Class	Before Fees		Total Return* 2003–2007		Annual Management Fees**	Net Return	Turnover Rate	Short-Term Capital Gains	Long-Term Capital Gains	After Fees and Taxes	
	Income (Yield)	Capital Appreciation	Gross Expected Return	Standard Deviation						Net Annualized Return	Net Real Return
Cash											
Short-Term Investments	2.60%	0.00%	2.60%	1.40%	0.20%	2.40%	100.00%	100.00%	0.00%	1.54%	–1.46%
Fixed-Income											
Municipal Bond Portfolio	4.50%	0.00%	4.50%	3.50%	0.40%	4.10%	50.00%	50.00%	50.00%	4.10%	1.10%
Taxable Diversified Bond Portfolio	5.65%	0.00%	5.65%	6.70%	0.40%	5.25%	50.00%	50.00%	50.00%	3.41%	0.36%
Equity											
Passive Large Cap Equity	1.50%	7.00%	8.50%	21.90%	0.20%	8.30%	15.00%	15.00%	85.00%	7.95%	4.54%
Active Large Cap Equity	1.50%	7.50%	9.00%	22.90%	0.80%	8.20%	50.00%	50.00%	50.00%	7.53%	3.79%
Passive Sm/Mid Cap Equity	1.20%	8.40%	9.60%	23.00%	0.25%	9.35%	25.00%	25.00%	75.00%	8.99%	5.41%
Active Sm/Mid Cap Equity	1.20%	8.90%	10.10%	24.00%	0.90%	9.20%	50.00%	50.00%	50.00%	8.49%	4.71%
Active International Equity	1.80%	7.70%	9.50%	23.50%	1.00%	8.50%	50.00%	50.00%	50.00%	7.80%	4.02%
Alternative Investments											
Private Eq/LBO	0.00%	16.00%	16.00%	35.00%	4.80%	11.20%	20.00%	20.00%	80.00%	10.72%	7.30%
Venture Capital	0.00%	15.00%	15.00%	40.00%	4.60%	10.40%	20.00%	20.00%	80.00%	9.95%	6.56%
Long/Short Equity Hedge	2.00%	13.25%	15.25%	11.00%	4.25%	11.00%	60.00%	60.00%	40.00%	8.85%	5.46%
Low Volatility Strategies	3.00%	7.25%	10.25%	7.00%	3.25%	7.00%	85.00%	85.00%	15.00%	5.03%	1.87%
Distressed Equity Hedge	1.00%	13.00%	14.00%	20.00%	4.00%	10.00%	95.00%	45.00%	55.00%	7.04%	3.23%
Real Estate											
REITs	6.00%	2.00%	8.00%	13.50%	1.00%	7.00%	60.00%	60.00%	40.00%	4.93%	1.82%
Real Estate Partnerships	6.00%	6.00%	12.00%	24.00%	4.00%	8.00%	30.00%	30.00%	70.00%	6.92%	3.76%
Expected Inflation	3.00%										

*CTC Consulting derived the forecasted risks and returns for these asset classes.

**The management fees reflect CTC Consulting's expected fee schedule for each asset class. Actual fees may vary by manager and by client.

NOTE: Table rates based on a $5 million account.

strategists exist who say they can predict what the future will bring. These people believe that you can put all your eggs in one or a few baskets. For the most part, they have not been proven correct.

Furthermore, we think that it is less risky to have a highly diversified portfolio than it is to own only the one least risky investment. For example, if you were to invest only in Treasury bills, you wouldn't encounter much risk in terms of your principal. Treasury bills are government-guaranteed so you don't have to worry about losing any money. But in 2003 you will only make about 1 to 3 percent on them, which means that, although you are not exposed to the risk of loss, you are exposed to the risk of inflation. In nominal terms, you can't lose money, but in real terms, you can, because if your Treasury bills earn 2 percent and inflation is at 4 percent, your money isn't keeping up with rising prices (and that's before taking taxes into account). If the purpose of money is to be able to buy things and the cost of buying things is going up faster than the value of your money, you will lose purchasing power (see Table 2.6).

TABLE 2.6   STOCKS, BONDS, T-BILLS (1926–2000)

	Zero Inflation	Low Stable Inflation	Rising Inflation	Falling Inflation	Entire Period
	1926–1945	1954–1965	1972–1981	1982–2000	1926–2000
			Average Return		
Treasury Bills	1.07%	2.55%	7.78%	6.23%	3.82%
US LT Government Bonds	4.72%	2.06%	2.81%	12.55%	5.32%
S&P 500 Index	7.13%	15.67%	6.47%	16.88%	11.05%
Inflation Rate	0.07%	1.43%	8.62%	3.29%	3.08%
Risk-free Real Rate	1.00%	1.12%	−0.84%	2.94%	0.74%

SOURCE: Ibbotson Associates and U.S. Trust calculations. The risk-free real rate is measured as the difference between the T-bill yield and inflation.

The fact is, you can't avoid risk. All investments are potentially unstable. In other countries, many of the most conservative investors who have saved money, built up their wealth, and invested in the least risky investment (such as their own government bonds) ended up losing all their money when their governments went broke or devalued their currency.

Time

Besides diversification, another element is important to consider while investing. That element is *time*. What is your time horizon? How long are you going to wait before you judge the success of your investments? Historically, U.S. Trust has taken a long-term view. We ask our clients to think in long-term horizons, which can mean five years and beyond.

Today, too many investors feel pressure to shorten their time horizon. They want to make money immediately. They want to work with an advisor who had the best record for the last quarter of a year. They want to see their investment rise within a few days. They want profits, and they want them right away. This attitude has meant that many portfolio managers are making decisions based on that constricted time scale. They face tremendous pressures to succeed quickly, which means they must shorten their time horizons.

Our insistence on using a long-term horizon differentiates U.S. Trust from other wealth managers, but for us, this stance has proven successful for 150 years. We have been able to adopt this longer horizon because we are among the largest institutions at which the majority of investment activities involve individual wealth, which is therefore taxable, as opposed to wealth that accumulates for charitable institutions and pension plans tax free. Because taxes are involved, we have incentives to avoid the pressure of short-term thinking. This is because a big incentive exists within the tax system to hold assets for a minimum of one year—it's preferable to pay a 15 percent capital gains tax instead of a 35 percent income tax. Also, the longer you hold an asset, the longer you defer your tax bill.

We also are able to take a long-term approach because the majority of our clients have been with us for a long time, and they're not looking to change investment advisors every time their portfolios dip. Smart investors learn over time that dips are inevitable, and that we are to be judged by long-term, rather than short-term, performance.

Still, there are risks involved in a long-term point of view as well. The world is changing at a much more rapid pace than in the past, and therefore we must stay abreast of current events, which can have a devastating effect on the markets. (This is not an endorsement of what's known as *market timing*, which in effect means watching the market on a minute-to-minute basis and trading because you believe you know where the overall market will be in the very near future. As mentioned, no one is clairvoyant, and that's what market timing needs to be uniformly successful.)

These days it can be tough to maintain a long-term perspective, especially with the daily barrage of media reports on the stock market. But most of these reports reflect the short-term picture, and merely explain what caused the market to go up or down that day. These momentary ups and downs don't tend to be worth monitoring. Think of it this way: In general, people are risk-averse. Although it would seem as though a $1 loss is equivalent to a $1 gain in emotional impact, the average investor is actually about 2½ times more sensitive to loss. So a $1 loss hurts as much as a $2.50 gain feels good. Or to put it in investing terms, if you invest a million dollars in the stock market, and it suffers a 20 percent decline, you've lost $200,000. To match or offset the negative feeling of losing $200,000, you'd have to make $500,000, or 2½ times the amount you lost, to feel equally positive (according to Amos Tversky and Daniel Kahneman, 1986). Psychologists have posited several theories as to why this is the case, but the bottom line is, it's not rational.

On any given day, the market is likely to go down close to 50 percent of the time. If you were very risk-averse, you would find that news painful. If you stretch your time period out to one year, however, the stock market will probably go down only a third of the time and up two-thirds. This more closely approximates the 1 to 2.5 ratio of good to bad that makes us as individuals feel okay. This means that if you look at the stock market more than a few times a year, you won't be happy. If you look at your statement just once a year, however, you'll feel better. If you looked only once every three to five years, you'd be even happier. Now we all know this sounds good in theory, but it will not happen in practice, nor should it, given the world in which we live.

FIGURE 2.4   RANGE OF EQUITY RETURNS

How time horizon affects asset allocation

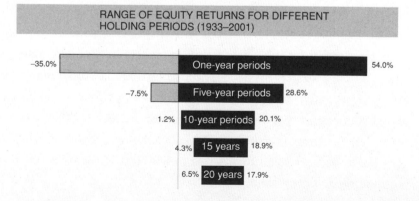

While stocks have the highest average return of any financial asset, they are also the most unpredictable over short periods. The chart below shows the range of returns for stocks held for various lengths of time between 1933 and 2001. Eighteen of the 69 years from 1933 to 2001 had negative returns, and the one-year returns during that period ranged from (–35.0%) to 54.0%. While the average return of 13.8% was high, few investors would tolerate that kind of uncertainty. Only three of the 63 five-year holding periods had negative returns. There were no negative returns for 10-year or longer holding periods.

RANGE OF EQUITY RETURNS FOR DIFFERENT HOLDING PERIODS (1933–2001)

–35.0%	One-year periods	54.0%
–7.5%	Five-year periods	28.6%
1.2%	10-year periods	20.1%
4.3%	15 years	18.9%
6.5%	20 years	17.9%

Long-term investing helps to protect against an irrational emotional response, just as a good advisor will protect us against similar emotional responses. People are overly susceptible to the emotions they feel when they lose money. But investments that give you good return over long periods of time involve short-term setbacks. The best investors tend to be those who don't worry about day-to-day fluctuations. They look at the long term. So should you (see Figure 2.4). That doesn't mean you can afford to be oblivious to day-to-day economic and geopolitical news, but you must view this news through the filter of a long-term investor with an appropriate asset allocation.

Investment Truisms

There are many truisms to live by in the world of investing. Probably the most important is simply to be sensible. Anything that seems too good to be true probably is. There are no real shortcuts. When some salesperson appears on television and promises that he or she can quadruple any investment in 30 days, the only person whose wealth is truly going to quadruple is that of the salesperson.

The most obvious and recent example of this maxim is the famous Internet bubble. Bubbles generally occur every 30 to 40 years, and it takes another generation to forget them. The generation that started investing in the 1990s, having never seen a bubble, grew up thinking that a 20 percent annual return was a reasonable expectation. For a while, it seemed to be. Everything was easy. You didn't need to hire a professional. Cab drivers were making money buying call options. The trend was up. These new investors didn't know about risk. They thought risk meant not placing 100 percent of their money in equities, and not having all of these stock holdings in the technology sector.

The problem with this sort of thinking is that a 20 percent return is not reasonable over a prolonged period of time, as anyone who has invested their money since March 2000 will tell you. Some investors who were around for the 1970s bear market and the collapse of those Nifty 50 stocks mentioned previously were reluctant to participate in the market of the 1990s. Instead, they sat on the sidelines, fully invested in fixed-income securities. And although these people missed the spectacular collapse, they were still worse off, because the returns for the last 12 years in equities still exceeded returns in the fixed-income markets.

Know Yourself

Know your financial objectives and investing goals. If you don't know what you want, you won't be able to achieve it.

Let's say you've just sold your business for $5 million. You feel richer than you ever thought possible. But what is your objective now? Do you want to preserve and protect your new wealth? Do you want to make it grow? Do you want to take risks? If you don't feel comfortable taking risks, then you have to invest very conservatively and be satisfied with lower returns. This may mean you'll have to adjust your standard of living to live within your investment returns now so you can save excess returns to negate the erosion of your purchasing power caused by inflation.

A major part of wealth management is managing yourself though the various phases in your lifecycle. When you first start out in life, you care mainly about paying your rent and buying a few luxuries now and then, like a fancy meal. As you get older, your priorities change. Perhaps you'll start a family or settle on a career that brings with it a variety of challenges and rewards. At each point, you'll need to create or modify your investment plan. In business, you need both a long-term and a short-term strategy. The same applies to individuals. People who are successful at accumulating wealth have such plans in place and know what they want to accomplish.

During our first session with our client Walter, he told us exactly what he expected his financial life to look like. At the time, he was making a good salary but he had yet to put any money away. Still, as a first-rate lawyer with a good firm, he was fairly confident of how his career would progress and how much money he would make. Walter knew himself as well as any client we've ever had; he knew how hard he wanted to work, how much money he would need to be happy, even how much money he wanted to give to charity. Fifteen years later, Walter is pretty much where he thought he would be.

Another client, Henry, came to U.S. Trust in 1998. Like Walter, he was confident that he could lay out his financial future. He had made a great deal of money as a venture capitalist and at age 40, was preparing to figure out what to do with his money and his future. But even as we were laying the financial groundwork with him, Henry's net worth decreased precipitously. We warned him that his assets were overly tied to one industry (technology), but he was convinced that he knew better than anyone the strength of the two companies in which he was heavily invested. Perhaps he did understand their technological workings, but he failed to see how the market would react during an industry-wide slump. Not long afterward, Henry's wife divorced him and gained custody of their two children. Within a relatively short time he changed from being the head of a wealthy family to a single man paying a great deal of alimony and retaining little income—and holding a fraction of the assets he had once held.

These stories demonstrate that before you can become a good investor, you must be able to answer a plethora of questions and then create an appropriate investment plan. What are your objectives? For example, how long do you want to work? Do you want to stay in the same career all your life? Where do you want to live? Do you want a second home? Do you want to marry, to have children? Remember, if your career path changes, you will need to alter your plans accordingly.

Plans are organic. Few people are like Walter, although few people are like Henry, either—most of us lead lives that take a middle course. Still, we all have to change our plans as our lives take unexpected turns. But it's not necessary to abandon your entire plan in the process. You'll simply need to modify it to match your life's new circumstances.

When it comes to planning, your age matters. If you're 60 and have sold your lifelong business, your goals will be very different from a person of 40. At 60, you may well want to preserve and protect your assets, while at 40, you may want to plow all that money back into another entrepreneurial activity. (If you did, we might counsel you to think it over. It's great that you've been so successful, but not everyone can repeat their success, and you probably don't want to risk everything. It is, of course, always your decision. But a good investment advisor helps you to see clearly what you truly want.)

Understand the lifestyle that makes you comfortable, and then structure your finances around your needs and desires. If what's most important to you is to live in a nice neighborhood, drive a nice car, and spend a month on vacation each year, how much money does that require? Don't kid yourself. Some people truly love the luxuries of life. There's no need to pretend you don't. You'd just be lying to yourself, and your investment advisor, if you said that you want to give a tenth of your money to charity when what you really want to do is take that money and buy clothes. The odds are that's what you're going to do anyway, so you need to plan on it.

Do you know your own risk tolerance? If you can't sleep because half of your money is sitting in the stock market, even if that's the most appropriate vehicle for it, investing in equities still might not be the best thing for you. For many people, knowing that their money is subject to the variable nature of the markets makes them too nervous to be good investors. We had many clients who started sweating when the markets went south in 2000. Some called us and asked if they should sell. We explained our long-term theory of investment. Some of them still wanted to sell everything, and we accommodated those wishes. It now seems that selling all your stocks might have been a very good decision, because the markets are down 40 percent from their highs. But clients who sold and realized capital gains had to pay a tax of 20+ percent and since it's hard to know when the markets will rise again and much of the forward momentum comes at the beginning of those upward swings, those clients may well be giving up potential gains. They may sleep better, but over the long term they will miss the rewards of investing in equities.

If you know you're not going to be able to stand the downswings of certain investments, you should be prepared to forego the wild upswings as well. There's nothing wrong with a conservative portfolio if it's what makes sense for you, both economically and psychologically. And you know what to expect from it, based on your investment plan.

U.S. Trust once had another client who received a $10 million divorce settlement in the late 1980s. She was very risk averse, and she put most of her money in bonds. Every time her stocks rose to represent more than a quarter of the value of her portfolio, she requested that we rebalance it by selling the remainder, and buying still more bonds. This required a great deal of work, because in the 1990s stocks kept rising and rising, and that meant we had to keep selling and selling. But even when faced with the possible earnings she could have enjoyed had she been more invested in stocks, she was happy. As she pointed out, she never had a year in which she lost money. That was all she needed to be content as an investor because, as she also pointed out, she already had more money than she needed—this was a relatively frugal woman who lived on $100,000 a year.

Be Willing to Let Go

Often, people who have created their own wealth have accomplished it through concentration. They owned a business, they drilled an oil well, or they held valuable stock options in their company. Their money has been based in one place, and they tend to have a large degree of control over it (that is, as much as anyone can).

One of the challenges for people who are business sellers, or those who have cashed out of valuable stock options, is listening to others tell them they should diversify. "Why should I?" they ask. "My wealth has been built up because I concentrated everything on one bet. It worked. Why change?" These people can feel very vulnerable when they surrender their assets to an advisor, who then surrenders the money to a number of different markets. They feel as though they have lost control. They can no longer make changes every minute, and they no longer have the power to control the direction of their assets.

One U.S. Trust client, Larry, started a business and ran it successfully for 30 years. Larry was a remarkably intelligent and resolute man, and he was used to telling people what to do. He came to us after he sold his business; he suddenly possessed a great deal of money, but no particular desire to spend the rest of his life managing it. He wanted to travel and sail, which was his new hobby.

Larry seemed to feel comfortable with us and he liked our investment philosophy. But the moment we began managing his money, we started getting phone calls. "What's my account doing today?" he would ask. "Is there anything I can do about it?" Any time the markets were down, Larry would call to fret that perhaps we should move his asset allocation toward bonds. When the markets went up, he worried that we weren't heavily enough into stocks. In his portfolio were 25 stocks, and if 24 went up, he wanted to know why we had ever invested in the twenty-fifth, and what we were going to do about it. Eventually, Larry did relax a little; he realized that if he was going to enjoy his retirement, spending it talking to us all day wasn't the key. But it took a while.

Letting go of control can take a while. But when you chose a good advisor, try to trust that advisor. Give that person time. You can't control the markets. You may not be able to control your emotions. But you can do well by letting go and diversifying out of the one thing you used to control.

U.S. Trust had another client, Vanessa, whose portfolio was heavily weighted toward stocks, and within that asset class, her holdings were mainly in General Electric (GE). Her grandfather had given her 15,000 shares of GE many years earlier and told her to hang on to it forever. When we started working with her, Vanessa refused to rebalance her portfolio. She felt that holding on to GE was the only right thing to do. Finally, after years of trying, we were able to convince her to let go enough to trust us and allow us to diversify her position. Luckily, we instituted this change in 1999, and when GE, like many other excellent stocks, soon lost more than half of its value, Vanessa thought we were geniuses. We weren't—we were simply holding true to the age old philosophy of diversification. We have had many similar experiences with clients over the years. Selling your favorite stock or your grandfather's favorite stock is difficult, but sometimes you have to do it.

Not everyone lets go so easily. We had yet another client who, in the early 1990s, decided that the world was going to hell, and that he would invest only in Treasury bills. We tried to make him change his mind, but he wouldn't. What we were able to do was get him to take the income from the treasuries and invest that, since to him it was free money. And because the bills were such a large part of his portfolio and we were buying stocks at early 1990s prices, eventually equities did become a large part of his portfolio—much larger than he had intended. So we arrived at our objective of diversifying in a manner that the client could live with. This is an example of "mental accounting," artificially segregating money into separate accounts purely for personal and psychological reasons.

Think Contrarian

Often the market coalesces around one particular investing idea, and you find that nearly everyone seems to be giving the same advice, touting the same stocks, or predicting the same future. The consensus isn't always wrong, but its very existence is a warning sign when the consensus gels into dogma. There's a reason why this consensus has occurred, usually because the arguments for it are so convincing. But too often, it's exactly such arguments that turn out to be wrong.

For example, in 1980, almost everyone predicted that the price of oil was going to rise to $100 a barrel. Books were written about the upcoming increase, analysts were in near accord, and stock brokers were all in agreement. It made sense—the world was running out of oil, and the price at the time, which was about $30 to $40 a barrel, seemed low. This was highly logical, fact-based conjecture. It simply turned out to be wrong. Oil didn't go to $100 a barrel—in fact, the price dropped below $30.

The problem with consensus is that it doesn't tend to gel until nearly everyone agrees with it. So in this case, everything was already priced under the assumption that the price increase would happen. When that phenomenon occurs, it's usually far too late to make a profit. Even if the price of oil had gone up $100, you still would have gotten only a paltry return on your investment because the oil stocks were already priced to assume this result. But if the price didn't go to $100, you stood to lose a lot of money—which is what happened to most people who jumped into oil stocks at the time. Indeed, oil stocks became too popular; their prices rose for a short time, and these stocks came to represent 35 percent of the S&P (Standard and Poor's) 500. Within five years, they were 5 percent.

It's said that history repeats itself. As we all know, the consensus in the late 1990s was that technology stocks could do no wrong. Everyone asked, "Why not invest in the future?" And so everyone did. And at the top of this boom, technology also rose to become 35 percent of the S&P 500. However, once the consensus had been achieved, everyone who was going to invest in these stocks already had, and the stocks couldn't go any higher. In fact, they dropped much lower. Today these stocks represent just 15 percent of the S&P 500. It's not that the consensus is always wrong. It's just that assets are already priced to accommodate it, so you have to be careful.

We have done very well by looking for financial vehicles that other people haven't liked, and picking them at a time when they were depressed. Like everything else we tell you, this isn't set in stone. For example, if you had bought Cisco stock in the early 1990s for $5 a share, and it rose to $100, becoming one of the world's most popular stocks, it wouldn't have been necessary to sell all of your shares. But peeling back on your holdings would have been an excellent idea. One of our better-selling disciplines at U.S. Trust is that when our successful investing idea results in one stock becoming a large part of someone's portfolio, we sell some. And in its place, we don't buy another stock like Cisco, but something different. This is where diversification kicks in again. The more diversified your portfolio, the less likely it is that you'll have to worry about the effects of consensus.

Which brings us to a related issue: *Don't fall in love with a stock.* There are times when you must sell a stock, even when you can't articulate a reason. Without meaning to pick on Cisco, we'll use it again because it's an excellent example to make the point. It is a good company, and in the late 1990s every single analyst seemed to agree on this fact, such that its excellence was already embedded in its price. If you had bought stock in it based on comments praising Cisco when it was selling at $85 a share, you would have seen it rise somewhat, but because everyone was already in agreement about that stock, you ultimately stood to lose more money than you'd win.

Even with Cisco, things could have turned out differently; perhaps their engineers could have come up with another ground breaking application, and the bubble would have continued. But if you had bought Cisco at $100 and it went on to grow earnings by 30 percent the following year, you would have made perhaps 10 to 20 percent, but you also might have lost 80 percent.

Be Patient

For centuries sages have taught that patience is a virtue. It's no different with investing. Many people, when they first invest in a stock, expect the stock to rise immediately. If it doesn't, they doubt their investment. But the true value of a company isn't always accurately reflected in its marketplace each day. The market is just that, a market, composed of a multitude of varying interests: people selling stocks because they need to raise cash, people buying stocks because they think the stock is worth more, other people selling stock because they think it is worth less, and/or people who are buying or selling because they think the economy in general is going down.

For example, today Microsoft's stock is selling at half the price it garnered two years ago. Does that mean it's worth half as much? Maybe, or maybe not. We only can try to predict what a company's earning growth may be and what valuation the market will put on that growth rate at any point in time. Where will interest rates be? Will there be inflation? There's no way to know. But with financial investments, people become impatient to know their precise worth at every moment. Do you reprice your home every day, or your artwork, or your jewelry? No, although in today's world it is tempting. But stocks are repriced constantly. That price can be influenced by a series of factors, not always reflecting the true value of the company or the franchise.

So be patient. If you believe Microsoft is a great company, don't sell it because it's dipped. Maybe the market doesn't agree with you right now, but maybe it does and there are other factors that are keeping Microsoft down, such as a general displeasure with technology stocks in general, or a fear that the economy is doing poorly.

FIGURE 2.5   HAZARDS OF MARKET TIMING

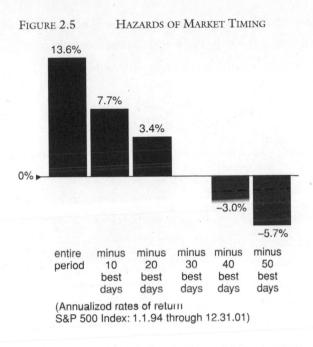

(Annualized rates of return
S&P 500 Index: 1.1.94 through 12.31.01)

As previously mentioned, some people believe in something called market timing, which nearly everyone seems convinced at one point or another that they can master (see Figure 2.5). Nearly everyone is wrong. It's tempting to think that you can predict when the market is going to go up or down. It's tempting to want to buy something the moment you hear good news about it, or sell something because you hear bad news. But no one really knows exactly when the markets are going to rise and fall. Yes, there were many people who predicted the market was going to go down in 2000, and they sold their stocks. But does that mean they know when to get back in?

Over the past century, the markets have often rebounded substantially before people began reinvesting their money. In October 1987 the market crashed 35 percent; many people claimed that they had sold everything just before. But how many of them also knew that within 18 months the market would have rebounded to higher levels? Every day of the week you can read expert predictions about the stock market. Some of these people predict the market will be going up, others promise it will be flat, and still others swear it will be down. Timing the market is a difficult, nearly impossible task.

Investing and Taxes

The relationship between investing and taxes is often overlooked by investors when planning their investment strategy (see Figure 2.6). It isn't just the rate of return that's important, but the rate of return after taxes—what you get to keep. (For more detailed information on this subject, see Chapter 3.)

Studies from the Securities and Exchange Commission, the government organization that monitors the markets, show that taxes can take 5.6 percent off the annual return of the least tax efficiently managed portfolios. On average, taxes reduce equity returns by about 2.5 percent a year. In 2000, investors paid more than $100 billion in capital gains taxes alone. Now 2.5 percent per year doesn't seem like much, but on an initial portfolio of $5 million, 2.5 percent over 10 years equals almost $1.5 million. The recently enacted tax act will modestly reduce the cost of taxes.

Any good investment advisor will also be a tax-intelligent investor. That doesn't mean that tax decisions drive investment decisions. Investment decisions should be made in light of investment objectives. But for most people, their main objective is to achieve the maximum return possible relative to the degree of risk on an after-tax basis. This means that you should know what the IRS permits and what it doesn't permit in terms of investments. You should be aware of when it is best to sell your holdings and the tax implications of doing so. Investing in various sectors through a number of "best in class" managers almost always means that you will be trading off tax management for hopefully superior performance even after taxes.

FIGURE 2.6   THE SUPERIOR PERFORMANCE OF EQUITIES

ANNUALIZED TOTAL RETURN AND THE EFFECT OF TAXES AND INFLATION
(1926–2001)

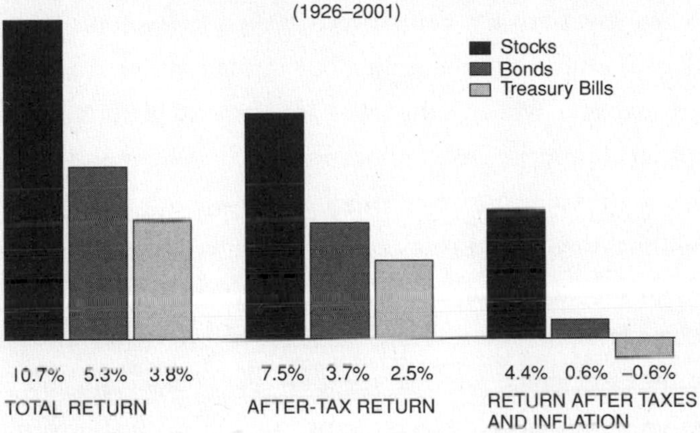

■ Stocks
■ Bonds
□ Treasury Bills

| 10.7% | 5.3% | 3.8% | 7.5% | 3.7% | 2.5% | 4.4% | 0.6% | −0.6% |

TOTAL RETURN   AFTER-TAX RETURN   RETURN AFTER TAXES
AND INFLATION

Assumptions:
Income Tax Rate: 39%
Capital Gains Tax Rate: 20%
Fees and Transaction Costs: 0.90%
Gains realized every 5 years
CPI Actual: 3.1% year

Source: Calculated by U.S.
Trust using data presented
in Stocks, Bonds, Bills and
Inflation® 2001 Yearbook,
©2001 Ibbotson Associates,
Inc. Based on copyrighted
works by Ibbotson and
Sinquefield. All rights
reserved. Used with
permission.

Investment Advisors

How Many Do You Need?

One relatively new question that intelligent investors must consider:
How many advisors are right for you? For most of the last century,
people usually worked with one investment advisor, who constructed
a portfolio that was designed specifically for them. But as investing
has grown more complicated, places like U.S. Trust have introduced
a system whereby specialized experts manage different segments of a
given portfolio to provide even more diversification and specializa-
tion. After all, can one investment firm be competent across all of
the investment sectors required of a well-diversified investment portfolio? The answer is probably no. Therefore, a new approach called *open
architecture* has emerged.

Open architecture allows an investor to enjoy the efficiency of dealing with one firm while enjoying the benefit of working with specialty managers. In this system, investors do not develop a relationship with all of the portfolio managers, but instead are serviced by a relationship manager whose skill set is investment planning; he or she develops an appropriate asset allocation for the client and then selects proprietary or nonproprietary products to fill the client's portfolio. Open architecture also allows clients to achieve greater diversification by having a choice of many more vehicles than they might ordinarily have. Over time, the relationship manager will rebalance the portfolio to keep the asset allocation in line with the financial plan, and will also review the performance of each sector to monitor the performance of the individual sector managers.

Based on the quantity of assets being invested, sector management can be accomplished via mutual funds or separately managed accounts. Clients receive similar performance with either vehicle, so the decision of which will be used is generally driven by expenses, along with certain tax considerations. Additional costs are usually associated with this new approach of sector management versus the traditional approach. Fees are generally higher because each segment manager charges an individual set of fees that don't take into account the size of an entire relationship. In addition, sector management can also be less tax-efficient, as the various managers may not communicate with each other vis-à-vis your tax needs, whereas with customized management, your portfolio manager will know your gain and loss situation well. Many new firms do not offer classic portfolio management services, but provide investment planning and help you select managers to meet your needs. These firms charge based on the assets they supervise.

Balance

Overall, the key to a good investment program is balance. A stock, a bond, a hedge fund, or real estate—each has unique investment characteristics. Each has seen a different rate of return over long periods of time, and each has a different impact on your overall portfolio if it goes up or down. It would be nice if we could predict exactly which of these vehicles are going to perform the best over the next decade and then simply place all of our money into it, make a fortune, and then shift the money elsewhere when we know another vehicle is going to rise.

Unfortunately, no one can do that. Still, over a long period of time, we think good advisors can achieve an excellent balance of all the possible investment vehicles. If your advisor can give you a good long-term return above the rate of inflation and can reduce the discomfort you experience on an interim basis, he or she has done you a great service. Although there will always be something working for you and something working against you in your portfolio, on average you will have smooth returns rather than big up-and-down spikes in the value of your portfolio and in the lining of your stomach.

Thus, you should beware of advisors who say they were number 1 on some list last year. The odds are excellent they will not be number 1 again this year, and you missed their great year. Frankly, we feel that anyone who can be above average year after year is an excellent advisor. Certainly, when you were in school no one urged you to be slightly above average, but think about it: If each year your advisor is able to beat the S&P 500 Index, that means that over the long term, you have found yourself an excellent advisor, because he or she has been able to do something that few people can—give you a steady return on your investment. Huge bets won't get you there. Balance will.

Active versus Passive Managers

When seeking an advisor, you probably will hear about both active and passive managers. If they are doing their job well, active managers apply disciplined analysis to find value in individual companies, sectors, or markets that other investors haven't spotted yet. Their goal is to outperform the market through solid strategies, research, and analysis. Active managers continually monitor the performance of the companies whose shares they own and even communicate with their management.

Unfortunately, statistics reveal that most active managers do no better than the performance of standard market indexes such as the S&P 500. When you take into account the fees paid to active managers, the disparity between their performance and the index grows more obvious. As a result, a new segment of the investment management industry became popular: managers who invest passively. Passive managers view stocks as commodities. Their goal is to replicate the performance of the market, and they purchase "market baskets" of stocks selected to reflect the composition of the market, such as those in the S&P 500 Index. Passive managers argue that it is impossible to outperform the market, so one might as well just own the market. Active managers generally charge fees relative to the size of the account; they may range from 0.5 to 1.5 percent. Passive managers generally charge fees of between 0.1 and 0.25 percent.

Certain risks are unique to passive investing. During the TMT bubble, investors in passively managed S&P funds suffered when those funds increased their holdings in TMT to 45 percent to match the indexes' exposure, and the index suffered when that bubble burst. Some individual managers invested in large-cap funds actually did much better than the S&P. Passive management is not always tax-efficient; however, passive management techniques have been refined to ensure more tax efficiency than in the past especially in separately managed passive accounts.

Whether to invest with active or passive managers is a debate that will continue. Many investors have determined that there is a place in their portfolio for both active and passive management.

Types of Investments
and Investment Terminology

Equities

Stocks, or equities, are sold through the stock market. When you buy common stock in a company, no matter how small your purchase, you are essentially buying an ownership position in it; together, all the stockholders own that company.

Return refers to how much money you make back on your investment. If you buy a stock for $10,000 and sell it for $15,000, your return is $5,000, or 50 percent.

Price/earnings (P/E) *ratio* is a common formula with which to judge a stock's value. It stands for the relationship between the stock's price and the company's earnings for the last four quarters. To determine the P/E ratio, you divide the company share price by the earnings per share. If a company has a P/E of 15, it means that its price is 15 times its annual per-share earnings.

Stock splits take place when a company decides that the price of its stock is too high, and it then splits, or divides the stock, usually in two (if you owned 100 shares before the split, you would own 200 after); sometimes companies decide to split the stock in thirds, or in fractions. Companies can also establish a reverse split when they think their share price is too low. In that case, if you owned 100 shares before the split, you would own only 50.

Dividends are paid to stockholders out of the company's profits. Not all stocks pay dividends, which tend to be small and are given out completely at the discretion of the company. This means that the dividends may well grow or disappear from year to year.

Large-capitalization and *small-capitalization* refer to the value these stocks possess, determined by multiplying the number of shares offered by the current market price of a single share. Large-cap stocks are those calculated at more than $3 billion of outstanding market value, and small-cap stocks are those whose value is less than $1.5 billion. In between, not surprisingly, are stocks known as mid-caps. Another category is micro-caps whose value is less than $100 million.

Growth companies are those that have shown faster-than-average gains in earnings over the past few years, which, it is hoped, will continue to grow at an above-average rate.

Value companies are those that haven't been doing as well as others in recent years, yet are considered to have value because they are inexpensive relative to their assets and are, it is hoped, ready to turn around and improve their profitability and growth rates (see Figure 2.7)

Blue chip stocks are those that have historically done very well compared to the rest of the market, are well managed, and enjoy an excellent reputation.

FIGURE 2.7   PERFORMANCE OF GROWTH AND VALUE STRATEGIES OVER THE LONG TERM

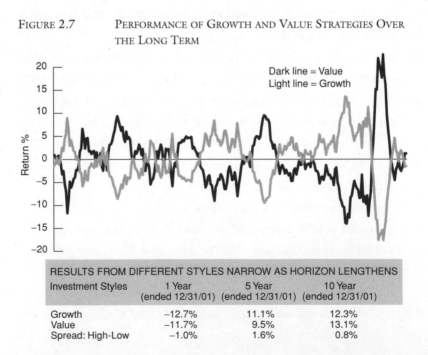

RESULTS FROM DIFFERENT STYLES NARROW AS HORIZON LENGTHENS			
Investment Styles	1 Year (ended 12/31/01)	5 Year (ended 12/31/01)	10 Year (ended 12/31/01)
Growth	−12.7%	11.1%	12.3%
Value	−11.7%	9.5%	13.1%
Spread: High-Low	−1.0%	1.6%	0.8%

Preferred stock has traits of both stocks and bonds. Like bonds, pre-ferred stocks pay dividends, and they can rise (or fall) like stocks. The downside is that the dividend doesn't rise even if the company's profits do, and the share price doesn't move up as quickly as its common stock.

Defensive stocks are those of utilities, health care providers, food companies, and other businesses that are considered less prone to mar-ket slides because the demand for their products continues even dur-ing lean times. The opposites of defensive stocks are *cyclical stocks*, such as airline or mining stocks, which can do very well when times are flush but perform poorly when the economy is shrinking.

Selling short is a strategy used when you think a certain company's stock price is going to fall. Essentially, you borrow the shares from your broker, sell them, and wait for the stock to fall. If and when it does, you then buy the stock at its new lower price, and repay your bro-ker the original amount. For instance, say you sell 100 shares of XYZ stock short at $50. When the price drops to $25, you buy 100 shares at $25, give them to your broker, and keep the $25 per share difference as profit (although you will have to pay a commission). However, if you are wrong and the stock doubles, you would lose your money.

Buying on margin means that you borrow money from your broker to finance a portion of the stock you are buying. If you want to buy $10,000 worth of stock, but only want to spend $5,000, the broker will put up the other $5,000. If the stock then goes up to $15,000 and you sell it, you must pay back your broker the $5,000, but you have earned a 100 percent profit. However, if the stock goes down, you, not the broker, absorb all the losses.

Real estate investment trusts (REITs), are a way of investing in real estate without actually buying real estate. Instead, you buy stock in a company that owns property, and the price of your stock goes up or down depending on the performance of the company (and there-fore the real estate market). There are many kinds of REITs, but the most common are equity REITs; also available are mortgage REITs, which invest in real estate loans, and blind REITs, which don't disclose their property holdings.

Bonds

Although most people who know a little about investing are aware of stocks, bonds are much less understood (see Figure 2.8). Bonds, or fixed-income securities, are an important component of any investment portfolio. With the exception of what are known as zero-coupon bonds, bonds provide a steady income stream, preserve principal, and add balance to your portfolio by reducing risk and volatility.

A *bond* is a loan to a company, state, municipality, or government. You are repaid interest and principal. Most bonds pay a fixed dollar amount of interest at regular intervals (usually every six months) until maturity. At maturity, principal (face value) is repaid.

Bonds involve two major risks: interest rate risk and credit risk. *Interest rate risk* is the risk that rising interest rates will lower the price of bonds. If you buy and hold a bond with a 5 percent interest rate and interest rates go up by 1 percent a year for two years, up to 20 percent of the value of your bond may erode. If you hold the bond to maturity, you will not lose any principal, but the yield you receive in the interim will be below market rates. Most bond managers manage interest rate risk by structuring a portfolio with bonds of "staggered" or "laddered" maturities.

Credit risk is the risk that the issuer of your bond will not be able to pay back your principal or pay interest. Most bond managers will select only high-quality bonds to minimize credit risk. They will need to have a research function to measure credit risk, because credit risk is a real risk even in municipal bond portfolios. For example, in the 1970s, investors in New York City bonds were painfully reminded about credit risk when their bonds were restructured. The city's fiscal

FIGURE 2.8   THE ROLE OF BONDS IN A PORTFOLIO

The short-term risk in bonds is rising interest rates, which
depress bond prices—particularly at long maturities...

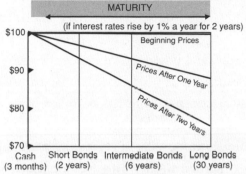

MATURITY

(if interest rates rise by 1% a year for 2 years)

$100

Beginning Prices

$90

Prices After One Year

$80

Prices After Two Years

$70

Cash   Short Bonds   Intermediate Bonds   Long Bonds
(3 months)   (2 years)   (6 years)   (30 years)

* Assumes beginning yields at 5% for three-month bills, 6.5% for two-year bonds, 7% for
  six-year bonds and 7.5% for 30-year bonds, with rates rising equally at all maturities.

... but if you're investing for just a year, fixed-income securities
are more secure than stocks.

RANGE OF ONE-YEAR RETURNS (1960–2001)

Worst Year   Best Year

−26.5%   U.S. Stocks   37.4%

−23.2%   Foreign Stocks   69.9%

−31.8%   Emerging Market Stocks   71.3%

−5.1%   Intermed. Bonds   29.1%

2.1%   T-Bills   14.7%

0.7%   Inflation   13.3%

Throughout this text, U.S. stocks are represented by the Standard & Poor's 500-stock Index—500
of the largest stocks, as measured by market value, of the 9,000 traded in the U.S. The S&P 500
is often used as a proxy for the U.S. stock market. Foreign stocks from the developed markets are
represented by the Morgan Stanley Capital International (MSCI, EAFE, Europe, Australia, and
the Far East) Index of major overseas stock markets, with countries weighted in proportion to
their gross domestic products. Foreign stocks from the emerging markets are represented by
the International Finance Corporation of the World Bank Global Index (IFC) from 1985 to 1987
and by the MSCI Emerging Markets Free Index from 1988 to 1995. Intermediate bonds are
represented by Treasuries with an approximate maturity of five years. "Return" refers to total
return: interest and/or dividends plus or minus price change (capital appreciation or depreciation).

Source: Calculated by U.S. Trust using data presented in *Stocks, Bonds, Bills and Inflation®
2001 Yearbook,* ©2001 Ibbotson Associates, Inc. Based on copyrighted works by Ibbotson and
Sinquefield. All rights reserved. Used with permission. International Finance Corp. (for emerging
markets, 1985–87), Morgan Stanley Capital International (for developed foreign markets, 1970–99
and emerging markets, 1988–99) and Standard & Poor's Corp.

crisis prompted it to renegotiate the terms of its debt arrangements, and bondholders were left with pennies on the dollar. Had the city defaulted on its debt, bondholders would have ended up with nothing. Investors in Orange County, California, bonds endured a similar situation in the 1990s.

Generally speaking, individual investors will place the majority of their fixed-income investments in tax-free or municipal bonds. Municipal bonds generally are exempt from federal income tax and also from state income tax for residents of the state in which they were issued. Because they are free from tax, the after-tax yields are quite impressive. Almost all investment firms now offer fixed-income vehicles to accommodate individual investors.

Size is very important in municipal bond investing. Unless your portfolio warrants investing several million dollars in bonds, you will be better off investing in bond funds, which enjoy the benefit of size when investing in the often inefficient municipal bond market.

Most individual clients have assets invested in tax-deferred vehicles such as a 401(k) plan. Fixed-income securities within those plans are usually invested in taxable bonds, most likely government-backed bonds or corporate bonds. Bonds backed by the federal government do not have credit risk, only interest rate risk. Corporate bonds involve a great deal of credit risk and also interest rate risk.

A *coupon* is the annual interest paid on a debt security, usually stated in terms of the rate paid on a bond's face value. The coupon is set at the time a security is issued. Coupon rates usually vary with maturity (the longer the maturity, the higher the rate) and with the issuer's creditworthiness at the time of issuance (the higher the quality, the lower the rate).

Total return consists of the bond's income as well as the appreciation or depreciation of its price. *Market risk* reflects the potential fluctuation in value a bond can experience when interest rates rise or fall after the purchase of a fixed-income security. If rates rise, the bond's price will decline so that its current yield reflects the new, higher rates. Conversely, if rates decline, the bond's price will rise. Lower-quality bonds generally offer higher yields than better-quality issues, but also may be more volatile. The higher yield compensates the investor for lending money to an issuer that is considered more likely to default, that is, not make timely interest or principal payments.

Types of Bonds

There are literally millions of bond issues in the United States alone. These fixed-income securities are defined by several characteristics:

- *Issuer:* U.S. Treasury, U.S. government agency, corporation, or state or local government
- Maturity: From 1 day to 30 years or more
- Credit quality: From high-quality U.S. Treasury securities to junk bonds
- Structure: Notes, debentures, or mortgage-backed or asset-backed securities

Treasuries are debt obligations of the U.S. government secured by its full faith and credit and issued at various schedules and maturities. The U.S. Treasury issues three types of debt: bills (with a maturity of less than one year), notes (2 to 10 years), and bonds (more than 10 years). Interest from U.S. Treasuries is federally taxable but exempt from state and local taxes.

Mortgage-backed securities are usually issued and/or guaranteed by a U.S. government–sponsored agency. The Government National Mortgage Association (Ginnie Mae) is backed by the full faith and credit of the U.S. government. The Federal National Mortgage Association (Fannie Mae) and the Federal Home Loan Mortgage Corporation (Freddie Mac) are chartered by Congress, but are owned by stockholders. These agencies buy qualified mortgage loans or guarantee pools of such loans owned by financial institutions. The loans are then securitized and distributed through financial institutions. Unlike most bonds, mortgages usually amortize principal over all or part of the bond's life, instead of paying it all at maturity.

Corporate bonds represent debt issued by corporations (financial, industrial, or service-related). Companies use the funds they raise from selling bonds for a variety of purposes, such as building facilities or purchasing equipment. Corporate bonds are subject to federal and state taxes.

Municipal bonds are debt issued by states, municipalities, and other government divisions to improve or build infrastructure, hospitals, schools, etc. The issuance of bonds allows local governments to borrow money to finance their capital expenditures. Municipal bonds are generally exempt from federal income taxes and income tax in the state from which they are issued (but they may be subject to the Alternative Minimum Tax).

Taxable bonds and *tax-exempt bonds* provide a steady income stream to an investor. The interest income can be either taxable or tax-exempt, (see Figure 2.9.) A taxable bond is a general obligation whose interest is subject to federal and/or state and local income tax. Examples include corporate bonds, U.S. Treasury bonds, money market funds, and bond unit investments trusts. A tax-exempt bond is a bond that is not subject to these taxes.

Deciding between taxable and tax-exempt bonds should take into account the investor's income tax bracket and the difference in the earnings between a taxable versus a tax-exempt bond. An investor in a high tax bracket may want to consider buying tax-exempt bonds as a way of receiving a higher income stream, whereas an investor in a lower tax bracket may consider a taxable bond. Another consideration with tax-exempt bonds is that you will need to account for any capital gains or losses if the bonds are sold prior to maturity.

FIGURE 2.9 FIXED-INCOME COMPARATIVE YIELDS (*as of May 12, 2003*)

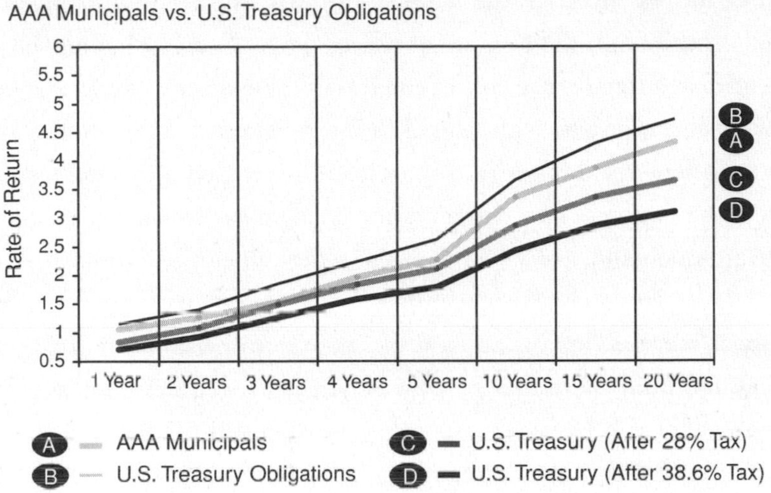
AAA Municipals vs. U.S. Treasury Obligations
Rate of Return
6
5.5
5
4.5
4
3.5
3
2.5
2
1.5
1
0.5
1 Year
2 Years
3 Years
4 Years
5 Years
10 Years
15 Years
20 Years
B
A
C
D
A AAA Municipals
B U.S. Treasury Obligations
C U.S. Treasury (After 28% Tax)
D U.S. Treasury (After 38.6% Tax)

Zero-coupon bonds are bonds sold at a deep discount; you don't collect interest, but instead get to buy the bond at a lower price than it will have when it matures (or comes due).

Mutual Funds

By buying mutual funds, you can invest your money without having to become an expert at picking individual securities. You and other investors are, in effect, pooling your money, and the fund's manager then makes the actual selection of stocks, bonds, or anything else appropriate for the portfolio. This way, $10,000 can be invested in a fund that may own stock in up to a hundred companies or more, instead of sitting in just one or two stocks or bonds. A multitude of funds are available to invest in, from large-cap to small-cap, from international to those focused on a specific sector (such as technology or health), from gold to silver, from bond funds to index funds (which track the performance of an index the mutual fund chooses to follow).

Open-end funds sell as many shares as investors want to buy. The more money invested, the more shares exist in the fund; if investors sell off the fund, the number of shares drops. You can buy or sell the fund depending on the cost of the fund's value on the day you want to do business, just as with a stock. *Closed-end* funds raise money only once, offer a fixed number of shares, and are traded on an exchange or over the counter. The market price goes up or down depending on investor demand, as well as changes in the value of its holdings.

Load funds charge a commission to invest in them; when you buy a *front-end* load fund, you pay your commission when you buy the fund (and there may be other charges as well). A *back-end* fund means that you pay when you sell your shares in the fund. A *no-load* fund is usually bought directly from the fund company itself, which charges no commissions (although that doesn't mean there won't be some other charges; management fees are charged on an ongoing basis, so make sure to ask). A *level load* means that the fee is deducted regularly from the value of your shares. Loads can run anywhere from 0.75 percent all the way up to 7.5 percent or more, so you should ask ahead of time.

Nontraditional Asset Classes

These assets include venture capital, private equity, real estate, and (more recently) hedge funds. A properly diversified portfolio will include representation from all of these sectors. Most of these asset classes involve more risk and higher returns. Their performance is not correlated to the general equity markets. Nontraditional assets should represent a meaningful (10 to 30 percent) allocation in your portfolio depending on your time horizon and risk parameters. As specialty investment classes, they are usually handled by specialty managers with whom you invest directly.

It is prudent to have more than one manager for each class, and in certain sectors, such as hedge funds, investing with up to a dozen or more managers may make sense. Because these managers require large minimum investments, only the very affluent can afford to invest directly with them. Therefore, a new kind of management vehicle has emerged called *the fund of funds*. This vehicle allows investors to invest in as many as 10 to 40 hedge funds (or venture capital funds or buyout funds) by investing in one commingled fund. The manager of the commingled fund is responsible for identifying the underlying managers and constructing a portfolio of those managers that makes sense. Funds of funds offer a compelling way for an individual to invest in nontraditional asset classes.

Hedge Fund Investing

Most equity managers invest by buying shares of stock in firms they believe represent a good value. Such managers are referred to as *long-only managers*. Some managers also identify securities that they believe are overvalued and sell shares of stock in those companies. Those managers are said to *short the stock*.

The short-selling process has many rules, but as mentioned earlier, the basic procedure is that the manager borrows the stock from a broker and sells it. The manager will repay the stock at some point in the future, presumably when the market has fallen and the stock can be repurchased at a cheaper price.

This process does have risks. To compensate, the manager will often "hedge" the short investment by buying the stock of a similar company the manager believes is also undervalued. By buying stocks in pairs, the manager mitigates risk, because if the entire sector to which the stock belongs, say pharmaceuticals, does well, the two positions will offset each another. While in the above example these stocks are in the same sector, not all managers hedge in pairs, which makes for a much riskier strategy. Hedging is a labor-intensive process and is often tax-inefficient for the individual investor. However, the best hedge managers have produced impressive risk-adjusted returns over time. This profitability means that for many, investing in hedge funds makes sense.

Within hedge funds, there is a wide variety of choices: hedged long short funds, hedged sector funds, opportunistic long short funds, arbitrage funds, and distressed funds. Hedge fund managers almost always use debt (or "leverage") to enhance the returns on their funds. This maneuver, of course, increases risk.

On occasion, hedge funds do "blow up." This happened to the fixed-income hedge fund Long Term Capital Management and cost individual and institutional investors billions of dollars. And in January 2003, Eifuku Master Fund, a $300 million hedge fund in Japan, disappeared in seven trading days. Because of events like these, investing in a variety of different hedge funds makes sense for most investors, as does investing through a fund of funds.

Investing and Business Owners

U.S. Trust Survey of Affluent Americans Results

A significant portion of the top 1 percent of all affluent Americans are business owners. In some respects, these people are quite similar to the other affluent Americans U.S. Trust studied, but there are some important differences.

Like the other respondents, most business owners did not inherit their wealth (and only 10 percent inherited their business). Eighty-nine percent described their background as poor, lower class, or middle class, and said they had begun working in a job such as delivering papers or babysitting as early as 10 years old. Not quite half attended college (46 percent), but 74 percent of those who did financed at least part of their education through a full- or part-time job.

The average age at which business owners held their first full-time job was 18. Just over half (54 percent) were corporate employees before ever owning a business, and 14 percent were involved in a failed business at some point. Although business owners decided to set up their own shop for many reasons, the most common cited were to make more money and to have more independence. The most common types of businesses involved real estate, produce and perishables, and construction, trucking, and machinery. Fifty-eight percent claimed average annual sales of between $6 and $10 million, another 29 percent had sales of $10 to $20 million, and 5 percent achieved sales of more than $40 million.

According to these business owners, the two major factors to which they attributed their success were a willingness to work hard (mentioned by 95 percent) and a willingness to take a risk (mentioned by 82 percent). Their greatest sacrifices were vacations (cited by 56 percent) and time to relax (55 percent). They stated that the most frustrating parts of their jobs were government-required paperwork (cited by 97 percent), taxes on business, obtaining raw materials, final products, or services (95 percent), and environmental regulations (82 percent).

Among those who ran a family business, the greatest sources of conflict were reluctance to turn the reins over to the younger generation (66 percent), disagreement among children involved in the business over business decisions (63 percent), children's belief that their siblings in the business were paid more than they are worth (60 percent), and disagreement between parents and children over how to run the business (59 percent).

Of married business owners, only 37 percent stated that their spouse was active in the company's management. Of those with kids, 39 percent said their children were active. Finally, 54 percent intended to pass ownership of the business to their children, 27 percent intended to pass it to a relative other than their children, 17 percent wanted to sell it to someone unrelated, 5 percent expected to dissolve the business, 4 percent wanted to pass ownership to their employees, and 10 percent hadn't yet given succession any thought.

Advice for Business Owners

Our experience at U.S. Trust has shown that one of the primary distinctions between those who own businesses and those who don't is that the business owners generally prefer that their finances unrelated to the business provide them with as much security as possible. They've taken so many risks to launch their own shop that they tend to be conservative with whatever extra money they possess. In practice, this means they prefer an asset allocation heavily weighted toward fixed-income securities, and they share a general skepticism about the stock market. "If I'm going to take risks," they say, "it will be in my business. Anything outside of my business will be secure."

For many of these people, their primary stock market experiences involve investments based on cocktail party and country club tips. Typically, they met someone on the golf course who recommended the XYZ company, and they bought the company's stock through a broker who's also a member of their club. Then, more often than not, the investments failed to perform. Thus, because they were basing their investments on informal advice rather than the expertise of a professional money manager, their stock market experience taught them that it's a gamble, and a bad one at that.

I know the CEO of a privately held financial concern whose company was one of the most successful entrepreneurial start-ups of the 1980s. He is worth more than $50 million on paper. He pays himself a handsome yearly salary that handily covers his bills, but ultimately, all his money rests in his own company. He owns no stocks or bonds. If any cash rolls into his life, such as a recent inheritance, he uses it to pay off the mortgages on his homes. He sums up his attitude this way: "As much as possible, I can control what happens to my company. I can't control what happens to any other company. Why should I risk investing in something that I have no control over?" This approach often holds even when business owners sell their business; they still don't want to buy equities or anything else that might put their capital at risk.

My recommendation to these people is to think about establishing some liquidity outside the business. What happens if you make a bad decision? Or if through no fault of your own something goes wrong at your company? That could mean the loss of all your assets, if you have no others. By putting all of your eggs in one basket, you place yourself at greater risk than investors who are willing to use asset allocation to create a diversified portfolio.

Concentrated Stock Positions

One of our clients, Ray, came to us with what we considered to be a fairly wonderful problem. Ray had been working at the same public relations firm for more than 30 years, and he had done very well. Starting as a junior member of a small company, he slowly advanced to a senior position, and when his company was bought by a much larger firm, he stayed on as an executive vice president. That company was then bought by a still larger firm and, defying all odds, Ray was named president of the new combined company. Ray's problem was that, due to generous corporate stock compensation programs, his stock portfolio, which was worth $5 million, was 90 percent concentrated in his own company. Ray was fully aware of the potential risk of having so much of his net worth tied to one company's stock, but he had been reluctant to diversify. He strongly believed in his company and always felt that selling its stock could be construed as a sign of disloyalty. He also was aware that if he did sell, he would have to pay a large capital gains tax.

This is hardly a catastrophic situation, because Ray's stock had helped make him wealthy. But it is a problem nonetheless, and represents a unique type of risk. Ray had become affluent, but if for some reason his company ever faltered, he wasn't going to stay that way. There is an old saying: Concentrate to become rich, and diversify to remain rich. We run into this dilemma fairly frequently; our clients usually face it for reasons similar to Ray's. Overconcentration of stock also occurs in a successful venture capital partnership investment in which someone has been given a great deal of stock in a single company. Sometimes it's caused by someone holding on to a very successful stock for so long that it has grown to occupy a disproportionately large percentage of his or her holdings.

Concentrations also occur when one particular investment proves to be a startling success. At U.S. Trust, many of our clients found themselves faced with this paradox in the 1960s because of the success of the already described Nifty Fifty. For example, many of our clients were early investors in IBM, which at the time performed so well that it soon represented more than 20 percent of many portfolios. Clients were reluctant to sell their IBM stock because they believed in the company and in its past results. Still, we counseled clients to sell at least some of their stock, and fortunately many did—much to their relief when IBM ran into a more difficult business environment in the 1970s and saw its stock languish.

Generally speaking, you must pay attention any time a particular holding represents more than 5 percent of your portfolio. If the holding represents more than 10 percent, it is an area of concern; if it is more than 20 percent, you've entered an area of risk. Yet, according to our surveys, most corporate executives keep more than 30 percent of their net worth tied up in corporate stock, and that is clearly a very strong risk. As we've noted, what happens if harm befalls that one company? Just ask all the dot.com executives who were worth millions of dollars in the late 1990s and now consider themselves lucky if they have any net worth at all.

One of the roles of a good financial planner and/or investment manager is to counsel clients on the risks of overconcentration, and to help them diversify. At U.S. Trust, the first step we take is to quantify the costs and risks associated with clients' existing concentrated low-cost-basis stock positions versus those of a diversified portfolio. The most important options to consider when moving to diversify are discussed in the rest of this chapter. These are not all easy to understand; your best bet is to trust in a professional to do it right.

Diversifying Concentrated Stock Positions

Outright Sale

The easiest and least complicated way to reduce holdings in a single stock is to sell it outright. This can be accomplished immediately and provides instant investment diversification. Such a sale is based on the current price of the stock, the capital gains tax is paid at the time of the sale (which means you give up any tax deferral), and you lose the use of the tax payment in the year of sale.

A slight variation on the outright sale is to sell portions of the stock on a preset schedule. For example, your stock could be sold in equal numbers of shares over a five-year time frame. This strategy affords you many of the benefits associated with dollar cost averaging, and also spreads out the capital gains taxes you must pay. When the desired quantity of stock is sold, you'll have a normal-sized position in that stock.

Sale of Covered Call Options

A call option is a contract between a seller who wishes to sell a stock at a particular price and a buyer who is willing to pay a premium to buy a stock in the future at that price. If the seller currently owns the stock in question, he or she would be selling a covered option. If the seller doesn't own the stock, this is known as a naked option.

By selling a covered call option, you increase your return by generating income—the premium—while waiting for the shares to reach a predetermined target sales price. If the stock reaches the specified price (the strike price), you're required to deliver the shares to the buyer of the option. In addition to being paid a premium, the benefit of this strategy is that you have established the price or prices at which you would like to diversify. If the stock does not reach the call price, the options expire, and you keep the premium and the shares; the process then can be repeated. The disadvantages are that you forego any appreciation beyond the strike price, and you have no downside protection if the stock falls, except to the extent of the call premium received.

From an income tax perspective, no taxable event occurs until the option expires (or is closed out by the seller) or until the underlying stock is delivered (i.e., sold) to the counterparty to settle the contract. If the call option expires unexercised, the seller will recognize a short-term capital gain in the amount of the call premium (less any commissions paid) at the expiration date (not when he or she received the premium). If the contract is closed out or exercised, it will be treated as a capital gain and taxed as such. Timing will depend on whether the contract is treated as part of a straddle for income tax purposes. As you can see, the tax consequences with respect to covered calls are complex; we recommend consulting your tax advisor before you sell under this scenario.

Zero-Premium Equity Collars

The opposite of selling a call option is purchasing a put option. This means you contract to purchase a stock at a particular price (the strike price) and pay the seller a premium for the privilege of exercising the option for a fixed term.

Sometimes we recommend that a client enter into a *zero-cost collar*; here you purchase a put option and sell a call option simultaneously to establish a minimum and maximum value around an equity position until the contracts expire. The cost of the premium paid to purchase the put option is offset by the premium received to sell the call option. By doing this, you ensure the value of your position below the put strike price, and receive future appreciation up to the call strike price—all while maintaining ownership in the shares, including voting rights and dividends.

Under a variation on this theme, you can use the low-cost-basis stock subject to the zero-cost equity collar as collateral for a loan. In turn, the loan proceeds can be used as capital for reinvestment in a diversified program. If the diversified portfolio outperforms the cost of the interest on the loan, you come out ahead and you have diversified your position from a single stock to a diversified portfolio.

From an income tax perspective, this move would let you achieve the protection described while deferring taxability until the contract expires (that is, as long as the contract is structured properly and not deemed abusive by the IRS). In certain circumstances, the contract may be repeated to continue the protection and tax deferral you seek. Generally, each option is treated as an open transaction until the contract is closed out, is settled, or expires. There are a number of ways to settle a transaction, each depending upon the underlying stock's price at the end of the contract as well as your individual tax situation and risk profile. As with covered call options, the tax treatment of zero-premium equity collars is complex; consult with your tax advisor.

Varying Forward Contract

This instrument is a privately negotiated contract that allows you to receive a large portion of your stock value in cash today with an obligation to deliver some or all of the underlying shares at a future date to the counterparty. This type of contract can be structured to come due anywhere from 2 to 10 years, depending upon your investment horizon. In a typical transaction, entering the contract you receive approximately 80 percent of the stock's value (subject to market conditions and the dealer's terms). Taxes on the proceeds are deferred until the contract settlement date, 2 to 10 years from now. The proceeds can then be reinvested at your discretion. At the end of the contract, you must deliver some or all of the shares to the counterparty. If the stock price is lower at the end of the contract than at the beginning, 100 percent of the shares must be delivered. If the stock price is higher, a lower percentage of shares must be delivered. If the stock appreciates by more than 20 percent during the contract period, generally no more than 85 percent of the shares must be delivered.

The benefits of a varying forward contract are that you will receive approximately 80 percent of the stock's value up front without any additional cash repayment obligations. Capital gains taxes will be deferred until the contract settlement date. You'll also retain voting rights and dividends on the shares during the contract period, and, importantly for the purposes of this discussion, you benefit from diversification. Although it's true that if the return on the diversified portfolio does not exceed the return on the underlying stock, you won't have done as well, you will have reduced risk in any case. In addition to the performance of the underlying stock and the cash reinvested during the term of the contract, other key determinants of the success of this strategy are tax-related, and include the effect of state income taxes and the impact of your tax profile, such as charitable contributions, on the various outcomes.

A disadvantage of the varying forward contract is that you will incur a discount to the cash payment up front (for which you obtain the access to the cash up front, downside protection, and tax deferral until the end of the contract), which you can recoup only through investment gains. (As you can see, the tax considerations with regard to varying forward contracts are complex, and once more we suggest you consult with your tax advisor.)

Tax-Efficient Diversification through Indexing and Loss Harvesting

This technique is tax-efficient (zero capital gains tax) and self-financing; it enables you to liquidate the concentrated stock while improving diversification and reducing risk. Here you invest in your own customized portfolio consisting of your concentrated stock and a customized index fund benchmarked to the Russell 1000 index (or another domestic equity index benchmark). You'll need free cash to implement this strategy—generally two or three times the figure represented by the concentrated position. (This requirement may prompt you to consider using an equity collar with a margin loan or varying forward contract in conjunction with your portfolio purchase.) Then the index fund manager will harvest capital losses, sell portions of the concentrated stock, and reinvest the proceeds into the index. Over a period of perhaps three to five years, all the stock will be sold and the proceeds invested in your customized portfolio.

In the end, you will have achieved a diversified portfolio without capital gains tax. The basis in the portfolio is equal to the cash originally invested and the basis in the concentrated stock. If you would like to sell off a low-cost stock position over a period of time and then reinvest in a broader, more diversified portfolio, you should consider this strategy.

Charitable Remainder Unitrust (CRUT)

If you are charitably inclined, a CRUT can be very appealing. Here you contribute your concentrated stock to a charitable trust. The low-cost-basis stock can be sold without the immediate payment of capital gains tax. The proceeds are reinvested and you receive an income stream for the term of the trust, or for life. The income stream is taxable to you (under a very complex set of trust accounting rules) based on the taxability of the investments in the CRUT portfolio. Offsetting this a bit, you'll get an upfront charitable deduction from your income tax (within limits according to your tax situation). At the end of the trust term (or your life), the remainder of the trust is paid to a named charity or charities, which can be a private foundation or donor advised fund. The trust is not subject to taxation in your estate.

If you would like a charity or charities to benefit upon your death (or at a point in the future) and you want to generate a tax-sensitive income stream while achieving a lower-risk profile today, the CRUT merits consideration. As always, careful tax planning is recommended before undertaking this strategy (as well as consultation with your legal advisor).

CHAPTER 3

Taxes

We don't pay taxes. Only the little people pay taxes.

—Leona Helmsley,
American businesswoman
sentenced in 1992 to four years'
imprisonment for tax evasion

If Patrick Henry thought that taxation without
representation was bad, he should see how bad it is
with representation.

—*The Farmer's Almanac*, 1966

Income tax planning and preparation allow you to conduct your financial activities in a tax-efficient manner. Rather than simply centering on April 15 each year, it should be a continuous process; reviewing income tax projections early in the year, as well as in the fall and just before year's end, makes good sense—as does timing these reviews to estimated payments if you are self-employed.

Income tax preparation is generally provided by certified public accountants, as well as by a few bank trust departments. Make sure your provider can efficiently produce your tax projections. Many CPAs also can perform a light audit of your broker or custodian to make sure you have received all of your interest, dividend, and principal disbursements. Your CPA's input is essential in investment, financial, and retirement planning.

U.S. Trust Survey of Affluent Americans Results

If presented with a tax cut, 58 percent of our survey respondents would invest the extra money, 21 percent would save it, 10 percent would spend it, and 8 percent would give the money to charity (see Figure 3.1).

Fifty percent of all respondents thought there should be no federal estate tax. But if there is to be an estate tax, the average respondent said its top rate should be 23 percent, rather than the current 50 percent.

FIGURE 3.1   WHAT THE AFFLUENT WOULD DO WITH
                MONEY SAVED AS A RESULT OF TAX CUT

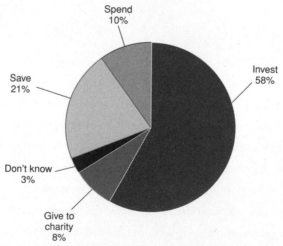

SOURCE: U.S. Trust Survey of Affluent Americans XX, June 2001

If tax codes were restructured, 38 percent said that the top federal tax bracket should be 21 to 30 percent, 20 percent said it should be 20 percent or less, 27 percent thought it should be between 31 and 40 percent, and 5 percent felt it should be 40 percent or higher. It is currently 35 percent for ordinary income and 15 percent for net long-term capital gains and dividends.

Tax Planning

One of our clients, Thad, a successful businessman in his late forties, hated taxes. In fact, he loathed them. Convinced that they were an odious governmental intrusion on his private affairs, Thad never let a financial planning session pass without commenting on the fact. This meant that Thad would do anything he could to avoid taxes—within the law, of course. He took every possible deduction (some of which didn't make complete sense), he gave to every charity he found (some of which he didn't even care for), and he invested in loser stocks so he could offset his capital gains with losses. Increasingly our meetings with him centered on taxes and nothing else. "I've got to get the government out of my life," Thad would say. "I made my money, they didn't. Let them make their own."

He particularly disliked paying New York City taxes, which he felt were an affront given that he had already paid federal and state taxes. "Why should I pay taxes three times?" Thad would ask indignantly. Anytime we were unable to reduce his taxes as much as he wanted, he would complain bitterly. Finally, his tax advisor suggested, with slight sarcasm, that if taxes bothered him that much, why didn't he consider anchoring his boat outside the 12-mile limit and living there? Thad took the remark seriously, thought it over, and although renouncing citizenship is a complicated and drawn-out procedure, Thad indeed managed to pull it off. Today he lives on his boat.

For the rest of us, if you are a U.S. citizen or live in this country, you will pay taxes. There aren't that many things in life we can count on, but as often has been said, death and taxes are certainly two of them. There isn't much you can do about death, but plenty of options are at your disposal to ensure that your taxes are as low as possible. Having a tax advisor isn't going to mean you'll never again pay taxes, but you may pay a great deal less.

The most important aspect of tax planning is always to have a current tax projection. This way, you always know where you stand, because even if you do no other financial planning or you couldn't care less about your money, you still will have taxes to think about whether your income is $25 million or $10,000. Don't wait until April 15; if you want to be smart about your taxes, you must think about them year round.

If the most important tool in planning is a solid projection for your annual taxes, the next most important element is a solid multiyear projection (see Table 3.1). Not everyone is in a position to do that, but if you have a sense of the direction in which your finances are moving for the next two three years, you can start doing some basic tax planning. These plans might include shifting deductions from one year to the next, balancing your income so that you don't earn a disproportionately large amount in any single year, or if you're a corporate executive with stock options, exercising those options at the right moment from a tax point of view.

Instead of viewing your tax return as a first step in organizing your year's finances, think of it as a restatement of all your tax planning. This will give you a sense of where changes can be made. For example, is your investment portfolio set up properly? Do you have high taxable income? How much of your portfolio is interest income? How much of that is taxable? Should you invest in municipal bonds? What about corporate bonds? Only careful scrutiny of your tax obligations can fully answer

TABLE 3.1   INCOME TAX PROJECTION CHART

	2001	2006	2010
Wages	$400,000	$400,000	$400,000
Interest & Dividends	35,000	35,000	35,000
Long Term Capital Gain	50,000	50,000	50,000
Adjusted Gross Income	485,000	485,000	485,000
Less: Personal Exemptions	0	(4,533)	(15,200)
Less: Charity	(10,000)	(10,000)	(10,000)
Less: Taxes	(57,010)	(57,010)	(57,010)
Less: Interest Expense	(30,000)	(30,000)	(30,000)
Less: Miscellaneous	(300)	(300)	(300)
Add: 3% AGI Floor	10,562	7,041	0
Taxable Income	398,252	390,198	372,490
Regular Tax	119,725	102,625	96,775
Gross Alternative Minimum Tax	117,100	117,100	117,100
Applicable Tax—Higher of the two	119,725	117,100	117,100
Savings Prior to AMT	N/A	17,100	22,950
Less: Savings Lost Due to AMT	N/A	(14,475)	(20,325)
Actual Net Savings	N/A	2,625	2,625

these questions. Are you aware of the best way to handle your charitable contributions? If you anticipate that next year you'll have a big spike in income, you may want to contribute more next year than this year to offset it (because, as you know, these contributions are tax-deductible).

Look at your stock options, capital gains, and capital losses. How can they work together? U.S. Trust has one client who made a three-year installment sale of securities from his privately owned company. This meant he had $1.5 million in capital gains in each of the three years. This year, he's struggling to get as many losses as he can. Even so, we won't be able to find a way to offset the entire gain (although having no losses to realize is not a bad position to be in). Another client of ours is a CEO who had sold his company for a great deal of money. As smart as he was about running his own company, he hadn't given his taxes much thought. Because he and his family were charitably inclined, we advised him to set up a private foundation, which he did with a bequest of $8 million. (This may sound like a large sum, but the man made $25 million a year in income alone.)

A caveat: In assessing each and every one of your financial transactions, give your taxes a vote—but not a veto. Too many people think that they need to make certain investments, incorporate, or take other steps for their taxes, because they have a vague concept of how taxes work but not enough to think through all the possible repercussions of their actions. For instance, one man told us recently that he needed to take out a big mortgage "for tax purposes." And yes, a mortgage would indeed lower his taxes, but it would also reduce his cash flow. Unless (or until) there is a 100 percent (or more) marginal tax rate, incurring mortgage interest will save you only the tax on that interest, with the net interest expense still coming out of your pocket.

Another point: Taxes and investments go hand in hand. Currently, home mortgage interest rates are near record lows, but so are interest rates on money market funds. Unless you need liquidity, regardless of the tax treatment, if you are paying more in interest on your mortgage than you are receiving from your short-term investments, you should consider paying off your mortgage rather than taking out another one.

Do not let the tax tail wag the investment dog. Back when the market crashed in October of 1987, one well-known company looked at its clients' portfolios and decided that so many of them had such huge realized gains in their portfolios prior to the crash that some "institutional tax planning" was in order. A decision was made across the board to identify nine stocks in the clients' portfolios that had large unrealized losses, and then sell those stocks and buy proxy stocks (in other words, they would sell a technology stock such as IBM and buy a similar one, such as Gateway). The idea was that the proxy stocks, being similar, would allow their clients to remain in the market in those sectors, but meanwhile the clients could harvest the losses from the original stocks.

Prior to year-end, the company sold the stocks, bought the proxies, and waited a month (you can't buy the same stock for 30 days before or after you've sold it or it is deemed a wash sale; for purposes of recognizing losses, it's as though you never made the sale in the first place). They then sold the proxies and bought back the original holdings. However, several people in the company had disliked this strategy and, to prove their case, performed some calculations on it. They found that, because the market rebounded, their clients would have been better served if they had stayed in their original stocks throughout and paid the taxes at the end of the year (part of this is because when they sold the proxy stocks, they had to pay a short-term gain to get back into their original picks).

This point is so powerful it bears repeating: Making decisions only for tax reasons is foolish. Tax considerations shouldn't drive financial decisions, but must be a factor in the analysis.

Tax Preparation

Most people don't prepare their own taxes—with good reason. Like nearly everything else in modern society, taxes have grown increasingly complicated over the last half-century. Finding an expert to prepare your taxes makes a great deal of sense. Unless you're willing to keep up with the constant changes in tax law, you're not likely to do as good a job.

How do you find a good tax accountant? The best way is probably word of mouth. Nearly everyone knows someone else who already has a good tax consultant. Ask around. When you find the person, make sure he or she is well qualified and preferably a certified public accountant (CPA): The word *certified* indicates that the person has passed a national exam and holds a license to practice accounting in a particular state. Also, CPAs must periodically return to school for re-education, which is necessary in a constantly changing tax environment. However, keep in mind that not all CPAs are individual tax specialists. Many of them practice as corporate auditors or tax advisors most of the year and will don their individual-tax-preparer hat only for a month or so before April 15.

Be sure that your CPA is well versed in the individual sections of the tax code. One indication of this competence is if the CPA is also designated a "personal financial specialist" by the American Institute of CPAs. This designation indicates a professional who has taken the time and training to become more deeply versed in all areas of personal financial planning, including taxes.

Even if you already have a competent advisor, it's important that you become thoroughly familiar with, and open about, your personal financial circumstances. This will enable your advisor to focus more attention on planning and/or reporting your taxes rather than wasting time hunting down your financial details.

Types of Income Taxes and Deductions

We encounter numerous taxes in all areas of life: real estate taxes, gift taxes, estate taxes, excise taxes, franchise taxes, and so on. But typically, when we discuss taxes, we usually mean income taxes. The other taxes tend to appear as additions to purchases, or as assessments from governmental units, and you're usually quite aware of them before they appear on the horizon.

The federal income tax is not as old as some people think. It's been around only since 1913, which means that some of you may have parents or grandparents who are older than income taxation. Within the income tax system, there are four things worth bearing in mind that will help you keep more of what you earn: gross income, adjustments and deferrals, deductions, and capital gains.

Gross Income

Gross income is the starting point in determining your tax liability. It accompanies almost everything and anything you can think of, or in IRS terminology, "income from whatever source derived": salaries, interest, dividends, net capital gains, rents, royalties, Social Security income, annuities, pensions, IRA distributions, and even alimony and unemployment compensation. Gross income is so powerful a concept that the government has used it on many occasions as legal grounds for areas far beyond your typical tax case. Perhaps the most famous example involves the notorious gangster Al Capone. When federal agents finally apprehended him and put him in prison, it wasn't because they were able to make murder or mayhem charges stick. He was convicted of evading taxes on his gross income.

Nearly every penny you make is considered gross income, but there are (as always) some exceptions. Four of the most significant ones are: inheritances, gifts, life insurance proceeds, and municipal bond interest.

When someone dies and leaves an estate, there may well be an estate tax imposed on the estate per se, but no income tax (some significant technical exceptions exist when the decedent had income that was tax-deferred; a tax is due upon his or her death). Whatever money you inherit is yours to spend. If your inheritance is in the form of a beneficial interest in a trust, however, you may have to pay taxes on the income generated by the trust if the income is paid or deemed to be paid out to you.

If you receive a gift, its fair market value is not immediately subject to income tax (although there may be a gift tax on the donor's

Checklist of Common Income Items (not all-inclusive)

- Compensation—wages, salaries, tips, etc.
- Interest income from taxable sources such as bank accounts and bonds
- Dividends
- State and local tax refunds that provided a tax benefit in earlier years
- Alimony received
- Self-employed business income
- Capital gains and losses
- Ordinary gains and losses
- Distributions from pensions, profit-sharing plans, and IRAs
- Rental income
- Income from flow through entities such as partnerships, S-corporations, and trusts
- Farm income
- Unemployment compensation
- Up to 85 percent of Social Security benefits
- Miscellaneous income such as gambling winnings, prizes and awards, and jury duty fees

end). But if the donor transferred appreciated property to you, you may incur capital gains tax when you sell the property because your tax cost basis in the property will be the same as the donor's.

Finally, when you buy a municipal bond and collect interest on it, this interest income also is not subject to federal taxes. Interest paid on bonds issued by your resident state also will escape taxation at the state and city level.

Adjustments and Deferrals

When you discuss your gross income with your tax advisor, he or she will mention *adjustments* and *deferrals*. Adjustments reduce gross income, and therefore your taxes. Deferrals delay the recognition of income to some time in the future, hopefully when your income will put you in a lower tax bracket.

The most significant adjustments are retirement-related; they include vehicles such as IRAs, Keoghs, and 401(k)s (see Chapter 5). Here you are able to put away a certain amount of money away, and in so doing reduce your taxable income. Suppose your gross income is $100,000 (and you have no other deductions). If you contribute $2,000 to your SEP-IRA (designed for the self-employed), you have reduced the amount of taxable income to $98,000.

Today a multitude of IRAs are available, and not every one gives you the same adjustment. However, the investment income all of them generate is deferred until you withdraw from the plan. And, with Roth IRAs, the income is not only tax-deferred, it is also tax-free if the account is set up and funded properly.

Deductions

Deductions also serve to reduce gross income, and therefore the taxes you pay. The rules on deductions have changed often since the inception of the income tax, and in 1986 a large number of deductions were altered. But significant deductions remain, such as on mortgage interest, charitable contributions, or fees paid for investment advisory or tax consulting services.

Mortgage interest incurred on debt up to $1.1 million on your primary residence plus one other residence is deductible. The debt must be secured by the residence(s), and the proceeds must be used to buy, build, or improve the residence(s). (Of that $1.1 million, up to $100,000 can be home equity debt that may be used for any purpose and still remain deductible, at least for purposes of the regular tax.)

Investment interest expense incurred on debt used to purchase or carry taxable investments is also deductible to the extent of your investment income. Any excess amount may be carried forward to future years as a tax deduction. Interest on business costs is typically deductible in full. However, personal interest, which comprises almost all the other forms of interest expense including that charged by credit cards and that which accrues on tax assessments, is not deductible.

Charitable contributions, which are discussed in more detail later in this chapter, are deductible as well. If you contribute cash to a charity,

---

Checklist of Common Adjustments to Income (not all-inclusive)

- Education expenses
- IRA (subject to income limitations)
- Student loan interest
- Certain tuitions and fees
- Archer medical savings account deduction
- Moving expenses (in connection with employment)
- One-half of self-employment tax
- Self-employed health insurance
- SEP, SIMPLE, and other qualified plans
- Penalty on early withdrawal of savings
- Alimony paid

Checklist of Common Itemized Deductions (not all-inclusive)

- Medical expenses (to the extent the total exceeds 7.5 percent of AGI
- State and local income taxes
- Real estate taxes
- Personal property taxes
- Home mortgage interest
- Certain points in home mortgage transactions
- Investment interest expense to the extent of taxable investment income
- Charitable gifts
- Casualty and theft losses (to the extent the total exceeds 10 percent of AGI)
- Miscellaneous itemized deductions (to the extent the total exceeds 2 percent of AGI), such as:
    - Unreimbursed employee expenses
    - Tax preparation fees
    - Investment management and custody fees for taxable investments
    - Union dues
    - Professional expenses
    - Safe deposit box
- Other miscellaneous itemized deductions
    - Gambling losses to the extent of gambling winnings
    - Federal estate tax on income in respect of a decedent

you can deduct the full contribution up to 50 percent of your adjusted gross income (AGI). However, if you give long-term-appreciated stock (stock held more than one year) to charity, you get a double bonus: You receive a deduction for the stock's full market value instead of its original cost, and you do not have to pay tax on the appreciation. Thus, if you have a 1,000 shares of XYZ stock purchased at $10 a share and today a share is worth $75, you may take a deduction of $75,000, rather than the $10,000 you originally spent to buy the stock. The total of all such contributions of appreciated capital gain property is limited to 30 percent of your AGI.

Miscellaneous deductions, such as investment advisory fees on taxable investments and tax consulting services, are deductible to the extent that the total of such deductions exceeds 2 percent of your AGI. (Technical rules apply regarding certain deductions. For example, if you incur a fee to manage your tax-exempt securities, that fee is generally not deductible because the income generated from those assets is not considered taxable income.)

Capital Gains

Another significant tax consideration, especially for investors, is capital gains. *Capital gains* are the profits you make from the sale of a capital asset, i.e., something you've sold that has appreciated in value. Using the XYZ example, if you didn't give your shares of stock to charity but sold them, your capital gains would be $65,000, or the amount of money the stock is worth now, minus your original investment of $10,000.

Capital gains are important for four reasons:

1. There is a significant spread between capital gains rates and income tax rates—at the moment, as much as 20 percent. The capital gains tax rate is currently 15 percent (for sales occurring on or after May 6, 2003) whereas the highest marginal income tax rate is 35 percent.

2. You, the investor and the taxpayer, can decide when you will pay the capital gains tax. Unlike a salary, which is taxable the moment it is paid, capital gains only become taxable when you cash them in. The dividend you receive when you have a stock, however, is immediately taxable—if that XYZ stock pays you a dividend four times a year, that money is recognized as ordinary income as soon as you receive it (at the new maximum dividend tax rate of 15 percent). But it's up to you if you want to hold on to the stock, in which case you don't have to pay any capital gains taxes, or sell it, in which case you will trigger the capital gains tax.

3. Capital gains can be offset dollar for dollar against capital losses. This also gives you a degree of control that you don't have as a salary earner. Let's say you decide to sell those thousand shares of XYZ stock and make a profit of $65,000. Assuming this is a long-term holding, you now have to pay a capital gains tax of 15 percent, or $9,750. However, let's say that at the same time you sell your XYZ, you also decide to sell a thousand shares of your ABC stock, which has not been performing very well over the last few years. You bought ABC at $75 a share, and now you are selling at $10. This means that you are taking a loss of $65,000. Lo and behold, that matches the profit you will make on the XYZ sale. As a result, because capital losses offset capital gains, you won't owe any money in taxes.

4. Capital losses are inevitable for most people—few investors have not at some point invested in a stock that went down. Over time, everyone will have some losers and (hopefully) some winners in their portfolio. The good news is that you can carry these losses forward, meaning that whenever you want to sell your winning stocks, and you incur capital gains, you can use capital losses to offset them.

Long-Term versus Short-Term Capital Gains

It's important to understand the distinction between long-term capital gains and short-term capital gains. Short-term capital gain refers to profits made from an investment held for less than one year; long-term capital gain applies to profits on an investment held for more than a year. Short-term capital gains are more expensive than long-term gains from a tax standpoint, because they are treated like ordinary income, and therefore subject to regular income tax rates. Again, if you bought that XYZ at $10 a share and in less than one year it shot up to $75 and you decided to sell it before one year-end, you would pay taxes on that money as though it was regular income.

Conversely, if you incur short-term losses, or losses from an investment that you held for less than a year, you can still use those to offset long-term capital gains. That's the one aspect of losses that's favorable—they can always be used to lessen the tax consequences of your winners.

Up to $3,000 in losses ($1,500 for married taxpayers filing separately) can be used to offset other income. Any losses in excess of this amount are carried forward indefinitely to future years to offset gains in those years. So mixing and matching capital gains and losses are favorite pastimes of investors planning their taxes between Thanksgiving and the New Year, when they clean up their portfolios and rid themselves of poor investments.

Taxation of Mutual Funds

Mutual funds have several advantages over individual securities. They provide instant diversification from dollar one (unless the fund is, by design, non-diversified). Managed funds offer professional management while index funds mirror the index upon which they are based. And, for smaller portfolios, funds are often a cost-efficient way to invest. However, they are a challenge from a tax perspective. The fund investor cannot easily control the tax timing of his/her fund investments. Essentially, the tax attributes of mutual funds flow out to the shareholders. In a personal portfolio, the investor may structure his/her investments to minimize taxable income or to time the recognition of capital gains and losses. But with fund investing, that is impossible. The portfolio is the portfolio, one size fits all. To the extent that taxable dividend or interest income is generated in a mutual fund, the shareholders will be taxed on that income. Similarly, if the fund incurs net capital gains for the year, the shareholders will be taxed on those gains. This is the case regardless of whether or not the shareholder reinvests those distributions.

Capital gains may be generated at the fund level and distributed and taxed to the shareholders, but this is only the first level of capital gains. When you sell mutual fund shares you will incur a capital gain or loss at the share level depending upon whether your net proceeds are greater or less than your tax cost basis. Many funds have significant unrealized gains in their portfolios, and if you invest in these funds you may have to pay capital gains taxes before you sell your mutual fund shares. You may even be paying capital gains taxes when the value of the fund has gone down. This happened to many unsuspecting mutual fund investors over the last several years. In 2003, many funds have unrealized losses, which could be advantageous. The rules for long-term and short-term treatment of mutual fund gains and losses are the same as for other securities—if you hold the asset for more than one year, any gain or loss is long-term and if you hold it for one year or less, the gain or loss is short-term. The trick with mutual funds is determining which shares to sell and their basis. Generally speaking, *specific identification* of shares will be most advantageous for most investors. You select the particular shares you want to sell in order to maximize a loss or minimize a gain (generally high cost first). If you take this route you should memorialize your decision in a letter to your broker or mutual fund company stating exactly which share you are selling—and

TABLE 3.2   TAX TREATMENT OF MUTUAL FUNDS

	Date	$ Amount	Share Price	# of Shares Purchased	Cumulative Shares	Avg. Cost Single Category	Avg. Cost Double Category
Purchase	1–Jan–01	2,500.00	10.00	250.00	250.00	10.00	
Dividend Reinvestment	30–Sep–01	75.00	10.75	6.98	256.98	10.02	
Purchase	1–Jan–02	2,500.00	11.20	223.21	480.19	10.57	
Dividend Reinvestment	30–Sep–02	152.25	12.01	12.68	492.87	10.61	10.61
Purchase	1–Jan–03	2,500.00	10.95	228.31	721.18	10.71	
Dividend Reinvestment	30–Sep–03	231.82	11.00	21.07	742.25	10.72	10.95

Assume all shares purchased in years 1 and 2 are long term and all shares purchased in year 3 are short term. 700 shares are sold at $11.50 per share. Sale occurs 10/15/03.

	Date	# of Shares	Selling Price	Proceeds	Basis	LT Gain/Loss	ST Gain/Loss	Total Gain/(Loss)
FIFO Method	1–Jan–01	250.00	11.50	2,875.00	2,500.00	375.00		
	30–Sep–01	6.98	11.50	80.27	75.00	5.27		
	1–Jan–02	223.21	11.50	2,566.96	2,500.00	66.96		
	30–Sep–02	12.68	11.50	145.78	152.25	(6.47)		
	1–Jan–03	207.13	11.50	2,381.98	2,268.06		113.92	
Total Gain/(Loss)		700.00		8,050.00	7,495.31	440.77	113.92	554.69
Specific Identification (High cost lots first)	30–Sep–02	12.68	11.50	145.78	152.25	(6.47)		
	1–Jan–02	223.21	11.50	2,566.96	2,500.00	66.96		
	30–Sep–03	21.07	11.50	242.35	231.82		10.54	
	1–Jan–03	228.31	11.50	2,625.57	2,500.00		125.57	
	30–Sep–01	6.98	11.50	80.23	75.00	5.23		
	1–Jan–01	207.75	11.50	2,389.09	2,077.47	311.62		
Totals		700.00		8,050.00	7,536.54	377.35	136.11	513.46
Average Cost (Single Category)		492.87	11.50	5,663.01	5,280.98	387.02		
		207.13	11.50	2,382.00	2,219.35		162.65	
		700.00		8,050.00	7,500.33	387.02	162.65	549.67
Average Cost (Double Category)		492.87	11.50	5,663.01	5,227.27	440.73		
		207.13	11.50	2,382.00	2,268.95		113.05	
		700.00		8,050.00	7,496.22	440.73	113.05	553.78

your broker or fund company should confirm this decision, in writing, within a reasonable period of time to you. If you choose not to use specific identification, you have a choice between the *"first in, first out"* method (FIFO—the default method of the IRS) or the *"average cost"* method. FIFO is exactly as it sounds. Shares acquired first are deemed to be sold first, with the actual tax cost basis of the shares used to calculate gain or loss. Average cost aggregates the tax cost of all shares to calculate an average cost that is then used for any sales of those shares. Of course, the average cost of your mutual fund shares will change over time as new shares are added and old shares are sold. Once you choose to use the average cost method for a particular fund method, you must use it for all subsequent sales of that fund. The double category average cost method requires you to separate all your long-term and short-term shares and calculate average cost for each category at the time of the sale while the single category method calculates one average cost for all your shares, regardless of holding period. (See Table 3.2).

Another advantage of mutual funds is that the fees charged by the funds and expenses are deducted at the fund level. This generally is more tax-efficient than fees paid for individually managed accounts where total miscellaneous expenses (including investment management fees) have to be greater than 2% of adjusted gross income.

Other Tax Issues

Alternative Minimum Tax

Yet another significant part of the tax code is something most people haven't even heard of. It's called the alternative minimum tax (AMT). The AMT is a separate and parallel tax system. It taxes a broader base of income, with fewer deductions, at an essentially a flat rate. It is the closest thing this country has to a flat tax.

The AMT is calculated at a flat rate of 26 percent on alternative minimum taxable income (AMTI) of $175,000 or less and 28 percent on AMTI above $175,000. The one exception to this tax rate is for dividends and net long-term capital gains incurred after May 6, 2003, which are taxed at 15 percent, the same as the regular tax. The AMT applies only when the amount you would owe under it exceeds your regular income tax. For example, if your AMT tax share turns out to be $75,000, while your regular tax is $50,000, you must pay an AMT of $25,000 in addition to the $50,000 regular tax for a total tax of $75,000.

A modest exemption of $58,000 for married couples filing jointly, $29,000 for married individuals filing separately, and $40,250 for single and head of household taxpayers applies against AMT, thereby limiting the exposure to AMT for lower-income taxpayers. The exemptions are scheduled to decrease by $13,000 for joint return filers and $6,500 for all others after 2004. Because of the new tax laws with lower marginal ordinary rates, there is a narrower spread than ever between the AMT and the regular tax, and the base numbers have never been adjusted for inflation, even though the average income has been rising. This means that many more taxpayers than ever will be subjected to the AMT.

The original intent of the AMT was to catch wealthy individuals who, with the right mix of deductions, paid little or no tax. From a social policy standpoint, the AMT made sense. But the way the law is written, it's now snaring people in its net who really weren't supposed to be captured. Any good tax consultant will put your taxes through both the usual system and the alternative minimum tax system, so although you may not know it, your alternative minimum tax is probably being calculated.

A great deal of esoterica is associated with the AMT, as there is in any governmental tax system. The AMT opens up a whole new set of tax accounting issues that have to be dealt with. For example, when you exercise incentive stock options, as opposed to nonqualified options, the spread between fair market value and strike price is not considered taxable income on a regular tax basis; however, it is taxable income under the AMT. You are also required to track the tax cost-basis of those shares in two different ways: the AMT way and the regular way. Thus, when you sell them, you have another adjustment to make. This rule makes the tax law three times harder than it needs to be.

It is unfortunate that Congress did so little about reforming the AMT under the 2001 and 2003 Tax Acts. U.S. Trust's own analysis shows that many people will find that the promised tax relief bestowed by the regular tax rates will prove illusory as the AMT impacts a greater number of taxpayers. Overall, the disadvantages of the AMT provide another good reason to make sure you do your tax planning in advance. For instance, if you have deductions you can defer into a higher-income year, you should do so in order to avoid the alternative minimum tax.

Charitable Giving Deductions

Charitable donation planning is another important component of tax planning. As previously mentioned, when you give securities to a public charity, you receive a tax deduction for the fair market value of the securities, and you don't have to pay capital gains tax. [The limitations here do not affect many taxpayers, but it is good to keep the basic ones in mind: With cash contributions to most charities, your deduction is limited to 50 percent of your AGI in any given year. Contributions of capital gain property, such as stock, are limited to 30 percent of AGI (and reduce, dollar for dollar, the 50 percent limitation on cash contributions). If you're very charitably inclined and exceed these limits, don't worry. Excess contributions can be carried over and used as deductions for up to five years. One caveat: Charitable contributions of

$250 or more require written verification from the charitable organization (and canceled checks no longer substantiate a charitable deduction.] In other words, when you give away that XYZ stock priced at $75 a share (which you bought at $10), you don't have to pay any capital gains tax, and you can write off the entire $75,000. Furthermore, the charity may keep the entire amount without having to pay tax, either.

There are other tax-sensible ways you can give. These include vehicles such as charitable remainder trusts, charitable lead trusts, donor advised funds, and private foundations. All these vehicles help you achieve your goal.

When you establish a *charitable remainder trust* (CRT), you are arranging it so your favorite charity will eventually receive whatever assets you wish to give away—but not at the moment. In the meantime, you, your spouse, or your children (or anyone else you wish) will be paid income from the assets in the trust. The assets don't belong to the charity until after the termination of the trust, which is often defined as your death. This trust makes the most sense for people who wish to give money to charity and who don't need the principal (the amount of money used to set up the trust) in order to maintain their chosen lifestyle.

A CRT offers many tax-planning opportunities, particularly if you want to retain an income. For example, say you own a great deal of stock in one company, perhaps because you worked there for many years. Over time it has appreciated significantly. And let's say that this stock represents the lion's share of your portfolio. If you sell it, you will be hit with a huge capital gains tax. But if you set up a CRT, the trust can sell the stock, pay no tax, diversify its holdings, and provide you with an income stream for the rest of your life—and give you an income tax deduction. On top of that, the best part is that your favorite charity will reap a great reward (for more on CRTs, see Chapter 6).

A *charitable lead trust* is the reverse of a CRT. As in a CRT, you can give to a charity and reduce your tax load at the same time. But here, instead of the charity getting all the money when you die, the principal is left to your children, your grandchildren, or anyone you wish. But while you're alive, the trust pays out an annual payment, and you receive an immediate one-time estate (or gift tax) deduction for the value of the money you are paying to the charity.

Donor-advised funds let you give money away and profit from it. Here you make an irrevocable contribution of cash, stocks, bonds, or mutual fund shares to a donor-advised fund. This generally yields a tax deduction in the current year. The fund then invests your contributions, and any investment growth that accumulates in your account is tax-free. You can advise the fund on how and when you'd like grants from your account disbursed to charities, and you can make more contributions to your account whenever you want. Being a public charity, a donor-advised fund is subject to more generous limits on tax-deductible contributions than contributions to private foundations.

Foundations are for richer clients. Their biggest advantages include ongoing control of your largesse and minimal federal excise taxation. Regarding control, your foundation board decides when and how much to pay to charity subject to a minimum annual payout of only about 5 percent of the foundation's fair market value. Federal tax on the foundation's investment income is 2 percent or less. Thus, by establishing a foundation, you can simultaneously remove a significant sum of assets from your estate (minimizing estate taxes), gain an immediate tax deduction without having to identify recipient charities right away, set aside some of the assets in a separate entity with minimal tax ramifications, and maintain control of the investment decisions about the money, as well as the timing of its ultimate disposition. There is a downside: Foundations are expensive to set up and maintain, and the tax form for foundations is a nightmare that makes filing an individual form 1040 look simple (see the discussion on foundations later in this chapter for details).

Stock Options

Another tax issue that must be considered is *stock options*. It's important to understand the best time to exercise them, and when it is best to take the tax hit.

U.S. Trust once had a client who had previously run into a great deal of tax trouble by making some bad financial decisions; she had exercised a large lot of incentive stock options, but the profits landed her smack up against the AMT. Here was a classic case of enjoying too much of a good thing at once, causing a massive tax hangover. We told her that what she should have done was exercise a small number of options each year, spacing them out to minimize the AMT impact. (Remember: Don't let the tax tail wag the investment dog. If it makes sense to exercise stock options for investment reasons, don't wait.)

You should find out which type of options (incentive or nonqualified) you own, if any. With nonqualified options, exercising the option is a taxable event, and the difference between the exercise price and the option's value at the time you exercise it is considered ordinary income. Note that because nonqualified stock options (NQSOs) are very flexible, they are the most common type of compensatory option. Generally, they have a limited life (frequently 10 years) and are often subject to a vesting schedule. Vesting is a form of golden handcuff: You must still be employed at the vesting date in order to exercise the option. After the vesting date, the option is yours whether or not you remain with your employer. However, there are no tax ramifications to owning stock options until you actually exercise them and buy the stock. At that time, the difference between the current fair market value and the option price (also called the spread) is taxable to you as additional compensation. Your employer will withhold taxes on the spread. Your basis in the stock is its fair market value on the date of exercise. When you sell the stock in the future, any increase or decrease in the value of the stock will give rise to a capital gain or loss.

Another variety of option, less common but potentially more valuable to the employee, is the incentive stock option (ISO). As long as all the rules are followed, ISOs do not generate ordinary income at the time you exercise them. Instead, the spread is treated as additional income for AMT purposes, which if the AMT is applicable, effectively causes the spread to be taxable. This AMT implication complicates the matter further with respect to the tax cost-basis of the shares, but in general, if you hold the ISO stock for at least one year from the date of exercise and two years from the date of grant, then any gain or loss on the future sale of that stock will be treated as a capital gain or loss. If you dispose of the stock prior to this holding period, then the spread will be taxed similarly to the spread on an NQSO as ordinary income. See example on page 250 in the Appendix.

In deciding how best to implement ISOs and NQSOs, consider their tax impact well ahead of time. ISO planning is more complex than NQSO planning. With NQSOs, as noted, when you exercise them the spread is treated as ordinary income, taxable in the current year. There are no AMT considerations with NQSOs. ISOs, on the other hand, may cause you to be subject to the AMT or make your existing AMT exposure that much worse. If you are fortunate enough to receive stock options as part of your compensation, then you should always update your multiyear tax projection.

Estimated Tax Payments

Individual taxpayers are required to pay their anticipated tax liability each year through payroll withholding or quarterly installment payments of estimated tax. Taxpayers who do not pay enough in a particular installment period may be subject to a penalty. For estimated tax purposes, the year is broken down into four payment periods: the period ending March 31, payable April 15; the period ending May 31, payable June 15; the period ending August 31, payable September 15; and the period ending December 31, payable January 15.

To avoid penalties for underpayment of estimated taxes, if your previous year's adjusted gross income was less than $150,000, you must make current estimated tax payments equal to 100 percent of your prior year's tax (this formula is known as the safe harbor or cover) or 90 percent of your estimated current year's tax liability. A special rule applies to individuals whose adjusted gross income for the previous tax year was more than $150,000 (or $75,000 for married individuals filing separately). In order to qualify for the prior year safe harbor for tax year 2003 and beyond, you must pay 110 percent of the prior year's liability rather than only 100 percent.

Foundations and Philanthropy

U.S. Trust Survey of Affluent Americans Results

The affluent in America have a long history of donating money to charity, as revealed in our 1998 survey. Almost every individual surveyed said he or she had contributed cash to charity. Eighty-three percent had contributed their time; 79 percent had given tangible assets and countless other types of contributions, from collectibles to stock or appreciated securities. Of those who gave of their time, 31 percent volunteered five hours or fewer per month, 22 percent gave 6 to 10 hours, 17 percent 21 or more hours, 13 percent 11 to 15 hours, and 11 percent 16 to 20 hours. On average, each person contributed about 8 percent of his or her after-tax income to charities; respondents' after-tax donations averaged $29,400.

Fifteen percent of those surveyed said that they had set up a charitable remainder trust, while another 25 percent intended to do so. And 7 percent had set up a private foundation, with 10 percent more stating they were likely to do so.

Seventy-nine percent said their desire to support worthwhile causes was a very important reason they gave to charity, while 69 percent said that they believed those who have been financially successful had a responsibility to share their good fortune. Sixty-three percent said they gave because of their desire to meet critical needs in the community, 50 percent wanted to help organizations than have benefited someone they already know, and 46 percent have given due in part to a desire to set an example for their children. A full 95 percent said they would give to charity even if it weren't tax-deductible, but 41 percent admitted that that they wouldn't have given as much if it weren't tax-deductible.

The affluent feel strongly that their children should be involved in charity: 69 percent had sponsored their kids in fundraising activities such as walk-a-thons, 67 percent encouraged them to do community service work, 60 percent include their children in their own volunteer activities, and 50 percent supported their kids financially so they could volunteer or engage in not-for-profit work.

The most common types of charities to receive aid from the affluent were those focused on human services, such as aid to the needy and disadvantaged (88 percent gave to such organizations), education (84 percent); children and youth services (76 percent), religious organizations (74 percent), health care research (69 percent), and cultural organizations (also 69 percent). Fifty-eight percent gave to charities that operate on the local level, 35 percent to national groups, and only 5 percent to international organizations.

Thirty-eight percent said that the most effective form of solicitation was through a personal request by a friend, 29 percent were convinced by a mailed letter, 22 percent in response to a personal request by a charity staff person, and just 1 percent responded to a telephone solicitation.

The reason the participants selected a specific charity for their largesse tended to reflect its reputation for integrity, or the fact that it met an important need, used its funds efficiently, or had benefited a friend.

Setting Up a Foundation

The word *foundation* can sound intimidating. But not only is having one more practical than you might think, you don't even need to be enormously wealthy to establish it. In fact, you can set up a foundation with almost any amount of money (and the initial costs can be less than $10,000, depending on your location). Still, starting a foundation doesn't really make sense unless you've got $1 million to allocate to it and preferably more than $3 million. It also doesn't take a great deal of time and effort. If you choose the right professional to administer the foundation, you won't have to do much of the work yourself, and once you've established your giving priorities and your organizational procedures, you can decide how proactive you wish to be in overseeing its activities.

There are several reasons to set up a family foundation. Advantages exist both during your lifetime and for your heirs. Among the most attractive advantages are the tax benefits: Cash contributions to a private foundation, if made before death, are tax-deductible up to 30 percent of your adjusted gross income. Gifts to a foundation of qualified publicly traded stock are deductible at their full fair market value (with a limitation of 20 percent of your adjusted gross income), and any unused portion of the charitable deduction can be carried forward for five years. Moreover, all bequests to private foundations made through a will are 100 percent deductible from estate taxes.

Broader reasons exist for creating a foundation. Instead of doling out money to various random charities, you'll have one consistent vehicle by which to further your and your family's values, and/or an entity that allows your children and grandchildren to participate together as a family. Of course, a foundation of your own allows you to exercise more influence over how your money is spent than when you give to public charities. Through the foundation you decide exactly who or what receives funding, the amount, and when they get it.

Not long ago a client named Jack came to see U.S. Trust for estate planning. As CEO of a manufacturing company in California, Jack had made a great deal of money over the last two decades—his estate was worth about $75 million. But Jack had yet to formulate a good retirement plan for the money or decided what to do with it after his death.

Jack was not new to philanthropy—he served on the board of a large state foundation that made large grants to the arts. After we discussed his interests and his family, he decided that he wanted to set up a private foundation as a vehicle for estate planning and income tax reduction, but also as a way to reunite his family (at the time his four children resided in four different parts of the country, from Seattle to Atlanta). He also wanted to teach them about the rewards of giving back.

Jack told us that in his work at the arts foundation, he noticed that a great deal of money was being given to large arts organizations, but that the smaller ones never even made it onto the radar screen. This was partly because either they didn't know how to apply for grants or they weren't significant or far-reaching enough for a large foundation to care about. Yet, Jack thought many of these modest arts organizations were doing excellent work, well worthy of funding.

Jack asked his children to meet him and his wife at their home in the Bay Area. He then sat them down and explained how and why he'd decided his money would be going into a private foundation, and that meant that the kids weren't going to inherit as much as they might have expected. But Jack made it clear that he wanted each of them to be actively involved in running the foundation. The children were delighted. All had successful careers, so none of them needed the inheritance money. And, since they all cared about the arts, together they came up with an inspired mission statement in support of local arts programs. The four children then divided the country into quarters, each taking responsibility for learning about the arts in his or her chosen area. Today the foundation is 10 years old and is successful in both its missions: helping community arts projects flourish, and keeping Jack's family united. The children used to get together only over the Christmas holidays, but now they meet four times a year to discuss their foundation work.

Because a foundation can unite an otherwise indifferent clan, some families, like Jack's, have created private foundations specifically to engage their children. And some have set them up to give their otherwise unfocused children a purpose. Some have even created incentives where a child can act as executive director and receive compensation.

Of course, these arrangements don't always work as planned. Allen and Mary are parents who came to U.S. Trust recently; they have three children who are not as functional as Jack's. Nor did the kids enjoy a good relationship with Allen, who was controlling, over both his family and his own computer company, which he had built from nothing. But as he grew to face his own mortality, Allen mellowed. He told us he wanted to set up a foundation to help educate underprivileged kids. He also had begun to yearn for a better relationship with his own children. To accomplish both dreams, he decided to create a foundation that they could run. His plan didn't work out; the kids, who harbored resentment against Allen, were unable to come together as a group. But it wouldn't be accurate to say that the foundation itself failed. It may not have served the immediate goal of uniting an unruly family, but the thousands of impoverished children who were able to attend school because of its work would still consider it an extraordinary success.

If you do decide you have the wherewithal and the passion to start a foundation, the range of missions is enormous. Any charitable function can work, from medicine to education to the arts. Some foundations have very specific mission statements—research in pancreatic cancer, say, or shelter for homeless women—but some are set up for purposes so general they could encompass almost any cause. One of my favorite foundations is the Seth Sprague Educational and Charitable Foundation, a wonderful organization in existence since 1939. Here's its mission statement:

> *The trust is created and shall be administered and operated by the Trustees exclusively for the benefit of, and the trust estate and the income therefrom shall be distributed by the Trustees exclusively in aid of, such religious, educational, charitable, and scientific uses and purposes as, in the judgment of the Trustees, shall in furtherance of the public welfare and tend to assist, encourage, and promote the well-doing or well-being of mankind, or of the inhabitants of any community.*

Under such a broad governance, this very successful foundation last year gave over $3 million to support a range of interests including public radio, inner-city scholarships, and children's health.

A few caveats are worth keeping in mind. As always, the IRS has rules governing foundations. Private foundations must qualify as tax-exempt organizations and comply with a multitude of tax regulations. For example, every foundation must make annual distributions of 5 percent of its net investments. And, a tax totaling 2 percent of the net investment income must be paid in annual quarterly installments (although this amount may be reduced to 1 percent, depending on various payouts).

The annual IRS deduction for charitable contributions made to foundations is lower than that for contributions made to public charities (20 percent as opposed to 30 percent). There are also costs associated with the annual filing requirement, and various penalties may be leveled, such as those associated with excess business holdings or prohibited transactions. If you have a good advisor, however, none of these rules should cause you any worry or discourage you from starting a foundation.

Giving

For people who don't want to deal with a foundation, or don't have as much money, there's a strong alternative: intelligent giving. There are many ways to be philanthropic: The most obvious is writing a check or making a gift of appreciated securities to the cause of your choice. But don't simply look at your checkbook balance for guidance as to how much you can afford to donate. Think about all the assets you own and the types of giving that make sense both for you and the recipient. Your gift doesn't have to be cash—you can donate pieces of art, coin collections, real estate, and so on. You'll need to examine the tax considerations for each gift type, particularly the difference between gifts of ordinary income as opposed to capital gain property. But these categories aren't hard to determine, and your tax consultant will know how to sort out any tax issues that might arise.

When you want to donate a large amount, a *planned gift* may be a good alternative to explore. Generally, this means an asset bestowed upon your death, usually through your will. But there are many other sophisticated strategies available for planned giving, including a wide variety of trusts, such as a charitable remainder trust, charitable gift annuity, or a pooled income fund. In most cases you arrange these trusts through an institution, such as your alma mater or a hospital. Also, many not-for-profit institutions now offer planned gift vehicles; in one type, called a *split gift*, the beneficiaries receive interest income during their lifetime; then, upon your death, or the death of your spouse, the corpus of the gift passes to the charity.

As mentioned previously, a charitable remainder trust (CRT) is similar, but does not have to be set up with an institution. Here you can create a trust in which the donor (you) or named beneficiary gets an income stream for life, and whatever is left over at the end of the term of the trust passes to the named charitable beneficiary. There are significant tax advantages to a CRT, especially in that the donor receives a current income tax deduction for the present value of the remainder interest. This type of trust also minimizes estate taxes— the trust is considered a part of your estate, but in some cases you are allowed to take a 100 percent tax credit on it (for more on CRTs, see Chapter 6)

Another popular giving vehicle mentioned previously is the donor-advised fund. Here you set up a fund or account at an institution—such as the New York Community Trust—or via a commercial vehicle—such as a Schwab Fund for Charitable Giving—and make an irrevocable contribution to a charity. The charity then sets up a donor advised fund in your name (or any name you choose). You then are entitled to make recommendations as to how the money should be allotted. These funds represent an excellent alternative to a private foundation for someone who intends to make a gift between $25,000 to the high six figures. There are limitations: You don't have control over the investments made with your donation, nor will you have total control over the grant making (although you will make recommendations to the fund's board). Nevertheless, our clients who have gone the donor-advised route have been very satisfied with the results.

Still another vehicle is the charitable gift annuity. Here you make an irrevocable gift to a charitable organization and receive the usual income tax deduction. In return, the charity pays you fixed-income payments for life.

Another suggestion is one we often forget: Sometimes the most thoughtful gift you can offer is yourself. Volunteerism is an excellent form of giving, and it obviously doesn't involve money. And we no longer live in an era where volunteering means addressing, stuffing, and licking envelopes. Interesting and innovative projects abound in which you can immediately and actively take part. You'll be in good company.

Avoid Taxing Mistakes

Becoming wealthy requires hard work and luck. *Losing* your wealth, however, usually involves making colossal mistakes. People generally make colossal mistakes when they get greedy.

At the height of the Internet bubble, my assistant came to my office on a few occasions holding a $100 bill. The bill was part of a direct mail campaign on how to avoid income taxes. The mailing invited the recipient to contact the sender to learn the secrets of avoiding, or minimizing, income taxes on either option exercises or large capital gains. I was delighted to pocket the $100, but I wasn't about to do business with anyone who would send it to me in the mail. I am a firm believer that although you must take chances in business to become successful, you have to be cautious when it comes to paying taxes.

Early in 2003, the popular press chronicled the problems of two very high-profile executives who made an enormous blunder. It's worth a moment to review their errors and offer some commentary. The executives were presented with a plan to minimize their income taxes on exercising stock options and on capital gains through an elaborate procedure designed to adhere to the letter of the tax code, but not the intent. The plan was presented by a major accounting firm that also happened to be the auditor for the executives' publicly held company.

The executives had to sign a nondisclosure agreement even to review the plan—and had to pay the accounting firm an extraordinarily large fee for tax advice (the fee for tax advice from accountants is usually based on the number of hours worked). The plan also received the blessing from a law firm that said the tax minimization plan should withstand IRS scrutiny.

The executives proceeded with the plan and although that in itself could be considered a mistake by many, their real mistake came when they decided that because they would not owe the anticipated taxes, they did not have to sell the stock in question, either—and could instead hold on to an undiversified position because they believed the stock was going to go up.

At this writing, the IRS has challenged the tax position and is now seeking the tax, plus interest and penalties, from these executives. The executives chose to hold the stock and they didn't sell enough to pay the potential tax, which would have been prudent. The value of the stock is now below the potential, or likely, tax obligation. Therefore, the executives' tax bill will exceed their net worth and they may lose everything.

If you insist on taking an aggressive tax position, I would counsel selling sufficient stock to cover the tax and keeping the proceeds invested very conservatively until the tax position has been resolved through an audit or the lapse of the statute of limitations. Sometimes you can win simply by not losing.

CHAPTER 4

Insurance

Insurance is an ingenious modern game of chance
in which the player is permitted to enjoy the
comfortable conviction that he is beating the man
who keeps the table.

—Ambrose Bierce,
American author

The insurance policy was a guarantee that, no matter
how many necessities a person had to forego all through
life, death was something to which he could look forward.

—Fred Allen,
American humorist

Insurance is a mechanism for transferring risk. For a fee (i.e., a premium), the financial risk of loss of property or life is shifted away from you to the insurance carrier. Shifting this risk of loss away from the individual to a much larger group (such as thousands of policyholders of a certain property and casualty insurer) benefits everyone, not just the insured person. Also, insurance policies enjoy compelling tax treatment.

Not long ago, one of our trust officers was working with Jacob, an elderly man who had been a U.S. Trust client for many years. Jacob was something of a recluse. He and his wife had married when they were both only 23 years old, but his wife died in an automobile accident just a few years later. They had no children, and Jacob didn't remarry. Instead, his job became his life, and he spent all of it working for a closely held, family-run manufacturing concern. Although the original family still owned and operated the company, Jacob rose to the highest nonfamily position, and through a combination of hard work and dedication, he retired a wealthy man at the age of 65.

When Jacob was 50 years old, he'd inherited his parent's home, a large and hauntingly beautiful Yankee mansion off the Massachusetts coast. There he lived alone among furnishings that had been in his family for years—people in Jacob's family seldom seemed to throw anything out until it could serve no utilitarian purpose.

During one particularly dry summer there was a small fire in the house. It was caught in time to prevent any serious damage; nonetheless, it was enough to prompt Jacob to call and ask us for guidance in reviewing his insurance needs. We had helped him obtain property insurance some years ago and talked frequently about possible changes, but we had never visited his home; we agreed to send someone up.

As our insurance representative walked through Jacob's house, he confirmed that Jacob's insurance covered almost everything. However, the man also noticed that nearly everywhere he looked, he saw walking canes: bamboo canes, wooden rods, delicate Asian poles, sturdy African walking sticks, and old American mahogany staffs. There were many of them, and they were quite beautiful. When asked about the canes, Jacob shrugged, and replied that he liked canes and that whenever he saw one he liked, he bought it. He didn't consider them a collection so much as simply a lot of canes. He didn't know if they were worth anything.

On a hunch, our insurance man contacted the insurance carrier, and asked them to take a look at Jacob's cane collection. After an inventory was made, we discovered that the collection was worth approximately $2 million. We advised Jacob to obtain an insurance policy as soon as possible to cover the canes, and we assisted him in obtaining coverage through Lloyds of London. Although the cost of this policy was several thousand dollars per year, the price was clearly worth it since the risk of loss of the $2 million cane collection was now transferred to the insurance company.

Although most of us are aware of the need for insurance and own at least one policy of some type, insurance requirements and the importance of insurance planning become more acute the more affluent you become. The most challenging element of insurance planning is, quite frankly, that most people feel about insurance the way they do about taxes—no one really wants to spend time focusing on it, or even talking about it, until it's too late.

Whenever we take on new clients, we always ask them to provide us with their existing insurance policies. What they usually give us is a jumble of papers representing a variety of different policies dating from different times in our clients' lives, rather than a coherent plan under which each part of a person's life has been analyzed and covered appropriately. Sometimes we'll find that clients are overinsured; others may be underinsured. We almost always discover that clients work with not one but several different brokers. This is partly because many people own more than one home, and they obtained coverage through a broker in each locale. However, there is much to be said for having a coordinated insurance plan—one set of eyes viewing all your assets—along with a risk management plan that considers all of those assets.

Strangely enough, we have found that clients more frequently tend to be overinsured than underinsured: In other words, they simply own too much insurance. We have seen many cases of double and triple coverage of the same risk, usually due to the fact that the various brokers are not communicating with one another. Not long ago we met a couple who had three houses: one in Connecticut, one in Florida, and a small apartment in Manhattan. The couple had insured each residence through a local broker, but hadn't realized that each policy also insured the other homes—meaning these people were triply insured. Obtaining insurance is an excellent idea, but overinsurance is simply a waste of money.

Many kinds of insurance are available to help mitigate various types of risk; following are very brief descriptions of each major type of insurance. Most of them are necessary for most people (and some of them are required). Books could be and have been written on each one of these areas. Consider this simply a primer so that when you do talk to an insurance agent, you possess a passing knowledge about each type of insurance you will need. As well, you can begin thinking about how you might coordinate your life insurance with other wealth management activities.

Life Insurance

The purpose of life insurance is to create or enhance an estate upon your death, thereby providing for the needs of your family or other beneficiaries. Life insurance can also provide liquidity and permit the orderly liquidation of a closely-held business or other illiquid assets. Life insurance planning is often the cornerstone of your overall estate plan. The number of types of life insurance policies available for purchase has grown over the years, mainly driven by changes in the economy, the tax laws, and the marketing opportunities identified by insurance carriers looking to sell as many policies as possible.

A *needs analysis* performed by a licensed life insurance agent or your financial planner can help you determine the type of policy to purchase and the appropriate amount. As stated above, life insurance creates an instant estate for the benefit of your heirs (or beneficiaries) upon your death. This estate helps your heirs pay your outstanding debts and funeral expenses, and can be sufficient to provide an income stream so that family members can maintain the standard of living to which they've grown accustomed (i.e., the standard of living with which you, the insured, provided them during your life). Bear in mind that you may not be able to purchase all of the insurance you might want and can afford, because ultimately the life insurance carrier (or, rather, its underwriting department) will determine the amount of coverage you will be permitted to obtain. In other words, a childless 60-year-old married male making $50,000 per year and renting a small apartment will probably be turned down for a $10 million, 10-year level-term policy (assuming he could afford the premiums) since clearly he has no need for this amount of life insurance.

Of course, life insurance planning is different for high-net-worth individuals. A needs analysis may not be an appropriate method for determining the amounts and types of coverage needed, since there may be no actual need at all, but rather a desire. For instance, let's say you are 35 years old, married with two children, each under 5 years old. You live in a $1 million home with a $500,000 mortgage, earn $1 million a year, and have saved $3 million. Clearly, you are very successful. How much life insurance do you need? How much life insurance do you want? This scenario is very different from the situation faced by an older middle-class couple who does not earn a million dollars per year and who has not accumulated as much in savings. The planning and analysis that go into determining the type and amount of coverage that would be appropriate for these people would be quite different from those to determine a millionaire's coverage needs.

Here are some situations in which you, as a high-net-worth individual, might require life insurance planning:

- If you are the income beneficiary of a large trust that does not continue for your spouse or other dependents after your death.

- If you have an annuity or pension payment that does not continue for your spouse or other dependents after your death.

- If you have an illiquid estate, and your heirs therefore have insufficient liquidity to live and to pay estate taxes.

- If you have created a charitable trust and want to make up to your heirs the assets that would otherwise pass to the charity upon your death.

If you elect to purchase such insurance, it is essential to coordinate it with your financial, retirement, and estate planning and gift-giving needs. You must also coordinate the investment attributes of your life insurance with your other investment activities. If these considerations sound complicated, they are. You will need to consult with your financial planner and/or a licensed life insurance agent. In particular, seek out someone with an industry designation, such as a certified life underwriter (CLU). To simplify the issue, it helps to understand the two broad categories of life insurance: less permanent, non–cash value life insurance, and more permanent, cash value life insurance.

Less permanent, non–cash value life insurance comes in several forms. One is known as *term* life insurance. This policy type provides coverage, is generally thought of as temporary, and does not accumulate a cash value. Term coverage is generally priced according to the cost per $1,000 of coverage (i.e., the cost of insurance, or COI) and increases annually as the insured ages. Term life insurance policies may be used to insure against the loss of life of a wage earner for a specific time period connected with a specific financial obligation, such as the 30-year term of a home mortgage or a child's four-year education. Some variations on term coverage are:

Annual renewable term: This is a term policy type in which the contract is renewable annually to some stated age, usually 75. Premiums increase annually (as the insured ages). Once the insured reaches age 75, the policy is no longer in force and the coverage ends.

Level term: This is a term policy type in which premiums stay the same for a specified period of time (e.g., 10, 20, or 30 years). The term or duration for which a level premium policy may be contracted is a function of the state in which the policy is purchased. Some states do not allow level premium contracts of more than 20 years.

Convertible term: What's known as *conversion* has become more of a feature than an actual policy type. Both annual renewable term and level premium term policies might come with a conversion feature that allows the policy owner to convert the policy to the more permanent, cash value variety, such as universal life or whole life (see below), but at a higher annual premium within a certain number of years (such as for the first 10 policy years, or until the insured reaches age 60). The major benefit of this feature is that the policy may be converted without additional (medical) underwriting, which is quite a significant benefit, especially if the insured is ill.

More permanent, cash value life insurance also comes in several forms:

Whole life: This policy type gets its name from the fact that policy premiums are generally payable for your entire, or whole, life. Premiums paid to the carrier are invested in the carrier's general funds. The investment return earned by the carrier, together with other factors such as the past year's mortality experience (i.e., how many covered people have died), will help to determine if the carrier will have a surplus of cash at year-end. If it does, it may declare a dividend (which is actually a return of premium or principal). Dividends can be used by policy owners in several ways, some of which include purchasing paid-up additional insurance, applying them toward the payment of the annual premium, or receiving them as cash.

Universal life: Universal life insurance is generally referred to as interest-driven insurance. Premiums are paid to the carrier, which then deposits the money in a separate accumulation account established for the specific policy. The account is then both credited with interest and charged with the cost of insurance, as well as mortality and expense charges, usually on a monthly basis. The balance in the accumulation account continues to earn tax-deferred and compounded interest. Periodically, the carrier may change the interest rate, which can go up or down over time, but which may not go below the contractual minimum rate.

Variable universal life (VUL): This type of insurance is similar to universal life except that instead of a cash accumulation account to which premium dollars are credited, premium dollars are allocated to mutual funds offered by the carrier for the particular variable universal life product. The funds invested in it are held in a separate account. Usually there are several (and there can be as many as 30) funds from which to choose and allocate investable premium dollars. The rate of return on the investments is what drives policy performance. As with a universal life policy, the separate account experiences gain (or loss, as the case may be) and is also charged with the cost of insurance, as well as mortality and expense charges, usually on a monthly basis.

Private placement variable universal life: This type of insurance is a variation on variable universal life and is essentially the same, except that investable premium dollars are placed with a private investment management firm (such as U.S. Trust) rather than invested directly in a mutual fund offered by the carrier of that specific VUL product. The two major advantages of this type of policy are that the policy owner has more control over the underlying investments, and the costs (such as COI), expenses, and commissions are generally lower. One caveat: Private placement VUL policies are generally structured with very high annual (or one-time) premiums (usually starting at $1 million).

The increase in cash value (by way of interest, dividends, and/or gain) of a cash value life insurance policy is untaxed until withdrawals are made from the cash value—and then only to the extent that these withdrawals exceed the premium basis, unless the policy is a modified endowment contract. In this case, the gain comes out first when withdrawals are made. The tax is at ordinary income tax rates, however, rather than at capital gain rates. Contact your attorney, tax advisor, and/or insurance agent for advice regarding taxation of withdrawals (and/or surrenders) from cash value life insurance policies.

Cash value life insurance policies may be considered suitable assets for long-term estate planning vehicles, such as irrevocable life insurance Crummey trusts. For example, a policy (or multiple policies) may be placed or purchased in an irrevocable trust, allowing the proceeds to escape taxation in the insured's estate at death, and providing income and principal for beneficiaries for many years.

Clearly, life insurance offers many advantages and is often the only way to instantly create an estate until you have created one through wealth accumulation, but few people enjoy paying for it. Several premium-financing options are available and elaborate mechanisms are also available to shift the payment of premiums to third parties. Through the use of *split-dollar* policies, insurance premiums may be paid for by a corporation. And through policy and promissary note sales to a defective grantor trust or via loans (or a promissory note), rather than with direct gifts to a trust (some or part of which may be taxable), the payment of premiums can sometimes be made more efficiently. (While these premium-financing options ought to be discussed in the context of your overall estate and gift-giving plans, they are extremely complex and should not be entered into without first seeking appropriate tax and legal advice.)

Life Insurance Policy

Reviewing how much insurance you need at any point, selecting an appropriate type, and making sure you have enough (and not too much) are all part of life insurance planning. You also must take into account that you will be subject to a medical exam that will determine your underwriting category (e.g., "preferred," "standard," "smoker," or "non-smoker"). Not every applicant for life insurance is extended an offer by the carrier. Health problems or even occupations and hobbies, such as piloting a private plane, may lead to your being uninsurable or being put into an underwriting class that is "rated," meaning the insurance will be very expensive (in comparison to the better underwriting categories).

As part of your life insurance planning process, you and your advisors may determine that an irrevocable life insurance trust is an appropriate estate and gift-giving plan. Creating an irrevocable trust, in which your trustees purchase a life insurance policy on your life within the trust, may have the net effect of allowing the life insurance to escape being taxed in your estate when you die. Life insurance trusts are a complex estate planning vehicle, but worthwhile because they may be considered triple tax advantaged, in that you may be able to escape:

- *Gift tax:* Gifts to the trust may qualify for the annual per donee gift tax exclusion.

- *Income tax:* Interest, dividends, and gain within the cash value of the policy may escape income taxes.

- *Estate tax:* The life insurance itself may not be included in your estate, as already noted.

Annuities

Annuities are another possible element of an insurance package that a good agent will discuss with you. Annuities are an investment vehicle that give you a guaranteed income for the duration of the policy. Similar to an IRA or a SEP, the earnings on your investment are deferred until you withdraw the funds. It is rare that an annuity program can outperform the investment opportunities available to an affluent individual, and annuities do not generally provide any of the estate planning advantages associated with life insurance. As with life insurance, several kinds of annuities are available. An *immediate annuity* will start providing you with an income as soon as you pay your one and only premium. However, you can never again withdraw that money, so you had better be sure that this is what you want.

A *life-only annuity* lets you receive payments throughout your life, but stops when you die. This means that if you are hit by a car the day after you've signed the papers, neither you nor your heirs will make another penny. A *10-year certain and life annuity* guarantees payments for a decade, even if you don't live that long, and then continues to pay you as long as you continue to live.

As with life insurance, annuities can be fixed or variable. If they are fixed, you'll receive the same payments every year, no matter what happens to the financial markets, even if there's unusual inflation. Variable annuities, however, are those in which your money is invested in equity funds, and your income rises or falls depending on the funds' performance.

Yet another type of annuity is a *deferred annuity*. Here, you are not paid when you buy the policy, but at a future date when you want to start receiving income. Deferred annuities can be fixed or variable.

Annuities provide you with an income for what could be a very long time, and as with retirement accounts, you do not pay taxes as they appreciate. However, just as with retirement accounts, you will be penalized if you withdraw the money before you are 59½ years old.

Disability Insurance

Many people who are otherwise very well covered for all kinds of insurance needs forget to arrange for adequate disability insurance. Although most people tend to believe they'll never be disabled, the odds are higher than you might think that some kind of disability may occur at some point in your life. If it does and you can't earn enough income to maintain your current lifestyle, you will very much wish you had purchased disability insurance.

The general rule is to buy insurance that will replace about 65 percent of your current pretax earnings, because these benefits are tax-free (as long as you've paid for your own insurance). As always, there are various policies available, and they can be expensive. However, you can actually save money if you buy disability insurance that covers you up to age 65 (because many people stop working after that, replacing salary is no longer an issue). Another way to save money in premiums is to increase the number of months you must be disabled before the policy begins paying you benefits.

Health Insurance

Unlike life insurance, which people without dependents may not need, health insurance is a must for everyone. Any good financial planner will insist that you be well covered, and if you're not, may be able to point you to an agent or broker. (For the most part, an insurance agent works for a specific company and offers products exclusive to that company, whereas a broker will show your products from many different companies and, theoretically, match you with the ones that best meet your needs.)

If you have an employer, most likely you're already insured. In fact, the concept of medical insurance was started by large labor unions as a way of obtaining a salary increase without having to worry about paying additional taxes. The unions asked for health programs, and their employers granted them because back in the early to middle part of the last century, health benefits were reasonably priced. Health insurance was far down on an employers' balance sheet. Today, however, it comes right behind salaries and rent. As we all know, American health costs have skyrocketed.

If you're not insured through your employer, you'll want to find individual insurance. If you do not, you'll have to accept the risk that if you're sick, you will fund whatever medical costs you encounter out of your own pocket. There was a time when this might not have been an unreasonable gamble, but current medical costs make this choice impractical. Of course, you may be required to spend as much as $30,000 a year covering your entire family with top-of-the-line insurance. But consider what might happen if you're not covered—a worst-case scenario could mean medical bills ranging into the high six figures. We've seen situations where they rose even above that. So why not transfer the risk from your own assets to those of the insurance company?

If you don't have an employer, try to be creative in coming up with a way to cover yourself. Recently, one of our clients set up a family foundation that is large enough to employ four younger members of his family. Because these children have real jobs at the foundation, they are paid like any salaried employees and receive W2 forms at the end of the year. By so doing, the foundation is permitted to—and has—set up a health plan for these family employees. Another U.S. Trust client family set up a foundation as a limited partnership, and at the end of the year, they receive a K1 form, or the equivalent of a W2 for partnerships. This arrangement also allows them to establish a health program. Keep in mind that for any of these group medical programs, there must be an employer/employee relationship. You can't simply bring a group together for the sole purpose of receiving medical coverage. The insurance company will investigate to verify withholding taxes, which prove that the covered individual is an employee.

Another health care–related issue that you must consider is long-term-care insurance. This type of policy is designed to help you look after yourself in the event of a prolonged illness. Such coverage has become important because, fortunately, we're living longer, but unfortunately, we seldom have sufficient assets to cover what may prove to be the enormous expenses associated with a long life. Many people don't realize it, but regular health insurance and government-funded Medicare do not cover these long-term health problems. For instance, the frequently changing Medicare rules currently specify that if you are confined for three days to a hospital and then enter a skilled nursing facility to be treated for the same problem, Medicare will pay 100 percent of the first 20 days of such care. Between day 21 and day 100, they'll pay all but $105 per day of these costs. After 100 days, however, Medicare pays nothing at all. To add insult to injury, if you didn't enter the hospital first, you would not have been eligible for any Medicare payment.

Although some employee programs do cover long-term care, most of them don't, so you will have to purchase it yourself. Long-term-care insurance is expensive, however. The younger you are when you buy it, the cheaper it is (generally, the rates start when you are 40 years old). At age 40, an average long-term-care insurance policy (standard, non-smoker rate) would cost you about $1,600 a year; at age 50 it costs about $2,100 annually; at 60, $3,600; and at 70, $6,500.

When purchasing this type of insurance, make sure it includes an inflation rider. What might look like a great deal of money today may not be in 30 years. You don't want your health care to suffer because of it.

Property and Casualty Insurance

This kind of insurance protects you against the financial consequence of having your property destroyed or damaged by a variety of perils. A partial list of policies insuring real and personal property includes homeowners, condominium, co-op, renters, farm owners, ranch owners, personal articles floater, automobile, water craft, airplane, and flood insurance.

Most policies provide coverage for loss or damage to property by including or excluding certain perils that may cause the loss. Under a typical property policy, a few of the excluded perils are neglect, earthquake, flood, intentional acts, wear and tear, and breakage of fragile articles. Thus, it is important to determine whether other types of insurance will be required.

Replacement-Cost Insurance

Your sofa may be beautiful, but the truth is that even if it cost $5,000 when you bought it yesterday, today you could probably sell it at only a fraction of that price. But if that sofa is destroyed, you'll want to buy something that's as good as the one you lost, and not a used piece. Therefore, when you're looking to insure your property, you'll want what's known as replacement-cost coverage, as opposed to no-replacement-value or depreciated-value coverage. Replacement-cost insurance is more expensive than other types, but it's worth it, and we recommend it highly.

Also, consider taking replacement-cost insurance on your property. We had a client who owned a famous home in California featuring very ornate oak carvings throughout. The house was struck by lightning and burned almost to the ground. It cost the owners $7 million to restore the house in the same condition. They would never have been able to afford to do this, complete with all its intricate carvings, if they hadn't owned replacement-cost insurance. Otherwise, their insurance would have paid only for standard features.

Most policies limit the amount of coverage for certain types of property. These limits include:

- *Contents:* Typically limited to 50 to 75 percent of the dwelling value.
- *Other structures:* Typically limited to 10 to 20 percent of the dwelling value.
- *Jewelry:* Typically limited to $1,000 to $5,000 per loss.
- *Silverware:* Typically limited to $1,000 to $5,000 per loss.
- *Furs:* Typically limited to $1,000 to $5,000 per loss.

- *Money:* Typically limited to $200 to $1,000 per loss.
- *Securities:* Typically limited to $1,000 to $5,000 per loss.
- *Additions and alterations:* Typically limited to 10 percent of the contents value.

Specific endorsements and/or policies can be purchased to provide coverage for excluded perils or limited property coverage. You may want to consider a personal articles floater, flood insurance, an all-risk endorsement, and/or earthquake coverage.

Automobile Insurance

Automobile insurance is fairly straightforward. When you buy a car, you also buy insurance for it—the process is ingrained into our heads at a young age. And unlike other kinds of insurance, automobile insurance is usually required; many states won't let you buy a car without it. But even if it's not required, you should make sure you are fully insured.

True, the cost of automobile insurance has skyrocketed over the last decade, but that doesn't mean you shouldn't be fully insured. As with health care, it costs much less than the potential out-of-pocket charges you may face in a worst-case scenario. In addition to purchasing the standard insurance coverage, you should also make sure that you are well covered for liability in case of bodily injury and property damage. If you or someone else driving your car plows over a curb and into a restaurant, the insurance will cover the costs of hiring an attorney to defend yourself against what could be an onslaught of lawsuits. Coverage will also pay for other court costs, as well as any judgments against you.

Liability Insurance

Personal liability insurance protects you from having to pay out a large sum of money from your own pocket in case your actions have caused someone else to suffer bodily injury or property damage.

U.S. Trust finds that liability coverage is the area in which most people are least capably insured. Although an increasing number of people are aware of the need for this kind of coverage, we still see clients who own many different properties but have failed to include all of them in a master liability plan.

If you are affluent, liability coverage represents your biggest exposure. If you own a house, you know its value and that of your personal assets. If they're destroyed, you have a good idea of what the dollar loss might be. Unfortunately, liability costs are virtually unlimited. Let's say a busload of medical students careens off the road and lands in a ditch in your property, and every one of them is hurt. There's no telling how many millions you may have to pay out in liability costs.

Unlike property damage, which can be anticipated to some extent, liability is hard to predict. Many years ago we had a client who owned land in the Northwest. Eventually, this property fell into a trust, held by various members of the family, but by the latter part of the 1980s the trust was terminated, its assets were sold, and all its distributions paid out. The person who purchased this land hired an inspector to check out the property. He discovered that a service station had been located on the property 60 years ago, and long-forgotten oil storage tanks had ruptured in the ground, polluting the earth and groundwater. The man then sued the trust because it had failed to maintain the property in good form. He won his case.

If you have a net worth of $5 million, $10 million, or $25 million, how much liability coverage is enough? This is a difficult question to answer, but generally speaking it is a question of balancing the cost of the insurance against your own comfort level and lifestyle. I think having a policy worth at least $10 million is essential for virtually all of our clients.

In addition to the liability coverage found in package policies, other types of policies provide liability coverage but are geared toward different exposures. Some of these policies include:

Professional liability insurance: This type of coverage can go by any of several names including D&O (directors and officers), E&O (errors and omissions), or medical malpractice. It protects you from being held liable when damage is due to your bad advice, errors, or omissions in judgments. People who would benefit from this type of coverage include corporate directors and officers, medical professionals, attorneys, architects, builders, etc.

Excess personal liability insurance: This type of policy is intended to provide additional coverage over and above primary policies, such as homeowner's insurance or automobile insurance. Typically written in $1 million increments, it costs roughly $100 per $1 million of coverage. This coverage is essential for anyone with substantial assets.

Worker's compensation: This insurance is for clients who have full-time employees such as maids, butlers, chauffeurs, and/or secretaries. It protects both the employer and employee, in that the employee cannot sue the employer for an on-the-job injury. Rather, the employee is guaranteed that his or her medical bills will be paid, and that he or she will be paid for most lost wages if he or she cannot work as a result of an on-the-job injury.

Other Insurance

There are a few other kinds of insurance available. Not all wealthy individuals will need them, but it's good to know they're available if you do.

Kidnap insurance insures you against the very unlikely, but not unheard of, possibility of kidnapping. Abductions don't happen in America as often as they do in countries such as Brazil or Italy, but even here people are occasionally taken for ransom. Let's say you've spent your life building up your assets, and then your teenage children travel to a foreign country and are abducted. The kidnapping insurance will not only pay the ransom, but will also pay for private investigators to track down the children. At U.S. Trust, only two clients have it as far as I know; each is insured for $5 million. You may not be likely to get or need this kind of insurance, but reading about it may pique your interest enough to prompt you to think about your life and whether it might be wise to buy some special type of coverage that most people don't need or want.

Directors insurance, once rare, has become much more common in the last few years. Before 2000, directors on corporate boards were seldom sued. That has changed due to the corporate scandals of the last three years, and we've recently been receiving many inquiries about it. If you ever serve on a board, you will want to make sure that you are well covered for liability, particularly if you're part of a team that makes what turns out to be a bad decision. Most boards have their own directors and officers (D&O) insurance, but with liability suits now reaching the hundreds of millions, some of our clients are concerned that they need more, so they take out a second (or third) policy against suits brought by shareholders.

Insurance Rules

One caveat to consider as you decide on the types of insurance you need: Different carriers have different rules. For example, the insurance company with whom U.S. Trust most often deals has a rule concerning the contents of one's home: They assume that the contents are worth 50 percent of value of dwelling. So if you have a million dollar house, they'll estimate you need $500,000 worth of contents insurance for your furniture, appliances, and so on. Other insurance companies, however, may have a 10 percent rule. Or, some companies only will insure silverware to $5,000, unless you have a special valuable articles rider on your policy. If your silverware is your pride and joy, you will need to let your broker know that—particularly since there are many people for whom silverware means little.

If you haven't resolved these issues up front, the worst that can happen is that you suffer some kind of loss and find that you are not covered to the degree you thought. Not long ago I heard a story about an executive at another company who had a beautiful vacation home in the Caribbean. That is an area where it can be difficult to get good insurance coverage because of the weather as well as potentially unstable political situations. In this case, a hurricane swept through the island and nearly destroyed his home. He thought he was fully insured, but when he called his insurance company, he found that his policy required them to pay only 75 percent of the damages. He had no idea.

Not every insurance rule is always as cut and dried. For instance, at U.S. Trust we have occasionally gone to bat for clients, trying to help them recover as much insurance as possible. Not long ago one of our clients lost one antique ruby earring which was insured under a valuable items rider. The standard in the insurance industry is that if you lose one earring and you receive compensation for it, you're required to give back the remaining earring to mitigate the company's risk. This client refused to do that. She said that the earrings had enormous sentimental value because they had been in her family for generations. The insurance company finally agreed. I don't think she's their favorite client, but she's pretty happy with them.

Finding a Good Insurance Broker

Now that you've considered your insurance requirements, you'll need to take the next step: finding a good insurance broker. It's probably smart to have one person handle all your insurance needs. A good insurance broker will represent a number of carriers and be able to make intelligent, informed recommendations as to which types of insurance are best for you, as well as how much to purchase.

A skilled broker will also make an effort to learn who you are and access your psychological profile. Are you risk averse? Some people are more willing to assume risks, and thus are more willing to take less insurance coverage. They may not cover their collections or other assets for as much and are willing to take the chance that, in return for little or no coverage, they will not need to pay out any money later to cover losses or liabilities. Once a broker knows your assets and has figured out your personality, he or she should be able to put together a plan.

The best way to find a broker is through word of mouth. I realize that insurance isn't something you talk about much, but if you need a good broker, ask around. When you have a few names, check their professional alliances, their degrees, and ask them for references. Any reputable broker should be able to steer you toward satisfied clients. If he or she can't, that should be a sign to look around some more.

If you still can't find someone with whom you're comfortable, remember that every state has its own professional hotline for dentists, lawyers, and insurance brokers. Contacting it may not always be the smartest idea, however, because some states are willing to list anyone who pays a small fee for the privilege.

Make sure your broker deals with multiple carriers. You don't want someone who represents just one carrier because this may mean that he or she is actually an employee of that company and will push only the company's products—and even the best insurance companies may not be appropriate for all your insurance needs.

Before you commit, visit with the broker. You want someone who is smart and who can answer your questions knowledgeably, but can speak in language that you can thoroughly understand. Ask as many questions as possible. Prepare a list of your assets ahead of time so you can give the broker an accurate picture.

Once you've set it up, review your insurance every year. Few people live static lives. You might have a baby, buy a new car, or build an addition to your house that adds to its overall value, which in turn means you must revise your insurance. Always be diligent about keeping track of what you own and remember that any time you add to your life, you might consider adding to your insurance.

And remember, you'll need to coordinate insurance services with the rest of your wealth management needs. Thus, the other wealth management professionals you use should be apprised of any changes, too, and considered part of the team that continually reviews your insurance solutions.

CHAPTER 5

Retirement

*You can be young without money but you can't be old
without it.*

—Tennessee Williams,
American dramatist

*Wealth is not without its advantages and the case to the
contrary, although it has often been made, has never
proved widely persuasive.*

—John Kenneth Galbraith,
American economist

Retirement planning allows you to retire based on a predetermined lifestyle at an age you decide. A subset of the
financial planning discipline, retirement planning should be reviewed regularly as part of your financial planning cycle, whenever
you contemplate a change in employment, and when retirement time
approaches.

Coordinating all of your retirement options is essential. To the
extent that you have a funded retirement plan, such as a 401(k), it
should be reviewed on the same cycle as your investments. Retirement

planning should be done by your financial planner, and similar guide-lines apply.

The real added value of a retirement plan is finding the solution that enables you to enhance as many other financial opportunities as possible. For example, with the right vehicle, you can make with-drawals from retirement plans that not only will solve your cash-flow needs, but also are highly tax-efficient, freeing up other funds with which you can do charitable giving.

Retirement isn't simply about turning 65—it's about making sure throughout your entire working life that you're ready for life when you're not working.

U.S. Trust Survey of Affluent Americans Results

At the rate they are saving, our survey respondents expect they can retire at age 60. But based on their actual savings habits, our calcula-tions show that 67 percent of respondents will fall shy of their retire-ment goals. The problem is that, on average, those surveyed are saving only 71 percent of the amount they need to reach their annual retire-ment goal (they want an average after-tax income of $166,394 in retirement; they are saving enough to have $117,507). Those who are 50 and older are saving only 58 percent of the amount they stated they want in annual retirement income—$126,064 in today's dollars, after taxes, versus the desired $218,300. This survey was conducted in 1996. Since that time, the S&P 500 is only up 5.73% on an annualized basis versus historical rate of return on equities of 10.29%. The lapse of time will only make saving for retirement more difficult.

Fifty-two percent of respondents said that planning for retirement is of utmost importance to them, and that they were sacrificing now to ensure their future comfort (see Figure 5.1). Fourteen percent admit-ted that there are too many other demands on their income now, and

FIGURE 5.1   HOW AFFLUENT AMERICANS PLAN TO FINANCE
                RETIREMENT

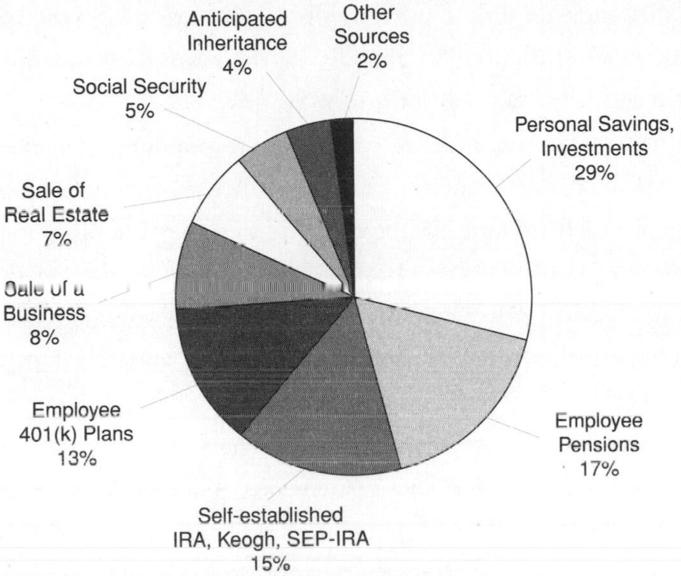

SOURCE: U.S. Trust Survey of Affluent Americans X, May 1996

13 percent said that they weren't worried because they would simply get by when the time comes.

Fifty percent of respondents began saving for retirement by the time they were 30. Twenty-three percent said they have already put away $1 million; 18 percent have between $500,000 and $1 million; 38 percent have between $100,000 and $500,000, and 20 percent have no more than $100,000. The average retirement portfolio is composed of 32 percent domestic equities, 24 percent domestic bonds, 18 percent cash, 10 percent real estate, 8 percent private business, and 2 percent venture capital.

What are the biggest retirement concerns of the affluent? Sixty-five percent said that they worry that inflation will diminish their retirement income; 52 percent worry that poor health will keep them from enjoying their retirement; 50 percent worry that after retirement, taxes will rise steeply, cutting their income; and 48 percent worry that Social Security will run out of money before they can collect everything that they are due. The younger affluent are more worried than the older about inflation, the inability to maintain their income, and a possible end or curtailment of Social Security.

When they retire, most of our survey respondents said their first priority is to spend as much time as possible with family (94 percent). Almost an equal amount, 93 percent, said that they intend to maintain basically the same lifestyle. Eighty-nine percent said they want to travel a great deal; 81 percent intend to pursue leisure activities such as golf, sailing, or tennis; 76 percent expect to do some kind of philanthropic work; and 75 percent are looking forward to pursuing hobbies such as gardening, photography, and needlepoint.

Regarding their future living situations, 40 percent said they plan to move when they retire, 39 percent plan to stay where they are, and 21 percent are unsure. Fifty-eight percent expect to maintain multiple residences. When it comes to choosing a place to live during retirement, the most important qualities, in descending order, are a clean, healthy, and attractive natural environment; interesting and stimulating cultural life; access to good health care; good weather; and proximity to children and/or grandchildren.

Retirement Scenarios

U.S. Trust once had a client, an older man named Carl, who arrived at our doorstep after years of working with a different company. Before we went over his financial information, we sat down and had a general conversation to get to know each other. Carl was a lawyer, and following years of corporate life, he had started his own firm. After hearing about the kinds of issues he dealt with, and how much he enjoyed his private practice, one of our advisors mentioned retirement plans.

Carl looked puzzled. He didn't need to depend on the money he made in his practice, he explained; he had money put aside. The advisor then asked him what he planned on doing when he retired, and if he had enough money to maintain those plans. We knew that Carl was an older man, but we were still surprised when he said, "I'm 82 years old. I'll be doing this until the day I die." Carl was correct. Not only did he look two decades younger than his age, he maintained a lifestyle of a much younger man until his death, which occurred while on his way downtown to file a will.

Not long after Carl came to us, Peter, the son of a client who had been with us for decades, called us up to discuss his retirement. Peter had worked very hard and made a great deal of money in the Internet boom, and unlike his peers, he had sold everything just before the crash, giving him a net worth of about $4 million. Peter wanted to come in and discuss how to manage his nonworking years, because all he wanted to do now was travel, learn to ski, and have fun. His age? He was 27. He felt that he'd worked enough for one lifetime.

Retirement Planning

Perhaps the changing of the times is more apparent in this area of financial planning than any other. In the past, people stayed at one job for most of their lives and then retired at the age of 65. Early retirement meant 62; few people worked past 70.

Following the recent bear market, many people have had to adjust their thinking about retirement. Not everyone now has the luxury of retiring early. Many are faced with having to work longer to meet their retirement lifestyle goals. The goal of retirement planning is to do your best to make sure that you don't make a meaningful mistake later in your career that can destroy or severely damage your retirement plans.

Another change: people used to start thinking about retirement savings when they reached their forties or fifties. Today, so many television shows, books, and radio programs have discussed the importance of saving that most people are getting the message. The number of Americans under the age of 18 with a Roth IRA has risen to more than 900,000. Saving for retirement has so permeated the culture that people take it for granted. Of course, you save for retirement—if you have the extra money to do so. My own personal philosophy was always to save in tax-favored vehicles even if I had to borrow to support my lifestyle.

We all know that we'll need money once we stop working. What we don't know is exactly how *much* money we will need. Plenty of planners ask you to estimate how much you'll need to budget for various expenses once you're retired, and they usually indicate that you'll want about 75 percent of what you live on now—but frankly, it's impossible to project your budget of 10 or 20 years from today. To achieve a comfortable retirement nest egg, you should consider maximizing your contributions to any and all of your retirement plans during your working years.

You also should monitor and adjust these contributions annually, based on your current liquidity, changing tax legislation, and available investment options. In this way, you can best ensure your retirement plan is targeted to meet your specific objectives. The fact is that unless you are monitoring these plans, you may make mistakes. You even run the risk of overfunding them. For example, in 2003 you're permitted to put up to $12,000 into a 401(k) plan (or $40,000, if you're self-employed). But is that too much money? Perhaps by contributing so much to your retirement fund, you might have to curtail your current lifestyle. It's smart to save for the future, but not everyone can or should follow my approach and borrow to live for today while saving for tomorrow. (We have found that doctors are among the most likely to overfund their retirement plans, but they're a special case: They do it because these plans are also asset-protection vehicles. In case of a malpractice claim, creditors generally can't get to the money within a retirement plan; it's not transferable. This rule does vary state by state and by the type of retirement plan, so if you're moving, your IRA or other plan may no longer be protected.)

There's another reason you should be saving for retirement, besides having money to live on later: tax advantages. Retirement plans allow you to put your money into tax-deferred savings, thanks to the many government-sanctioned vehicles for accumulating money. Not only can you defer taxes on the interest generated by a retirement account, but your contributions will generally be excluded from your taxable income, as will contributions made on your behalf by your employer. The earlier you start thinking about taking advantage of these tax-deferred vehicles, the better off you will be in future years.

Tax Savings

The impact of tax deferral on retirement savings is impressive. The sooner you start saving, the more dramatic the results. If you contribute $3,000 each year to an IRA (the new maximum, as of 2003) and it receives an 8 percent annualized return, after 20 years the balance would be $148,000; after 30 years it grows to $367,000; and after 40 years you would have saved $839,000. Although $3,000 may seem like an inconsequential amount, it does grow to a substantial sum if you start early and stay the course (see Figure 5.2).

FIGURE 5.2   FUTURE VALUE OF ANNUAL IRA CONTRIBUTIONS

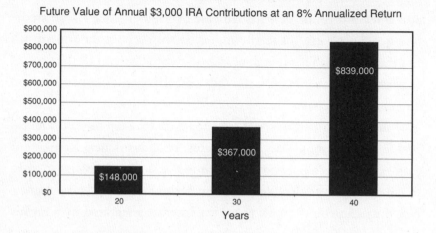

Future Value of Annual $3,000 IRA Contributions at an 8% Annualized Return

Individual Retirement Accounts

The number of available individual retirement vehicles is extensive, but they are also limited. Tax codes specify how your money may or may not be taxed, how much money you can contribute to individual retirement plans, and what portion of those contributions is tax-deductible. Your choices are discussed in the following paragraphs.

Individual Retirement Accounts (IRAs) provide tax-deferred growth and, in some cases, a current income tax deduction. In order to be eligible to contribute to an IRA, you must have earned income. For tax year 2003, you could contribute up to $3,000 of your earnings. You also may contribute an additional $3,000 for a nonemployed spouse, raising your total household contribution to $6,000. For taxpayers over the age of 50, starting in 2002, you will be able to make an additional catch-up contribution of $500 per year for tax years 2002 to 2005 and $1,000 per year for tax year 2006 (adjusted for inflation starting in 2007).

If you qualify, you may be able to deduct all or part of your IRA contribution from your taxable income. For example, you can deduct the entire amount if neither you nor your spouse is covered by a qualified retirement plan. Otherwise, as your income increases, the amount available for deduction decreases and is eventually phased out entirely. However, tax law restrictions have made it impossible for many individuals to fund individual retirement accounts on a fully tax-deductible basis when they are considered "active participants" in employer-sponsored retirement plans and have an adjusted gross income (AGI) over specified levels.

For married couples, the active participation of one spouse in an employer-sponsored plan is enough to trigger possible limitations on IRA deductions for both spouses if AGI limits are exceeded.

Nonemployed Spousal IRAs

If one spouse actively participates in an employer-sponsored plan and the other does not, the nonparticipant spouse may make a deductible IRA contribution of up to the maximum allowable for that year if the AGI on the joint return is $150,000 or less. The deductible amount is phased out with AGI over $150,000, with full phase-out at $160,000. The current law does not index these AGI limits for inflation.

Nondeductible Traditional IRAs

Individuals (and nonemployed spouses) with $3,000 of earned income in 2003 whose AGI exceeds the aforementioned limits may choose to make contributions to a nondeductible IRA.

Nondeductible Roth IRAs

Although no tax deductions are allowed for Roth IRAs, they offer a feature that may be even more attractive than an upfront deduction.

Specifically, withdrawals after age 59½ will be tax-free provided the Roth IRA has been in existence for more than five years. Also, you are not required to take minimum distributions at age 70½, as you would with most other retirement plans. As with traditional IRAs, contributions to a Roth IRA may only be made by individuals whose earned income is at least equal to the contribution amount. A Roth IRA contribution may also be made on behalf of a nonworking spouse. The allowable contribution will phase out for single taxpayers whose AGI is between $95,000 and $110,000 (or $150,000 to $160,000 for joint filers).

Any child can contribute to a Roth IRA, assuming he or she has some earned income and adjusted gross income of no more than $110,000, which is probably a good assumption for most children (still, 14-year-old Daniel Radcliffe earned exactly $110,000 for his starring role in *Harry Potter and the Sorceror's Stone;* however, for his next movie, *Harry Potter and the Chamber of Secrets,* he made $3 million). Yet, many kids earn money from doing chores, delivering papers, or babysitting, and some manage to find summer jobs that can be fairly lucrative, on a small scale. All these can count as earned income (the money can't be dividend income—the child must truly work for the money).

A gift also can be made in order to help someone else build up a nice retirement fund. For example, let's say your college-aged daughter made $10,000 this past summer during her vacation; you can give her $3,000 to set up a Roth IRA even though she's already spent all the money she made. The government doesn't care how she spent the money; it simply requires that she made enough money to establish the contribution (this assumes that you already haven't given her the full $22,000 gift allowable under current rules).

Although they may not be able to make contributions to a traditional IRA, individuals who continue working after age 70½ may continue to make contributions to a Roth IRA, provided the income limitations are not exceeded. Roth IRAs do not require minimum distributions. Therefore, if you are retired and don't need income from your Roth IRA, you have the option of allowing your money to continue compounding tax-free. This tax-free growth also may be passed on to Roth IRA beneficiaries. Unlike the original Roth IRA owner, the beneficiaries of a Roth IRA must withdraw the account's funds over time and according to IRS regulations.

Traditional versus Roth IRA

Investors who can participate in the new Roth IRA may receive significantly more after-tax income during retirement from that account than from traditional IRAs (both deductible and non-deductible).

In general, the longer the period of investment before retirement, the greater the advantage of the Roth IRA, since earnings compound tax-free over a longer period of time. If the IRA assets will not be used during the investor's lifetime and will be passed to the next generation, the greater the advantage of the Roth IRA, since there are no required minimum distributions to deplete the Roth IRA account during the contributor's life.

Be aware that this comparison hinges upon certain variables, such as tax rates at the time of your contributions and when you retire, the length of time remaining until withdrawal, and projected rates of return. If you do qualify for a Roth, fund it to the maximum extent allowable.

If a Roth IRA has been in existence for less than five years, withdrawals are presumed, for tax purposes, to come first from contributions (as opposed to earnings). Since contributions are considered a return of capital, no tax or penalty is due on contributions regardless of when they are withdrawn. However, earnings withdrawn before the age of 59½ from a Roth IRA in existence less than five years will be subject to both income tax and a 10 percent penalty (as always, certain exceptions may apply).

Rollover to a Roth IRA

Note that a traditional IRA may be rolled over into a Roth IRA if your AGI is $100,000 or less. This $100,000 AGI limit applies to both single and married filers. Income taxes (but no penalties—unless the Roth IRA is not held for at least five years) will have to be paid on the rollover, however. Such rollovers may be a good idea, depending on current and future tax rates and whether you have non-IRA funds available to pay the taxes due. If you have low or depressed stock values, consider it a good time to convert a regular IRA into a Roth IRA because when you do, it becomes taxable income, but you'll have no future capital gains to worry about.

If the value of your traditional IRA account is not depressed, it may not make sense to convert from a traditional IRA to a Roth IRA. As noted above, doing so will accelerate income tax with respect to your IRA assets. Therefore, the decision to convert a traditional IRA into a Roth IRA must be carefully examined. Some of the key factors to consider in making this decision include:

- How much time you have until you begin taking the money out, and how long you expect to be making withdrawals after retirement.

- The total amount you might convert, since you would have to pay taxes on the taxable portion of the rollover.

- Your current tax bracket and projected tax bracket after retirement.

- For those over age 70½, whether you have made the proper distribution elections, and if a spousal rollover is possible.

Other Retirement Plans

Qualified Plans

These include pension plans, 401(k) plans, profit-sharing and savings plans, Keoghs, employee stock ownership plans (ESOPs), qualified annuities, and stock bonus plans. Such plans can be divided into two broad categories: defined contribution plans and defined benefit plans. Each type of plan is distinct in its characteristics and tax rules. In general, however, you need to know which of your company plans are qualified and the distribution options available for each plan, such as a lump sum or annuity payment.

401(k)s

As with other retirement plans, the 401(k) lets you place a portion of your pretax salary into a retirement account. Not only do your savings grow tax-free, but many employers will match some or all of your contributions. At a minimum, you should make contributions to the extent your company matches all or some of them. Failing to take advantage of this option is like turning down a small bonus. The amount contributed by you and your company is not taxable until withdrawal. Although your company's matching contribution may not be yours to keep if you end employment before the contribution vests, your prior contributions and their earnings always belong to you.

Defined Benefit Plans

These plans pay a fixed monthly amount of income at retirement period. The benefit payable to you is based on a complex formula, taking into account your earnings and years of service. Contributions to these plans are almost always made entirely by the employer. The most common defined benefit plan is an employer pension plan.

Annuities

Most defined benefit plans pay out in the form of an annuity although some provide for a discounted lump sum payment. An annuity is a stream of payments usually lasting for the life of the retiree (called by the legal-sounding term *annuitant*). If you choose to take a reduced annuity payment, a second or joint annuitant (usually a spouse) also can receive a payment if he or she outlives you. Typical joint annuitant options include 100 percent joint and survivor (J&S), in which each person receives the same payout, regardless of the order of death; 50 percent J&S, where the surviving joint annuitant receives 50 percent of the annuitant's payment; and other options. You also can guarantee the number of payments (called a *term certain* option).

The more protection you provide for the joint annuitant (e.g., your spouse), the smaller the payment to the annuitant (you). In the case of a married couple, the greater the sum of assets owned by the couple, the lesser the need to protect the surviving spouse with an annuity. If necessary, an estate can be augmented with life insurance on the life of the retiree (but as we've discussed, life insurance can be very expensive when you buy it at retirement age). An annuity may be attractive if you seek a safe, secure, guaranteed stream of level payments during the life of the surviving spouse.

The risks of an annuity are twofold:

1. An annuity offers inadequate protection in an inflationary environment.

2. The family may suffer a financial loss if the annuitant dies early in retirement and there is no joint annuitant, or if both annuitant and joint annuitant die early in retirement.

For more on annuities, see Chapter 6.

Profit-Sharing Plans

These plans allow employees to share in the company's profits, although showing an actual profit by the company is not necessary for a contribution to be made on your behalf. Each year the company can designate a varying percentage to be set aside for the benefit of its employees. Often, these funds are controlled by the company, not the employee.

The 2001 Tax Law

The 2001 tax law has created significant changes to retirement planning vehicles. For instance, since 1981 there has been a $2,000 limit on contributions to IRAs; beginning in 2002, the new law permits contributions of up to $3,000, and the allowable contribution amount increases gradually to $5,000 by 2008. To help those closer to retirement, the new law contains a catch-up provision, allowing those age 50 and older to save more. For instance, in 2002, they can contribute up to $3,500 to an IRA, and the catch-up provision increases gradually to $6,000 by 2008. After 2008, these amounts will be adjusted for inflation in increments of $500.

As always, remember that there will be complex participation and coverage rules.

Savings Incentive Match Plan for Employees (SIMPLE)

Companies with 100 or fewer employees (and no other plans) can establish this inexpensive retirement plan. Employees can defer up to $7,000 of their income into these plans (the figure increases annually after 2002). Employers, too, generally must make contributions on behalf of their employees, usually 2 to 3 percent per employee. These plans operate like a no-frills 401(k) plan.

Nonqualified Plans

Nonqualified plans are often used to supplement benefits that are otherwise limited by IRS rules. They can be broken down into two broad categories: the employee elective plan and the excess or supplemental benefit plan. In the employee elective plan, your company takes money from your upcoming bonus (or deducts money from each paycheck) and puts it into a retirement plan; this money is not considered income and will continue to grow. These plans are generally available only to a select group of employees, such as highly compensated executives or senior management.

The excess or supplemental benefit plan also applies to highly compensated employees. Let's say 15 percent of your compensation up to $200,000 is taken into account for a company's qualified retirement plan, but you earn $350,000; a percentage of the excess ($150,000) can be contributed to a nonqualified benefit plan.

Nonqualified plans that are not available to all employees and are usually designed for senior executives or highly paid employees are (naturally) not qualified (under IRS rules) and are not eligible for favorable tax treatment upon distribution or rollover to an IRA. On distribution, nonqualified plan payments are subject to ordinary income tax (and in some cases Social Security taxes), but are not subject to any minimum distribution rules or age distribution rules.

A variety of nonqualified plans exist, including elective deferred compensation plans, long-term incentive plans, benefit equalization plans, excess (additional) pension plans, and restricted stock plans, to name a few. The decision to defer within these plans or to continue deferral upon an award maturity is usually made during employment. You must be aware of when your plan assets will be distributed and what investment allocation choices, if any, are available within your plan. If such plans are pegged to company stock performance and paid in the form of shares of stock, they are subject to ordinary income tax upon distribution.

The advantages of these plans are that they are nontaxable in the year of deferral, offer compounded tax-deferred growth, can be paid out when you're in a lower tax bracket, and may not be subject to state tax if you do not reside in the state at the time the funds are distributed to you. The disadvantage of these plans is that they generally are not funded. In other words, if you elect to defer a portion of your salary, say $1,000, and earmark it for this plan, your company won't pay that amount to you, but also won't necessarily set it aside for you, either. Your employer must keep track of it as if you actually made a deposit, and promises to pay you that sum plus the hypothetical return on it. But the money doesn't physically exist in an account for you.

Nonqualified plan assets are also unsecured, which means they're subject to the company's general creditors in the event of insolvency or bankruptcy (although there are various trusts the money can go into that can protect part of it). These plans are also subject to rescission if management decides to terminate the plan, or if there is a change in control and new management makes that decision.

Certain irrevocable trusts (so-called *rabbi trusts*) can be used to lessen the risks associated with nonqualified benefits, but complete protection of your money from a company's general creditors is virtually impossible without causing the funds to be taxable to you on a current basis. As with regular qualified plans, the payouts from nonqualified plans are taxed as ordinary (compensation) income when you withdraw them; moreover, the money may be subject to the FICA (Social Security and Medicare) tax at that time. That is, if you retire and take the payments over a period of time, they may be subject to FICA taxes, whereas when you were working they may well have been over the FICA limit.

Lump-Sum Distributions from Qualified Plans

Depending on your specific personal financial situation, you might prefer to elect the lump-sum option from a qualified plan. Here the monies from an entire fund are distributed within one calendar year. A taxable lump-sum distribution like this will be taxed in full in the year you take the distribution. A tax-free lump-sum distribution can be achieved by rolling the money into an IRA account or another qualified retirement plan, such as a 401(k), within 60 days of distribution.

If you roll it over from trustee to trustee, no tax will be withheld. If you want to take the money and then put it into a new plan within a 60-day period, the plan administrators withhold income taxes. Any distribution not rolled over will be subject to taxation. However, favorable tax treatments may still be available for the amount not rolled over, providing you participated in the plan for at least five years, and you were born prior to January 1, 1936 (or were at least $59^1/2$ at the time of distribution).

The rules concerning the favorable taxation of lump-sum distributions are varied and complex. They include such concepts as 10-year averaging, 20 percent capital gain treatment on pre-1974 allocation ratios, and special treatment for in-kind distribution of employer stock. Consult a tax or financial professional about tax treatment of your lump-sum distribution before you dismiss it in favor of an IRA or other rollover.

IRA and Qualified Plan Beneficiary Designations

Just as important as putting money into a plan is making sure that you withdraw it correctly. You'll want to ensure that your IRA beneficiary designations—the forms you complete specifying to whom the money will go upon your death—are completed properly. In doing so, you'll assure that your account is transferred in accordance with your objectives. For instance, if your will directs that your property be divided for and distributed to trusts for your minor children, then your beneficiary designation should be arranged in the same way. One of the most common estate planning mistakes we encounter is lack of coordination between a well-drafted will and retirement plan beneficiary designation forms.

The beneficiary designations that you have on file with the trustee or custodian of your IRA determine not only to whom the account will pass, but also how required minimum distributions (RMDs) will be calculated during your life as well as after your death. Thus, it's important to ensure that the beneficiary designation form you have on file with your IRA trustee [or 401(k) administrator] is not only consistent with what we call your *wealth-transfer objectives*, but also is drafted in a tax-savvy manner. You should revise the form as often as is necessary to reflect changes in your personal circumstances or personal financial situation.

In general, the RMD rules require you to begin taking minimum annual distributions from IRAs and other qualified retirement accounts starting no later than April 1 of the year following the year you turn $70^{1}/_{2}$ (in most instances you can defer it longer if you are still actively working at that age). The amount of your RMD is calculated based on the ending balance of the IRA as of December 31 of the previous year divided by the appropriate life expectancy factor. For example, if your IRA has a balance of $400,000 as of December 31, 2002, your RMD for 2003 would be $16,194.33, assuming you are 73 years old ($400,000/24.7). You are always free to take more than the RMD amount. However, if you take less, the shortfall is subject to a 50 percent penalty. If assets remain in your plan at death, the beneficiaries you designate in your beneficiary designation form will determine to whom and how the benefits are paid.

You may name two types of beneficiaries for your IRA:

1. A *primary beneficiary* is an individual, group of individuals, or a legal entity to whom your IRA will pass upon your death.

2. A *secondary beneficiary* becomes the designated beneficiary if the primary beneficiary is not living at the time of your death, or if the primary beneficiary disclaims all or a portion of your IRA.

Careful consideration of the beneficiary allows you to take advantage of significant planning opportunities. Consider the executive who wanted to give half of his 401(k) assets to his family foundation and half to his children. He named his estate as beneficiary and then executed a will with the foregoing dispositions described. Unfortunately, by taking these steps, he caused his entire 401(k) assets to become taxable income after his death, which meant that after taxes, a much smaller amount than he intended will pass on to his family foundation and children.

By simply taking the right steps, he could have benefited both his family and his charity. Instead of naming his estate as the beneficiary, the executive should have divided his IRA into two separate accounts during his lifetime. For one of his IRA accounts, he should have designated his children as equal beneficiaries; for the other, he should have named his family foundation as sole beneficiary. By doing this, the income tax owed after his IRA passes to his foundation would be taxable to his foundation, rather than to his estate. Since his foundation is a tax-exempt entity, it is not required to pay income tax, so the IRA funds it receives are entirely tax-free. His children, too, would have benefited from the ability to withdraw the other one-half of the IRA over their life expectancies—something they would not have been able to do had the foundation been a beneficiary of the same IRA.

Retirement Plans for Small Business Owners

Recent tax legislation regarding retirement plans can provide excellent tax-saving opportunities for small business owners. In addition to the contributions allowed to a SEP and Keogh, small business owners can now make an additional contribution of up to $11,000 (or $12,000 if you are over 50 years old) using the new solo 401(k) plan. This plan gives you investment flexibility, and permits participants to borrow up to $50,000, or one-half the balance, whichever is less. Existing SEP and/or Keogh retirement accounts may be consolidated into the solo 401(k) plan.

Let's say you have $50,000 in self-employed income and can contribute up to $9,291 to a SEP or a Keogh. With this new plan, you can contribute up to $20,291 (or $21,291 if you are over 50). You cannot exceed $40,000 in contributions to all your plans (unless you are over 50, in which case, again, you can add another $1,000). The solo 401(k) plan must be set up by December 31 or the last day of the proprietor's fiscal year.

Retirement Plan Options for the Self-Employed

If you are self-employed, you may have not thought much about employee benefits. If so, you are missing out on providing the advantages of a retirement plan to one of your most valuable employees: yourself.

As previously discussed, the advantage in establishing a retirement plan is that contributions and investment earnings grow tax-deferred until distributions from the plan begin. Withdrawals generally begin at normal retirement age, by which time you may be in a lower tax bracket than during your younger years. Even if you're not in a lower tax bracket, the tax deferral afforded over many years can significantly increase your wealth.

Generally, you can establish a retirement plan if you have nonwage income from performing personal services, including director and consultant fees. A plan can be established regardless of whether you are self-employed part time or full time, or even if you participate in a plan offered by your full-time employer (subject, as always, to certain restrictions). Profitability is not required to establish a plan. However, you must have some net self-employment earnings to make annual contributions, depending on the type of plan you establish. The maximum annual earnings taken into account for plan contributions were $200,000 for 2003, and will be adjusted annually for inflation.

Your choice of retirement plan should be based on your objectives. Depending on the type of plan you choose, your maximum annual allowable contribution can vary; this is usually the key consideration in selecting a plan. Other considerations are flexibility in making contributions, costs involved in establishing and maintaining the plan, annual filing requirements, and withdrawal obligations and limitations. It also is important to note that if you have employees, you may have to make a contribution on their behalf once they satisfy the eligibility requirements outlined in the plan. Very strict nondiscrimination rules and coverage tests must be followed in order for the plan to maintain its qualified status. Please consult with your tax advisor to determine if this applies to your situation.

The most common retirement plans for self-employed individuals are defined-contribution and defined-benefit plans, otherwise known as Keoghs. Contributions to these plans are based on net self-employment income earned. The plan must be established by your taxable year-end, but contributions do not have to be made until your tax-filing deadline, including extensions.

In the paragraphs that follow some tax-deferred plans available to self-employed individuals are described. Contributions to these plans are fully deductible. However, limitations and restrictions may apply if you maintain more than one plan.

Defined-Contribution Plans

A defined-contribution plan is a qualified plan that provides an individual account for each participant; benefits are based solely upon the amount contributed to the participant's account. The most commonly established defined-contribution plans for the self-employed are *profit-sharing* and *money purchase* plans.

Profit-Sharing Plan (PSP)

This type of plan allows you to contribute up to 25 percent of compensation (capped at $200,000 for 2003) or $40,000, whichever is less, on a discretionary basis from year to year.

Money Purchase Pension Plan (MPPP)

An MPPP allows you to contribute up to 25 percent of compensation or $40,000, whichever is less, with a fixed contribution percentage determined when you set it up. Unlike the profit-sharing plan, contributions to an MPPP are mandatory in any year that there is earned income. Prior to 2002, MPPPs were often set up in conjunction with a PSP. With the changes introduced by the 2001 Tax Act, however, there is seldom any need to establish an MPPP with a PSP.

Defined-Benefit Plans

The annual contribution to a defined-benefit plan is based on the amount that must be put aside today to provide you with a fixed benefit at retirement. The contribution amount is calculated using actuarial data, factoring in your current age and projected retirement age, current annual income, the required annual benefit (limited to a per-centage of earnings), and the projected investment growth rate.

The annual contribution limit to one of these plans may be much higher than with a defined contribution plan, and the amount will be tax-deductible. Also, these plans can be funded to provide a benefit at retirement equal to 100 percent of average annual compensation up to $160,000 (indexed each year for inflation). That arrangement allows for a quick buildup of retirement assets, particularly for older partici-pants, but once the benefit formula is determined, the annual con-tributions are mandatory. However, these plans can be expensive to administer.

Simplified Employee Pension (SEP)

A SEP is a retirement plan that allows you to contribute up to 25 percent of compensation (limited to $200,000 in 2003) or $40,000, whichever is less, on a discretionary basis from year to year. The plan must be established and funded by your tax-filing deadline (plus extensions). A SEP is similar to a profit-sharing plan in that you can choose whether to make a contribution, and how much, on a year-to-year basis. However, it is easier to maintain because there are no on-going IRS filing requirements as with qualified plans. Still, a penalty is applied to excess contributions.

Savings Incentive Match Plan for Employees (SIMPLE)

These plans are a relatively new option for small employers; here a self-employed individual is considered both as an employee and em-ployer. As an employee, you can elect to contribute up to $7,000 (adjusted for inflation) to the plan every year. In addition, as the employer, you must make annual contributions in one of two ways:

1. Through matching dollar-for-dollar contributions up to 3 percent of net earnings from self-employment for the calendar year, up to $7,000. This figure may be reduced to a percentage of not less than 1 percent in any two out of five years.

2. Through making nonelective contributions equal to 2 percent of net earnings from self-employment, regardless of whether any employee contributions are made, allowing for a current maximum contribution of $4,000.

Generally, a SIMPLE does not provide the maximum benefit if you do not have employees who also need to be covered. This is because the contribution limits are generally lower than those under other plans, and the SIMPLE must be your only plan.

Insurance

Investors interested in retirement vehicles have shown a resurgent interest in sophisticated life insurance products, such as private placement variable life insurance products, or using insurance as a "wrapper" for investing in hedge funds or marketable securities (for more information on life insurance, see Chapter 4).

One especially popular product is variable life. Here you pay cash premiums into a life insurance policy, and then determine how that cash is to be invested. The options include several nonpublic mutual funds, among other choices. Unlike the case of mutual funds, however, you don't handle the money; the manager does, and you have no control over his or her actions, although you can have a say in who it is. For instance, you can ask that a place like U.S. Trust handle it, and the life insurance company will then contract with U.S. Trust to perform the specified task. That money is now inside an insurance product, so all the gains and taxable elements are tax-free.

Charitable Remainder Trusts as Retirement Plans

A note on charitable remainder trusts (CRTs) is in order. We'll talk more about CRTs in Chapter 6, but they are also a retirement plan possibility. With a CRT, you bestow your money or other assets on a favorite charity that you wish to receive whatever asset(s) you eventually give away—but not at the moment. In the meantime, you, your spouse, or your children (or anyone else you select) will be paid a fixed dollar amount or a percentage of the value from the assets in the trust.

There are many ways to structure these CRTs that may help you retire well. One way is through a net income makeup CRT (NIMCRT). As with a regular CRT, you place property into a CRT, retain a stream of payments from the trust, and at the end of your life, the balance goes to your selected charity. You can structure this in such a way that it will pay out the lesser of the income generated by the trust, or the stated percentage payout. Assuming that payout is 6 percent, but the trust has no current income, there is nothing available with which to pay you, so the trust "owes" you the payout. In this way, you can accumulate assets inside these vehicles, letting them grow and compound tax-free, and then change the investment allocation to produce an income later on, when you need it.

The IRS allows this arrangement in part because it's legal, but also because you do risk a downside. If you die during the period you are accumulating the money, then all of that money goes to your charity.

CHAPTER 6

Estate Planning

The day is not far distant when the man who dies leaving behind him millions of available wealth, which was free for him to administer during life, will pass away "unwept, unhonored, and unsung," no matter to what uses he leave the dross which he cannot take with him. Of such as these the public verdict will then be: "The man who dies thus rich dies disgraced." Such, in my opinion, is the true gospel concerning wealth, obedience to which is destined some day to solve the problem of the rich and the poor.

—Andrew Carnegie,
American industrialist and philanthropist

Money is better than poverty, if only for financial reasons.

—Woody Allen,
American filmmaker

Estate planning allows you to meet your objectives for the disposition of your assets during your lifetime, and after your death. Often associated with making a will, this kind of planning can involve intergenerational wealth transfer and philanthropic planning. As with financial planning, estate plans generally need to be reviewed about every five years, or whenever there is a significant change to your personal situation, or when there's a change in the laws affecting your overall wealth management situation.

U.S. Trust Survey of Affluent Americans Results

Eighty-four percent of estate planning respondents surveyed have already drawn up a will, while 70 percent say that they have a formal estate plan. Forty-nine percent have reviewed their wills in the last five years, and 53 percent review their wills every three years.

Eighty-nine percent of married respondents have discussed their estate plan with their spouse, and 86 percent have named an executor. A spouse was the most common executor/trustee (cited by 47 percent of respondents).

Thirty percent of respondents estimate that their estates will be valued at somewhere between $1 and $5 million at the time of their death. Another 29 percent estimate their estate to be worth between $5 and $10 million; 25 percent assume their estates will be larger (see Table 6.1).

Fifty-nine percent plan to donate at least part of their estate to charity, 58 percent will give money to colleges or academic institutions, 45 percent to health-related organizations, 34 percent to religious institutions, 24 percent to charities related to public issues such as the environment or politics, and 20 percent to libraries or museums.

Eighty-four percent of respondents said that they will treat their children on a totally equal basis in their wills. But certain circumstances

TABLE 6.1   ESTIMATED VALUE OF ESTATE AT TIME OF DEATH

Estimated Value of Estate at Death	Percentage of Respondents
Less than $1 million	5%
$1 million to less than $5 million	30%
$5 million to less than $10 million	29%
$10 million to less than $25 million	17%
$25 million or greater	8%

n = 155
SOURCE: U.S. Trust Survey of Affluent Americans XIX, December 2000

warrant a reevaluation, and 74 percent said that the child's mental health is extremely or somewhat important in determining what a child will inherit, 70 percent said the same for a child's physical health, 53 percent said a child's ability to manage money wisely is important, and 51 percent said a child's ability to get and keep a good job matters. The least important issues cited were the age and sex of a child, and which child the parent feels closest to.

On average, respondents thought the age of 29 years is the youngest at which a child should be entrusted with a significant inheritance. The average respondent felt that a child would have to inherit $3.4 million before the size of the inheritance would have a detrimental effect on his or her values.

Estate Planning Scenarios

Not long ago we had a very successful client who had made many millions of dollars in several different companies, all of which he had started himself. He also owned five cars, a plane, three homes, and was the father of two teenage children. Unlike most of our clients, the order of the items in that list seemed to represent their importance in his heart. For whatever reasons, when it came time to take care of his estate planning, he wasn't interested.

"I don't care about making a will," he said, "I made my own money. My kids will have to make their money, too." We told him that he certainly didn't have to leave his children everything, but that it might be nice for them to inherit at least something. He said he would think about it, but that since no one ever left him anything, he didn't see why he should have to leave anyone anything.

His reaction to the next question was a little more discouraging. We asked his preferences concerning a guardian for the kids in case anything were to happen to him. "I don't care," he said. "The court can appoint someone." Once again, we engaged him in a conversation. It's not our job to change people's values, but we do want people to be fully informed when they make these kinds of decisions. Eventually, after hearing about the difficulties that can occur with court-appointed guardians, he rethought his plan and made a sensible guardian selection. But he continued to refuse to leave his children any money.

Another wealthy couple who came in to see us recently had a different attitude. They had begun their estate planning many years ago with another advisor and appreciated the power of giving money to their two children while they were still alive (currently an individual may give up to $11,000 and a couple may give up to $22,000 per recipient each year without incurring a gift tax).

This couple couldn't have been nicer and more considerate. Their only problem was that they had given away so much of their money that they now had to ask their kids to give some of it back. It wasn't that they needed the money to live on because they had already taken those expenses into consideration. But this couple had established a lifetime habit of donating to charity, and had come to realize that they no longer had enough money to continue giving as they wished. The situation was embarrassing for them, although their children— grateful for everything their parents had done for them—had no problem with the request. The couple just hadn't thought through their planning carefully enough to determine the cash flow they really needed to give to charities in the manner to which they had grown accustomed.

The Importance of Estate Planning

As these stories illustrate, estate planning is the most subjective of the wealth management and financial planning disciplines. Decisions often must be made without the benefit of empirically correct answers that are available when balancing issues surrounding, say, income taxes or retirement. Think of all the personal questions that must be addressed:

- Do I leave my assets outright to my spouse or in a trust? If I don't leave them in a trust, how do I know my spouse will leave my assets to our children?

- At what age should my children receive their inheritance? Should it be in a trust or outright?

- Who should be my executor and trustee?

- Who should be the guardian of my minor children?

For estate planning to be successful, you must be able to answer these and other difficult questions as you work with your estate planner to draw up a plan that is both sound and tax-efficient.

As mentioned earlier, many people procrastinate when it comes to financial planning. They procrastinate even more over estate planning because it's uncomfortable to focus on death. They're involved in running their lives, building their wealth, and advancing their careers. Few people look forward to taking the time out to discuss their mortality. But if you don't attend to estate planning, all those assets you've spent your life accumulating may wind up somewhere that might make you turn over in your grave.

Good estate planning begins with a few dispassionate questions asked from an appropriate distance. Think of it as if you were standing on top of a mountain, looking down on your life. From this perspective, ask yourself:

- What are my assets?
- Who are the objects of my affection?
- What are my goals and objectives?

Once you understand the answers to these three general questions, you can work out the specifics of what else needs to be done. If you can't answer them yourself, any good estate planner will sit down with you and try to gain some insights into who you are, what you care about, and what your concerns are. For example, are you philanthropic? What type of relationship do you have with your family? What do you think money should be used for? Your response to these subjective issues will help your estate planner home in on more concrete objectives.

Each family has distinct concerns that will affect its estate planning choices. For instance, one of our clients, Ben, emigrated to the United States as an impoverished young man. With the help of a government agency he'd been able to set himself up in a small business; eventually, it grew to the point that Ben became a terrifically wealthy man. He felt very indebted to the government for his success and as a result, Ben didn't think there was enough he could do for this country, and paying taxes was the least of it. This sentiment had a powerful impact on his estate planning, because every time we showed him how to lessen his tax bite, he objected. Ben did want to make sure that his children and not the government received his business, but he didn't care how much they had to pay in taxes to get it.

Then there was the case of Dolores, a single mother who had lost her husband many years ago and never remarried. She had two children, a son with whom she remained on good terms, and a daughter, Christina. Dolores and Christina had fought many years earlier, and outside of a frosty exchange of Christmas cards, they had barely any contact. Dolores was wealthy enough to leave a significant estate. She knew her son could handle the money well—he was a successful lawyer with a family of his own—but she was worried about Christina, who never had any money, and whose soft heart might make her an easy mark once she inherited Dolores' wealth.

Dolores had never given her children as much as a penny. So, as part of her estate planning, we suggested that she should give her daughter cash gifts to the maximum allowed, which at the time was $10,000 a year. This way she could see how Christina handled it. Dolores did as we asked, and she received a gracious thank-you from her daughter. Over the next decade Dolores continued to give Christina the maximum allowable tax-free cash gift, and slowly, the two women began to establish an uneasy but constant relationship. Furthermore, Christina turned out to be quite smart about managing her newfound money.

Obviously, no boilerplate formula can take into account all situations like these. Your life circumstances are as particular to you as your fingerprints. What do you want to do with your wealth? Other than your family, whom do you want to inherit your assets? Industrialist Paul Mellon left several million dollars to his horses, as well as several million more to his dogs.

To make sure your estate planning is complete, don't just jot down a general list of your assets. Take a complete and specific inventory: your bank and investment accounts, insurance policies, company benefits, IRAs, tangible personal property, real estate, etc. If you have already begun this itemization process through financial planning, you can use the same information you've already gathered. This may sound easy enough, but it requires work, and we've found that clients often encounter some difficulty pulling together all the data. Furthermore, many clients simply don't want to do it because they value their privacy and are loath to reveal their whole financial picture to anyone.

You also need to decide who will be the recipient, or beneficiary, of each and every asset, and make sure that you have all your beneficiary designations completed and ready for review—your IRA, your life insurance, your property ownership, and so on.

You also should consider how you wish your instructions to be interpreted. Often, people really can't anticipate precisely what the next generations will, much less should, do with their inheritance. U.S. Trust once administered a trust that provided for the beneficiary, Carola, to receive payments to provide for her "health, education, maintenance and support." At a certain point in her life, Carola wanted to build a small gymnasium in her basement so she could exercise more often. Funds for a gym weren't expressly granted in the trust, but one member of our staff had known the original family well, and it was clear to him that the decedent's intentions were such that she would approve, so we obtained a letter from Carola's doctor stating that it would be to her medical benefit to have the gymnasium.

Such situations are why we recommend using the broadest possible language in wills, trusts, and the like. If you make the language flexible, you give the document the ability figuratively to live and breathe over time. The more restrictive you are about the way your

---

Six Things You Must Know about Estate Planning

1. If you die without a will, state law will determine who will receive your property, which may not be in accord with your wishes.

2. The marital deduction provides that you can transfer unlimited amounts of property to your spouse (providing he or she is a U.S. citizen) without incurring gift or estate tax at the time of the transfer (see the sections on QTIP trusts in this chapter).

3. You may give a gift of up to $11,000 a year without incurring gift tax. This is known as the *annual exclusion*.

4. In 2003 (assuming you have not made any taxable transfers during your lifetime), you can leave up to $1 million to persons other than your spouse without having to pay any federal estate tax. This amount will increase incrementally until it reaches $3.5 million in 2009.

5. The Federal estate tax will be eliminated in 2010 and reinstated in 2011.

6. Trusts are not only for the very affluent.

assets can be used, the greater the possibility that you will hamstring the recipient. Not that some people don't have that exactly in mind—they make sure that their wishes will be remembered from the grave. We've seen wills that tell people whom they can or can't marry, and after whom they should name their children. One man who felt his children weren't serious enough about getting an education created an inheritance reward program hinged on how far the kids advanced in school—they received so much money if they graduated from college, more for earning a professional degree, and even more if any of them obtained a Ph.D. We had another client who didn't seem to trust his son, and in his will dictated every detail of how the inheritance could be used, from where the son could buy a house to what kind of car he could drive.

Choosing an Executor

However large or small your estate, it's important to make sure that you pick a responsible executor for your estate. An executor has many duties. He or she must locate the will and make sure it is properly probated, i.e., that the will is proven to be legally valid.

Next, all the assets specified in the will must be collected and appraised. Although some people keep meticulous records, making their estates easy to compile, others have assets scattered all over the world, some of which no one—not even the deceased—was ever aware of (if you select a competent wealth manager and keep up with your financial planning, that shouldn't be a problem for you).

The role of executor can be a difficult one, particularly if he or she has to dole out unpleasant or surprising news to unsuspecting heirs (or those who thought they would be heirs, but aren't). Occasionally, the executor may be given the rather odd job of telling the heirs details about the deceased that may surprise or disappoint them. We had a client who was a Boston-area schoolteacher; his wife was an accountant. Together they had one daughter, one dog, and one Chevrolet they drove into the ground. The family lived in a small home outside the city, and seldom spent any money.

Isabelle, the daughter, grew up expecting little, although the family had made sure she received an excellent education. She then became a high school teacher, and a single mother when she and her husband divorced not long after their baby was born. Isabelle's parents sent her a small sum of money now and then, and she made enough to support her child.

However, when the parents died, Isabelle learned the truth: They had been excellent investors, and over the course of their lifetime had accumulated about $5 million. Isabelle was thrilled to inherit such a large amount of money. But it seemed a slap in the face to learn this only courtesy of the executor, and wrestle with why her parents hadn't been more generous to her or their granddaughter while they were alive.

The executor may have to perform several other duties. For example, it will take time for the deceased's house to be sold or transferred, so mortgage payments on the house must be continued. Bills for water, heat, and electricity must be paid (unless you want to inventory the contents in the dark). Insurance premiums must be kept current (in case the house is burgled before the division of assets is complete). The executor will have to change the name of all of the decedant's accounts to estate accounts and open a bank account for the deceased's estate so that fees and payments are covered and there is a repository available for any money that may still come into the estate, such as dividends, bonuses, and salaries. Finally, the executor is responsible for preparing the decedent's final income tax returns, preparing the estate tax returns, and paying all funeral expenses, debts, and administration expenses.

Once the administration of the estate is complete, the executor distributes the estate's assets. When making your choice of executor, remember that the tasks with which you charge this person may have a strong, sometimes negative impact on those who receive (or don't receive) your assets—and the executor may bear the brunt of these feelings.

Trusts

One of the most prevalent estate planning tools is the *trust*. A trust is simply a contractual agreement requiring the administration and disposition of property. The typical parties to a trust are the grantor, the trustee, and the beneficiaries. There are two types of trusts: a *testamentary* trust, which you establish in your will, and an *inter vivos* trust, which you create during your lifetime. An *inter vivos* trust may be *revocable*, which means that it can be changed, or *irrevocable*, which means that it cannot be changed. A testamentary trust is not effective until you die, and is irrevocable thereafter. This is because you can change your will as many times as you wish before you die; you can't afterward.

One advantage of a revocable trust is that you can avoid probate. The probate process means that a will may become a public document, which anyone then may ask to see. A revocable trust is not public, so it can provide confidentiality. Note, however, that this confidentiality is not absolute. Some states require that a copy of the revocable trust be filed along with the will, if the will contains a bequest to the revocable trust.

Another advantage of a revocable trust is that it provides the ability to avoid delays in the administration of your estate. Until your will is admitted to probate by the court, your executor or personal representative has no authority to take any actions with respect to the assets of your estate. But if the bulk of your assets are held in a revocable trust at your death, any delay encountered in probating your will will have no effect on your trustee's ability to administer the assets therein. Revocable trusts are quite popular in states such as California, where the probate process is particularly onerous and time-consuming. Most people do not own all of their assets through a revocable trust, however. Accordingly, even if you choose a revocable trust as your vehicle, you must still execute a will in order to dispose of those assets that you don't own through your revocable trust. The final advantage of a revocable trust is that in the event of your disability or incompetence, someone else can step in and take over for you, allowing continuous management of your property.

If your estate is going to include a trust, you should appoint a *trustee*. A trustee will be the person or institution who will take responsibility for the trust, administering it in accordance with the trust's terms. He or she either hires a professional to act as agent or invests assets, makes distributions to beneficiaries, and files tax returns alone. In return, the trustee receives a fee for his or her ser-vices. You must make sure that your trustee is someone in whom you have complete confidence. In many cases, an institution such as a bank is your best choice for a trustee, because it has both the procedures and the experience to administer a trust and invest the assets. Moreover, the institution will be there to serve multiple generations. I personally believe the best solution is to involve an institution and a trusted individual or family member to serve as executor and trustee. The individual executor or trustee, either alone or in connection with the beneficiaries, should also be able to remove a corporate fiduciary and replace them with a different corporate fiduciary. In addition, the beneficiaries should have a similar right to remove and replace corporate, as well as individual, trustees. In this case all beneficiaries should agree with the action in order to have this right. There may be adverse tax effects if this provision is not drafted appropriately in the trust or will. Once you have set up a trust and selected a trustee, again, make sure that the language in your will is flexible so the trustee can make necessary changes as contingencies arise.

U.S. Trust had one case in which a grandmother created a trust for her daughter and her daughter's two children, a boy and a girl. According to the terms in the trust, the mother was able to access the capital only for medical emergencies. The grandchildren, however, were able to use it for "support" and "lifestyle." For the most part, all went smoothly, until the female grandchild decided that she wanted to have a baby. Unfortunately, for various medical reasons she was not able to become pregnant except through in vitro fertilization, which can be extremely expensive, especially if the first attempt doesn't work. She was looking at bills of upward of $50,000. Theoretically, according to the trust, this woman could not claim medical reasons for dipping into her trust principal.

As trustee of the will, we sat down and had a long discussion. Ultimately, we decided that the woman's ability to have a child could be considered part of her general support and lifestyle. And, of course, we were certain that her grandmother, who had selected us to be the trustee in the first place, would have loved her granddaughter to have a family of her own. Taking care of her heirs was truly the concern of the trust in the first place. We made a decision to distribute the funds, and our client eventually had her baby.

Power of Attorney

A *power of attorney* offers you a relatively simple and inexpensive mechanism by which you can appoint one or more persons to act on your behalf in a variety of financial and legal affairs. These powers may be broad or limited, depending on your wishes. For estate planning purposes, you also can allow this person to make gifts on your behalf.

A *durable power of attorney* is one that remains effective even if you become incompetent. In such a situation, the durable power may let you avoid a situation in which a court appoints a guardian to manage your property. In this context, the durable power also serves as a simple substitute for a revocable trust, which can also provide for the management of your property in the event of incompetence. Upon your death, the power of attorney ceases.

As with selecting an executor or trustee, since the power of attorney confers significant authority on the agent, you must take care in choosing the right individual. If you don't want to confer immediate authority, you can use a *springing power of attorney*. This means that the power takes effect only upon the occurrence of a specified event, such as disability.

Why You Should Have a Living Will

A living will does not dispense assets or establish trusts; it expresses your wishes in case you need life-sustaining treatment, or any other urgent medical care for a serious condition. As such it should be viewed as part of estate planning.

Let's say you've been in a terrible accident and can only be kept alive with artificial life support. You may not wish this kind of treatment, but you're in no condition to say so. Only through a living will can this kind of decision be made by someone else—a decision informed by your wishes. As mentioned, a health care proxy is the document in which you choose an agent to make these decisions; in turn, the agent is guided by what is in the living will.

A piece of advice: Let the person whom you've picked to make these life-and-death decisions know ahead of time what is expected. It can be quite a surprise to find out that you're responsible for a choice that might have to be made in a matter of hours.

As with power of attorney, you should use a lawyer to draft these documents. Make copies of the living will and the health care proxy, and make sure that they're accessible when needed. You also might want to consult with your physician about your choices, particularly if you have a chronic health condition. In fact, it makes sense to give your doctor copies of these documents when they are drafted.

Although power of attorney is a useful option for handling financial and legal matters, it is generally not used to convey medical decision-making authority. In order to authorize someone to make your medical decisions, you should use a *health care proxy*. This document is typically executed in conjunction with a living will, which contains a statement of your wishes regarding life support and similar measures. The laws regarding powers of attorney, health care proxies, and living wills vary from state to state. Consult with your attorney to make certain you are in compliance with applicable law.

Tax Laws and Estate Planning

Now that you understand the broad considerations of estate planning, you can make specific financial decisions that will be most tax-advantageous and financially lucrative for you and your beneficiaries. Changes to the tax laws are an important consideration.

In 2001 the government made sweeping changes to the federal transfer tax system. From 2002 to 2009, the estate, gift, and generation-skipping transfer tax will be reduced. In 2010, the estate and generation-skipping transfer taxes will be repealed, although the gift tax will remain in effect. Beginning in 2011, the estate, gift, and generation-skipping transfer taxes will revert to their form before the 2001 legislation (see Table 6.2).

In light of this, as previously noted, one of the best and most tax-efficient strategies for estate planning, if you want as much money as

TABLE 6.2   GIFT AND ESTATE TAX CREDIT

Calendar Year	Gift Tax Credit	Estate Tax Credit	GST* Tax Exemption
2002	$1 million	$1.0 million	$1.1 million
2003	$1 million	$1.0 million	$1.12 million
2004	$1 million	$1.5 million	$1.5 million
2005	$1 million	$1.5 million	$1.5 million
2006	$1 million	$2.0 million	$2.0 million
2007	$1 million	$2.0 million	$2.0 million
2008	$1 million	$2.0 million	$2.0 million
2009	$1 million	$3.5 million	$3.5 million
2010	$1 million	(Tax repealed)	(Tax repealed)
2011	$1 million	$1 million	$1 million**

*Generation-skipping tax.
**To be adjusted for inflation.

possible to go to loved ones, is to start giving gifts of money. Individuals are permitted to give away $11,000 per recipient annually without paying gift tax; a married couple can give $22,000. The earlier the gift is made, the greater the potential tax savings may be. Suppose you give $22,000 to your child when he or she is very young, and that money grows to more than $250,000 by the time you die. That $250,000 is not considered part of your estate. So no estate tax will be due on the money.

Under current tax law, you will have to pay a gift tax if you give away more than $1 million worth of property during your lifetime (not including the annual exclusion, gifts to a U.S. citizen's spouse, another person's tuition payments or medical bills, and charitable gifts). If you are married, each spouse may make the gift of $1 million. There are many vehicles available to you to maximize the value of that $1 million exclusion, such as family limited partnerships, grantor retained annuity trusts, and charitable trusts, discussed below.

Estate Planning Options

Based on the current transfer tax laws, the estate and gift tax can be viewed as a voluntary tax. By that I mean that there are so many techniques available to minimize transfer taxes that you can go a long way toward eliminating transfer taxes. There are trade-offs in order to accomplish this goal, the most significant being the transfer of your assets from your own name into trusts or other vehicles. Most people are not willing to make that trade-off. They enjoy the control and the power and therefore still end up with very large estates.

Here are a few basic estate planning vehicles that you may want to consider as you prepare your own estate planning (see Table 6.3) (these definitions are abbreviated for easy reading—to learn about each in full detail, please consult with an expert on the subject):

Estate tax credit: Full use of this credit avoids taxation of the property in the surviving spouse's estate when he or she later dies. To obtain the maximum advantage from this credit, each spouse should have assets in his or her own name equal in value to the unified credit. This estate planning technique is most commonly accomplished by a will provision using a formula.

Marital deduction and the QTIP trust: This technique allows estate tax to be deferred until the death of the surviving spouse. If he or she is a

TABLE 6.3   BENEFITS OF TRUST

Trust	Benefits	Timing
Charitable lead trust	• Income tax charitable deduction • Excess appreciation to non-charitable beneficiaries	Lifetime or at death
Charitable remainder trust	• Income tax charitable deduction • Deferral of capital gains tax if assets sold	Typically lifetime
Children's trust	• Management of assets • Control over distributions • Creditor protection	Lifetime or at death
Generation–skipping trust	• Avoidance of estate tax in child's estate • Creditor protection	Lifetime or at death
Grantor retained annuity trust (GRAT)	• Excess appreciation removed from estate	Lifetime
Life insurance trust	• Avoidance of estate taxation of insurance proceeds	Lifetime
Qualified personal residence trust (QPRT)	• Transfer of residence for less than fair market value	Lifetime
Qualified terminable interest property (QTIP) trust	• Deferral of estate tax until surviving spouse's death • Control over distribution at surviving spouse's death	Typically at death
Revocable trust	• Property management in case of disability • Avoidance of probate at death	Lifetime
Unified credit trust	• Avoidance of estate taxation in surviving spouse's estate	Lifetime or at death

U.S. citizen, the marital deduction is unlimited in amount and can be obtained by making an outright bequest or by placing assets in a qualifying trust, usually a qualified terminable interest property (QTIP) trust. The surviving spouse must receive all the income from the trust and may receive discretionary principal payments. The QTIP trust has the advantage of allowing the first spouse to control the ultimate disposition of the property.

Tuition and medical exclusion: Tuition payments made directly to an educational institution and medical care payments made directly to the provider are exempt from the gift tax. This exclusion is unlimited in amount, and does not affect the gift tax annual exclusion.

Life insurance trust: This technique avoids estate taxation of life insurance proceeds in the estates of both spouses. In order to implement it, an irrevocable trust must be the owner and beneficiary of the life insurance policy. The grantor (the insured) may not be the trustee of the trust. At the death of the insured, the proceeds of the policy are paid to the trust and disposed of pursuant to the trust terms. (Table 6.4 illustrates the savings from an insurance trust stragety.)

Grantor retained annuity trust (GRAT): Through a GRAT, a grantor transfers property to a trust and retains an annuity for a chosen term of years. If the trust is structured properly, the creation of the GRAT generates little or no gift taxes. For this technique to succeed, the grantor must survive the trust term. If the trust property appreciates at a rate in excess of the IRS prescribed interest rate, the excess appreciation passes to the remainder beneficiaries free of gift tax.

Personal residence trust: This technique allows an individual to transfer a personal residence for less than its full value. The individual transfers a residence to a trust for a term of years and retains the right to live in the residence. At the end of the term, the residence passes to the trust beneficiaries. If the individual desires to remain in the residence after

TABLE 6.4   SAVINGS FROM AN INSURANCE TRUST STRATEGY

Estate Tax Calculation

Year of Death – 2003	Current Plan with Credit Shelter Trust		Proposed Plan CST Funded and an Insurance Trust	
	Client	Spouse	Client	Spouse
Gross Estate	$10,000,000	$5,000,000	$8,500,000	$5,000,000
Inheritance From Spouse	—	8,800,000	—	7,330,000
Funeral and Admin. Expenses (2%)	(200,000)	(276,000)	(170,000)	(246,600)
Adjusted Gross Estate	9,800,000	13,524,000	8,330,000	12,083,400
Charitable Deduction	0	0	0	0
Marital Deduction	(8,800,000)	0	(7,330,000)	0
Taxable Estate	1,000,000	13,524,000	1,000,000	12,083,400
Post–1976 Taxable Gifts	0	0	0	0
Federal Estate	1,000,000	13,524,000	1,000,000	12,083,400
Federal Tax Per Schedule	(345,800)	(6,427,560)	(345,800)	(5,721,666)
After 1976 Gift Taxes	0	0	0	0
Unified Credit	345,800	345,800	345,800	345,800
Federal Tax + Max Credit	0	(6,081,760)	0	(5,375,866)
State Death Taxes—Max Credit	0	820,120	0	704,872
Total Federal Death Taxes	0	(5,261,640)	0	(4,670,994)
State Death Taxes Per Schedule	0	(820,120)	0	(704,872)
Net Income Tax on IRD	0	(135,000)	0	(135,000)
Total Death Taxes	0	(6,216,750)	0	(5,510,866)
Family Share	1,000,000	7,307,240	1,000,000	6,572,534
Family Share—Both Spouses	—	8,307,240	—	7,572,534
Irrevocable Insurance Trust	—	—	—	1,500,000
Total Family Share		$8,307,240		$9,072,534

Benefit of Irrevocable Life Insurance Trust: $765,294

the end of the term, he or she must pay full fair market value rent to the trust beneficiaries.

Valuation discounts: Here you can transfer assets to a family limited partnership (FLP) or limited liability company (LLC). As the general partner or managing member, you retain control of investments and distributions. You give interests as gifts to family members, either outright or in trust. Because these interests are not marketable and are not controlling interests in the FLP or LLC, valuation discounts are available for gift tax purposes.

Charitable remainder trust: In a CRT, you transfer property to a trust that makes payments to one or more individuals for an initial term, after which the remainder is paid to charity. The tax advantages are an income tax charitable deduction for the value of the remainder interest and deferral of capital gains tax if the appreciated property is sold by the trust.

Charitable lead trust: Property is transferred to a trust, and payments are made to a charity for a term of years, after which the remainder is left to one or more individuals (an income tax charitable deduction is available at the trust level, as long as there is an upfront deduction for the charitable payments). If the property appreciates at a rate greater than the IRS prescribed interest rate, the excess appreciation passes to the remainder beneficiaries free of gift tax.

Generation-Skipping Transfer Tax

Another tax you should know about is called the *generation-skipping transfer tax.* This applies to any transfer you make to a person two or more generations below you such as a grandchild or more remote descendant. The generation-skipping transfer tax applies to transfers of property directly to a grandchild as well as to transfers from a trust to a grandchild. This tax is imposed in addition to any estate and gift tax that may have to be paid, and it may result in a combined transfer tax rate of approximately two-thirds.

The generation-skipping transfer tax is a flat rate, equal to the maximum estate tax rate. Like the estate tax, the generation-skipping tax will be repealed in 2010, and then return in 2011—unless Congress takes further action. The good news here is that each individual may take a generation-skipping transfer tax exemption, which for 2003 is $1,120,000 and will, like the estate tax exemption, increase incrementally over time.

Keeping Your Estate Planning Options Up to Date

Remember to review your estate plans any time a major life event occurs, such as if you move to a new state, if your economic or family situation changes, or if there is a change in the tax law. Even if none of these occur, you should examine your plan about every five years. And make sure you hire a qualified attorney to guarantee that your plans reflect what you want to do and are in compliance with current tax laws.

Also, remember that although there are cut-and-dried laws concerning your estate and the taxes you will pay, there are no fast rules concerning your emotions. An estate planning session can resemble a therapy session—most people, like it or not, take stock of their lives while summing up their possessions, beneficiaries, and chosen guardians for their children. We have seen many people go through remarkable transitions while considering how to handle their estate.

Not long ago we met with a client, Ted, who was an inventor. For most of his life he made little money, but when he was in his late fifties one of his inventions succeeded—he was able to patent it and then sell it for a great deal of money. Suddenly, his family, which had always lived modestly, was now very wealthy. Ted had three children. Two of them led successful and happy lives, but Josh, the third and youngest, was something of a problem. When Josh was 18, he was caught selling drugs and sent to prison. Upon release, he was sent to a halfway house; there he had a child with another resident.

When Josh found out that his father had become very wealthy, he brought the mother of his child and their new daughter to Ted and asked him for help supporting his new family. Ted refused. He explained to us that Josh had always been trouble and it was too late for any reconciliation. Ted's wife tried to intervene, but Ted was adamant. He felt he had given his son plenty of chances and now he had drawn a line he didn't want to cross. When Ted came to us to do his estate planning, we suggested that he might want to consider making provisions for Josh's daughter, his only female grandchild. Ted replied that he would never give Josh or his daughter a penny. And that was how he drew up his first will.

Meanwhile, Josh was killed in a terrible automobile accident. The little girl, who had become an adorable child, was living with her mother. She sent Ted a photo of the girl every year along with a progress report on how well she was doing. By the time she was 5, when Ted came in to revise his will, his heart had melted. This time, as he went over his charity bequests and the trust funds he was setting up for his three other grandsons, he included the little girl—not in the same league as the others, but nonetheless, it was an enormous step.

Every year Ted sent out a Christmas card with photos of everyone in his family. The year following the revision of his will, we noticed his granddaughter was now in the picture on the card. And when Ted came in to revise his will a few years after that, he included the girl as an equal to his other grandchildren. Despite Ted's initial determination to ignore the child of his prodigal son, the blood ties were too strong for him to do this.

Children

Stitched into the pillows that sit on my office sofa are the following quotes: "Money isn't everything but it sure keeps you in touch with your children," by Milton Berle, and "Always fly first class. If you don't, your son-in-law will," by an unknown wit. Virtually all of our clients who have seen them have smiled in a way that indicated they got both the jokes and the reality behind them. Our surveys reveal that, indeed, one of the joys of becoming affluent is the ability to share life's luxuries with your family. At the same time the affluent worry about what we call *affluenza*, or the condition that can arise when too much wealth distorts children's values and robs them of initiative.

U.S. Trust Survey of Affluent Americans Results

Our survey on parents and children found that, like all parents, the affluent worry about their kids—but sometimes over a different set of issues. Because of their personal wealth, 61 percent of the respondents worried that their children will place too much emphasis on material possessions, 57 percent thought they will be naïve about the value of money and how hard it is to earn, 54 percent suspected they will spend beyond their means; and 47 percent worried that their initiative will be undermined by their material advantages.

There is something affluent parents don't worry about: Only 18 percent think that their kids will have big shoes to fill and will fail at it. Most of the affluent parents aren't concerned whether their children follow in their footsteps. A majority said that the most important financial goals for their kids are that they find a satisfying career, earn enough money to support a family, and are able to support themselves entirely with their earnings. Sixty percent of parents said that as long as their children are happy, they don't care how much money they earn.

In order to teach their children values concerning money, 88 percent set up a savings account for them, 85 percent provided an allowance, 65 percent helped kids develop a budget for personal expenditures, 63 percent set up a checking account, 54 percent set up a brokerage account for them, and 45 percent helped them get a credit card for which the children themselves pay the bills.

To teach good work habits, most parents expected minor kids to complete chores—99 percent of kids must clean up their bedrooms, 85 percent must take out the trash, 83 percent had to set the dinner table or do the dishes, 77 percent had to take care of family pets, 65 percent had to babysit a younger sibling, 60 percent had to do lawn work, and 58 percent had to do laundry. Seventy-seven percent of parents expect that their kids had or will have a part-time job during junior high or high school or during summers. The average age for kids of affluent parents to start working is 15.

Although 76 percent of affluent parents were willing to pay or have paid for their kids to attend a private undergraduate college, only 59 percent were willing to kick in for graduate school. Regarding extra-curricular activities, 91 percent said they will give their children music, art, or dance lessons; 87 percent will send them to summer camp, 86 percent will encourage them to participate in sports such as tennis, golf, skiing, karate, or gymnastics; and 83 percent intend to provide them with international travel.

Children and Money

Concerns about children's welfare often arise early in a marriage. One of the first disagreements among couples we counsel in the wealth management process is over whom to name as a guardian for young children. Should it be his parents? Should it be hers? Oh no, she says, his are too old; he thinks hers are too permissive, and so the chorus goes. Too often, I have seen this discussion bog down, leading to a delay in completing estate plans, leaving clients without wills and allowing the possibility that local laws and not their own wishes will determine who will receive their assets, as well as who is appointed guardian of the minor children.

The stress continues over choosing the best time to let your children have money. Are they too young? Should we wait until they're adults? Is there ever a good time? Or should all the money go to charity? Unfortunately, there are no cut-and-dried answers to these questions. How a child will handle money, whether it's $50,000 or $5 million, is impossible to predict. There are too many factors to consider.

In answering our surveys, affluent parents expressed concern about making wise inheritance decisions regarding their children. Eighty percent of the parents plan to establish trusts for their children to ensure their offspring will control no assets nor receive their inheritance until they are at least 28 years old. We believe this is a desirable strategy. Most of our clients use discretionary trusts as a vehicle for managing their heir's monies. Discretionary trusts grant power to a trustee to make distributions from the fund's current income or from capital (principal). Such trusts can be on behalf of a single beneficiary (one child) or a class of beneficiaries (all of your children).

Some of the advisors at U.S. Trust recommend that parents conduct a test: Give your children access to some money when they're young and see how well they manage it. If they squander it all, that's useful information to consider when you might otherwise have been planning to give them more. Indeed, many trusts are set up in a staggered fashion, providing kids with the chance to be the steward of their own assets while giving their parents a chance to see how they perform at various ages.

The power vested in the trustee of a discretionary trust gives him or her a choice whether to pay, when to pay, whom to pay, and how much to pay. Trustees can be empowered to exercise their discretion based on your family's objectives. Factors to be considered include the beneficiaries' well-being, health care, education costs, support for daily expenses, capital needs such as to purchase or maintain a home, and so on. By specifying provisions under which the trust is to be administered, you can provide some degree of control from the grave to discipline your beneficiaries.

For instance, you can specify that funds are to be withheld under conditions such as family abandonment, matrimonial problems, divorce, use of abusive substances, and other situations. You can even arrange to protect spendthrift beneficiaries from their creditors, provide them with tax savings or deferrals, and insulate trusts in such a way that elderly beneficiaries will not be disqualified from receiving governmental benefits. Thus, the discretionary trust, when administered by wise trustees, is one of the great tools of estate planning. Our clients use the discretionary trust for many reasons, and it is critical for the person creating the trust to let the trustee know the terms of discretionary distributions of income or principal.

One of our senior relationship managers recently met with certain clients, a man and his second wife (who was not the mother of his children). The client was in the process of creating a trust under which his current wife would be his primary beneficiary during her lifetime, with complete discretion vested in the trustee to pay income or principal. Upon the wife's death, the property was to go to the children of his first marriage, who happened to be close in age to their stepmother. While exploring how flexible the client expected us to be in exercising the discretionary powers he would grant us as trustee, the relationship manager asked the client, "If your wife asked us to buy her a helicopter, how would you want us to respond?" The husband said: "Buy her two."

Another client, Adam, needed to discuss the terms of trusts he planned to create for his children. He expressed concern that a very large fund might damage his children's incentive to become productive members of society. Adam recognized that some of his children were more deserving than others of his trust assets, whether because they needed more money or would be better able to put it to productive use, or simply because they had better moral character than their siblings. Adam also believed that distributions should be paid out when the children reached specified ages, with one-half the principal paid to each child at age 25 and the balance at 30. However, Adam expressed the wish that if one of his children became a member of a cult or anticipated an acrimonious divorce, then the trust assets be withheld from distribution even though the child had reached the required age. Criteria such as these are possible under a well-crafted discretionary trust. In a nutshell, trusts will protect your beneficiaries from inability, disability, creditors, and predators.

Trusts and similar plans require maximum flexibility because even in the same family, results can differ. We worked with a wealthy family in which the mother and father had built a highly successful business together. They had two boys, whom they hoped would take over the business. When the boys graduated from college, the eldest started at the family company, but was lazy, failed to show up for work every day, and constantly begged for extra money to buy a larger house or a faster car. The couple eventually asked him to leave the business. In light of this, we helped the parents set up a performance trust that states he must be gainfully employed before he can collect the benefits (it seems to us that this is the only reason he has ever taken a job). The younger son, however, worked hard at the company, never asked for special treatment, and got along well with the other employees. He will eventually inherit the business. The couple had no idea ahead of time that this pattern would play out as it did.

Another of our clients, Bill, started off life the son of a foundry worker; he married Dotty, a grade school teacher, and had three kids, a girl and two boys. While in his thirties, Bill invented a mechanical device that made him a great deal of money. The children were raised knowing the family had no financial worries, but they were not aware of just how affluent they were. Bill grew up with a serious work ethic, and he truly hoped to inculcate his kids with the same values.

When Bill was in his late fifties he asked us to help plan his estate. After reviewing the family's situation, one of our recommendations was that Bill and Dotty start giving their kids some of the money. Bill felt uneasy with this, even given the tax bonuses associated with such gifts. All three of his children were working, and all had careers they liked. Bill feared that the thought of too much extra money might derail them.

Eventually, Bill decided to start giving his kids money when they were 35 years old, a point at which he felt their characters would have formed. So we called a family meeting, and the children were informed of the situation. Bill also announced that he wanted to create a small foundation, and he was pleased when his daughter, who had been working in public policy, wanted to be actively involved.

Bill still held back on telling his kids just how much money was involved. He didn't know if the kids, the foundation, or other charities should receive all or part of the wealth. He asked us to come up with various scenarios, which we did. Ultimately, his confidence in his children's maturity led him to explain to them the full nature of the situation. "What do *you* want me to do with the money?" he asked. He was startled, but pleased, when the kids told him that they didn't want it. The work ethic had taken hold, and instead, the family decided to place the money into the foundation.

At U.S. Trust we spend a great deal of time working with the second and third generations of the affluent for an obvious reason: They inherit the money. We work together as a unit with their parents, helping to educate the children financially, sharing with both the kids and the parents what to expect.

Through this experience, we have developed a strong belief that openness about money is the best policy and more often than not produces a better adjusted young adult. But sometimes we will run into those who strongly believe in the opposite strategy, or what we call the mushroom theory: Keep the kids in the dark about their money. Despite owning multiple residences, yachts, and jets, these clients still try to convince their children they are not affluent, in order to protect them. But kids aren't stupid—it's not hard for them to see the truth.

Although we are not supportive of this strategy, it is an individual's choice. However, if you aren't open with your children all along, counseling them at key times can be difficult. For instance, when your child has found his or her life partner, more often than not we will counsel the child to create a prenuptial agreement. A prenuptial agreement is a contract between the bride and groom, executed before the marriage, that sets forth property rights. If the marriage doesn't work out, it specifies which property belongs to whom, and simplifies divorce proceedings. Many families feel that bringing up a prenuptial agreement interferes with premarital bliss. In addition, a proper prenuptial agreement generally requires full disclosure from each party, along with separate legal representation. If you haven't shared family financial information with your child up to that point, this can become an awkward situation.

Ultimately, even mundane issues such as geography can play a role in determining how you treat your children vis-à-vis money. New York City, where I live, is a particularly baffling place to resolve these issues. Here, a one-room apartment for a young college graduate can rent for $2,000 a month, or $24,000 a year. Many young people just out of college won't make that much salary in an entire year, no less have it available for rent. So do we help our children? Do we give them an apartment? Do we help them pay their rent to make sure they can live in a good neighborhood? Some affluent parents tell their children they're on their own and that's that. Others continue to support them indefinitely. One of our elderly clients has a 50-year-old son who has never worked a day in his life. The mother believes it's her job to give him whatever he wants, and what he has wanted is her money. Another of our clients has adopted the attitude that his children must have to provide for their own necessities, but he will help them afford life's luxuries.

My own philosophy is that if you are fortunate enough to have kids on the right path, helping them can bring you joy. Other people might feel differently. As with most parental decisions, there's no right or wrong, as long as whatever you do springs from love and respect.

CHAPTER 7

How to Choose a Financial Advisor

Put not your trust in money, but put your money in trust.

—Oliver Wendell Holmes,
American writer and physician

In those days he was wiser than he is now; he used frequently to take my advice.

—Winston Churchill,
former British Prime Minister

Becoming wealthy is the result of a lifetime of hard work and dedication, whether you do it alone or with a spouse or partner. Managing your wealth requires a similar discipline, as well as a great deal of knowledge and, most often, the right advisor(s). During my career I have observed that most of our clients have gravitated toward that one individual whom they have chosen as their trusted advisor. This person—usually a paid professional but sometimes a friend or relative—becomes an integral part of their family's financial plans, and often their personal plans as well, working closely with the family's other advisors.

This role carries enormous responsibility. For example, in October 1987, when the stock market suffered a steep decline over two days, one of U.S. Trust's portfolio managers was vacationing on a cruise ship. He ended up spending all his days and nights on the telephone with clients—not because he had to, but because he wanted to. After all, his clients trusted him to be there for them, no matter where he was.

You are fortunate if you already have a trusted advisor. If you don't, how do you find someone to help you with your financial, estate, and income tax planning, as well as investments, retirement, and your insurance needs? A good advisor generally has expertise in one subject but also enjoys sufficient knowledge of others to provide useful advice. The advisor can also help with the coordination of multiple services, such as private banking, custody, trading, and record keeping. Generally speaking, the more affluent you are, the more complicated are your wealth management needs, and the more likely your trusted advisor will have to be joined by a team of specialists. To use an architectural analogy, you become your own general contractor, subcontracting out all of the services you require and then coordinating them to build your financial "house." Or, you can find an advisor to serve as that coordinator.

The extremely affluent will often assemble a family office to oversee their wealth management needs, but to pursue that route effectively, your family should be worth a minimum of $100 million. Some people do act as their own advisor, which can work if they have the time and the wisdom. But more often than not these people ultimately end up with a professional because they realize as they get older (and perhaps wiser) that the advice of others can be invaluable. If you are fortunate to grow very old, or unfortunate and lose your mental acuity early in life, you can't act as your own advisor. Finding your trusted advisor when you are on top of your game is essential and best enables you to work together efficiently.

Prerequisites for a Financial Advisor

Trustworthiness and integrity are absolute prerequisites for any advisor. Recommendations from friends who are satisfied clients are worth considering, but you should still do your homework about the firm in question. Check references thoroughly. Explore any public sources, such as reports from the regulators who oversee the firms. Figure 7.1 shows the results of the U.S. Trust Survey of Affluent Americans, concerning desirable attributes of an advisor.

Because of the many corporate scandals in recent years, virtually every industry has been tarnished, and the financial services arena is no exception. In every field of financial planning, investment management, accounting, and law we've seen well-publicized examples of system breakdown. All the more reason, then, to make sure you trust your advisors, as well as the firms in which they work.

As you sort through the myriad of firms and individuals available to choose from, here are some thoughts and questions to pursue:

- You will be selecting both a firm and an individual within the firm to be your advisor. In the case of a small firm, this can be one and the same. If you were referred to a specific individual within a firm, but discover that service will also be provided by other members of his or her organization, make sure you are comfortable with them. As in any relationship, your chemistry with the advisor will influence the success of the service as much as any other aspect.

- Consider whether it is important to you that if you die or are incapacitated, the person and/or firm you choose has the ability (and continuity in management) to provide advice to your surviving spouse and family.

- Make sure your advisor and the firm's team will be available to give you the level of service you require. You should inquire

FIGURE 7.1   IMPORTANT ATTRIBUTES OF A FINANCIAL ADVISOR

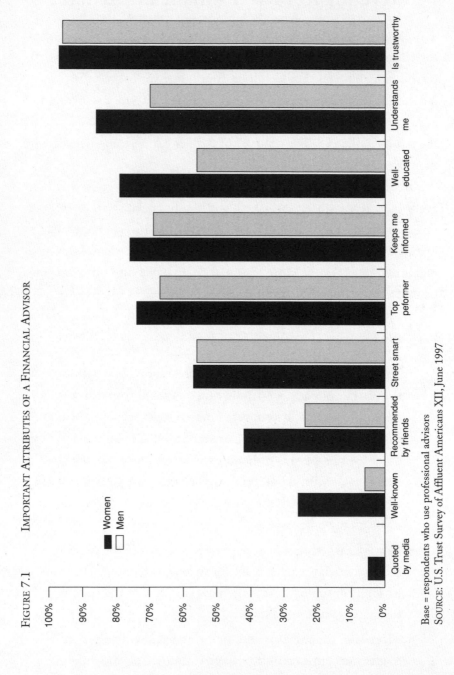

Base = respondents who use professional advisors

SOURCE: U.S. Trust Survey of Affluent Americans XII, June 1997

about how many clients they handle and the quality of their backup. People managing hundreds of other relationships may have a difficult time giving you the amount of time you want and need.

- Understand how you will receive your advice. Will it be in person? Over the phone? By mail? Over the Internet? How frequently can you expect to have meetings? When you have a question, whom should you call?

- What type of statements and reports will you receive? Ask for samples. If the samples don't meet your requirements, find out if the firm can produce the type of reports you need, and how much this will cost.

- Don't let fees be your primary concern. Examine firms without regard to fees and then select your finalists. Only then should you examine their fees and compare them to the alternatives to make sure they are reasonable. Try to understand how all the fees are calculated. For example, consider the investment of cash in your accounts: Almost every firm uses money market funds to invest cash awaiting investment because these funds offer competitive yields and provide instant liquidity. Most large firms use proprietary funds to meet this need, giving them an additional (but reasonable) form of compensation. But on occasion, a firm may use money market funds unfairly to increase their compensation by charging higher-than-average fees. You must do your homework to find out what you'll be charged for, and why.

- In addition to understanding the firm's stated fees, make sure the fee payment method does not set up insurmountable conflicts of interest. If you choose an investment manager who trades through a captive broker-dealer, not only will there be a fee charged for managing your portfolio, but also a fee to the firm on the trading activity itself. This is business as usual; you'd pay a similar fee to another firm. However, if the trade involves buying or selling the inventory of a broker-dealer, such as municipal bonds, it should be closely scrutinized.

- Make sure all clients pay similar fees. If you sense that a firm discounts its fees, ask if they will guarantee that you will receive the lowest fee available for similar services.

- If you are looking for premium service and competitive results, you must be willing to pay appropriate fees.

- Understand the management of the firm and its culture. If major changes in management occur while you are a client, investigate further. For example, does the new management have appropriate experience in the business of the firm? Firms involved in mergers or acquisitions also require additional scrutiny. Why was a firm sold or why did it merge? Do the reasons for the merger support your interest in the firm? Will the principals remain active? Usually, mergers make sense for everyone—clients, employees, and shareholders—but sometimes they fall apart, and the upheaval can adversely affect your finances.

- Find out how your professionals are compensated. Are their interests aligned with yours? Could they make money at your expense?

- Don't be timid. Ask questions. No question is too dumb. How your questions are answered, both in terms of content and the respondent's demeanor, will give you insight into the firm's culture.

Virtually every firm in the personal financial services business has positioned itself to help clients in the investment planning process. This process is centered on driving clients to the appropriate asset allocation decisions based on their particular circumstances. According to many studies, asset allocation alone is responsible for more than 90 percent of portfolio performance.

As it prepares plans, a firm gathers information about you, including your resources, personal circumstances, time horizon, age, income needs, liquidity requirements, and tax concerns. The firm also spends time understanding your return expectations and risk tolerance, and then uses its modeling tools to formulate the strategy it feels is best for you.

You must find out if the firm is willing to educate you along the way. Firms that simply ask you to fill out a form and then hand you a plan probably haven't spent sufficient time to understand you and your needs. Most firms in the investment management business don't charge for this personal analysis, because it helps bring in clients so they can sell them their main offerings. As previously mentioned, there are new firms that specialize in investment planning combined with some version of financial planning. They charge a supervisory fee for providing the service and placing the assets with independent (from them) portfolio managers.

Become aware of the products and services you are likely to purchase from your chosen investment firm; that knowledge will help you interpret the advice they give. For example, if the firm is in the investment management business and they suggest that you only need to invest in the value sector (stocks that are known for their steadiness, as opposed to growth stocks, which are riskier but potentially more profitable), this may be a danger signal. Pushing a specific type of investment indicates they may be biased—particularly if it turns out the firm has a stake in the value stocks or the product they are recommending.

You also should inquire whether the firm will take into account your other assets, such as corporate benefit plans. Will they help you make decisions within those plans, even though the firm will not be managing those assets nor receiving a fee?

Some investment consulting firms offer investment planning, manager selection, and performance measurement for a fee, but do not get paid for providing investment services per se. This type of arrangement was generally provided only to the very affluent because the cost of the service is based on time spent and is usually not justified unless the asset base (the amount you invest with them) is large. However, today many advisors provide this service to investors with as little as a few hundred thousand dollars; the fee is based on a minimum and a percentage of the assets under supervision. This combined fee is often high, but may well be the price to be paid to receive unbiased advice. Also, if you are a self-directed investor, you can find many new tools and services on line to guide you through this process.

Still, most likely you will be dealing with brokers, registered investment advisors (RIAs), or banks and trust companies. Their fees are typically based on the value of your assets under their supervision, and will vary based on asset class and the use of proprietary products versus nonproprietary products (products that they own versus products managed by another firm). Some firms will charge a minimum fee for investment planning and then additional charges if they also help you implement that planning. Or, they may apply the initial fee against future fees if you purchase additional services. Let's look at the various types of financial advisors.

Types of Financial Advisors

Brokerage Firms

Brokerage firms, which buy and sell stocks, bonds, and other products, may or may not charge separately for investment planning. Historically, they have billed for their services on a pay-as-you-go basis. In other words, you pay a fee to the firm for each transaction. In turn, the brokerage firm pays the broker a percentage of the transaction fee as compensation.

Recently, both brokers and clients have come to realize that paying by the transaction can give the appearance of a conflict of interest: The client may perceive the broker's advice to be motivated by a desire to generate transaction-based revenue. Therefore, many brokers now offer managed accounts in which you pay the broker a percentage of the assets under supervision; in exchange, the broker will provide you with both proprietary and nonproprietary products as appropriate.

Such investment vehicles can include individually managed accounts or mutual funds, as well as a variety of alternative investments, including access to hedge funds and venture capital products. These asset-based fees, which cover most services, can run as high as 3 percent to as little as 0.50 percent—the larger the pool of assets under supervision, the lower the percentage fee charged. These fees also may cover additional free services, but some of the underlying products (such as alternative investments) may carry their own fees. Thus, it is important to understand what is and isn't covered in the fee proposal.

The larger brokerage firms have begun positioning themselves to offer a much broader range of options, from trust services to banking services. You need to investigate whether what appears to be a one-stop shop has actually devoted the requisite resources to be able to deliver these services competently and in a personalized fashion. If it has, you can feel confident their traditional broker, now called a financial advisor, is in a position to serve as trusted advisor and wealth manager.

Registered Investment Advisors

These advisors come in all shapes and sizes, from large national firms with substantial resources to single practitioners. After registering with the Securities and Exchange Commission, all an advisor need do is hang up a shingle and go into business. Recently, their ranks have begun to include accountants, lawyers, financial planners, insurance agents, and all of their firms. RIAs can serve as investment counselors, actually investing your assets directly, or consultants, helping you to choose other managers. These days almost all advisors will help you find other managers or products that complement their own particular investment management style. Many people choose to do business with small RIA firms because the principals are actively involved in the business, and/or because they don't like dealing with the size and bureaucracy of a large broker or bank.

If you decide to do business with a small firm, you must think about what would happen if the principal became unavailable, as well as what kind of record-keeping and backup systems the firm maintains. You also should be concerned with the depth and quality of the research the firm provides, given such limited resources. Many small firms subscribe to wonderful services and can effectively replicate the resources of large firms. As well, most RIAs affiliate with brokerage firms or banks to hold their clients' assets and to provide record keeping. If you have assets with multiple custodians or brokers, your registered advisors can employ technology that will take feeds from the various custodians and brokers and consolidate the record keeping.

RIA fees are usually based on the size of assets under supervision. Underlying fees for custody, trading, and asset management are generally passed on to you, the client. Many fee arrangements are unique to dealing with RIAs, so you should thoroughly investigate both the direct and indirect charges involved.

Banks and Trust Companies

Today there is little difference between the operations of banks and trust companies and brokerage firms because of recent changes in legislation and regulation that have made it possible for the appropriate divisions of banks and brokerages to trade securities, offer financial advice, take deposits, and make loans all under one roof. There also is little difference between fees charged by banks, brokers, and RIAs. The difference in fees is on a firm-by-firm basis rather than by category of firm.

Historically, banks and trust companies have charged an assets-based fee for services that included investment planning and investment management services. Until recently, they only used proprietary investment products, but now almost all banks and trust companies offer a mix of proprietary and nonproprietary products.

Banks and trust companies have generally kept their clients' assets in custody in the bank rather than in brokerage accounts (see the section on custody, Chapter 1). Another subtle difference between bankers and brokers is that banking has traditionally been a relationship business, while brokerage has been a transaction business. In other words, bankers have tended to develop client relationships and charge fees, but not call clients to push products; however, brokers do push products. However, this distinction is blurring with changes in legislation, regulation, and the business environment.

Selecting and Working with Investment Managers

Managing your managers is another consideration. When you have completed your investment planning, you will need to select investment managers to implement your strategies. You can do this on your own, but more likely than not you will use the services of one of the firms discussed in the previous section.

Whether you use a firm or do it yourself, the process will involve quantitative and qualitative research. You will want to choose experienced managers who are capable of producing consistent, first- and second-quartile risk-adjusted returns within their asset class, who have disciplines that allow for tax efficiency, or risk-adjusted after-tax returns (in the case of hedge funds), and who agree with their firm's investment process, compensation structure, and culture.

Once you select a firm, you should track it to spot significant changes in any of the above criteria. For example, changes in the firm's investment process may be a danger signal that its current policy is not working. If you selected the firm because of that very policy, you may wish to switch.

Fees

Fees are another important consideration when you are selecting and working with managers. Table 2.6 on page 61 provides average fees for different asset classes for separately managed accounts. It is based on a $5 million account. Smaller accounts may have higher percentage fees and larger accounts lower percentage fees. Fees are calculated differently for nontraditional asset classes, such as venture capital and hedge fund management. For these asset classes, managers receive a management fee of about 1 percent, and also receive a carried interest or a share of the profits.

Many venture capital and hedge fund managers charge a fee known as *1-and-20*, or 1 percent for management plus 20 percent of the profits. As shown in the above chart, most traditional equity managers receive only the 1 percent fee. However, if a hedge fund produces a 12 percent return, the manager will receive the 1 percent management fee plus a carried interest of 2.4 percent, for a total fee of 3.4 percent. Hedge fund and venture capital managers receive this carried interest because traditional wisdom has it that the few managers who possess such specialized skills can charge a higher fee.

Similar fee arrangements, including management fees and profit sharing (but usually at lower levels), also apply in the real estate and leveraged buyout asset classes. For example, a real estate investment fund may share in 20 percent of the profits—but only after the investor receives an initial 8 percent return. The 8 percent minimum return before profit sharing is known as the *hurdle rate*. In that case, if the investment produced an annualized return of 12 percent per year after the 1 percent management fee, the manager would receive, in addition to the 1 percent, a carried interest of 20 percent of 12 percent, or 2.4 percent. However, the returns were less than 8 percent, the manager would receive only the 1 percent management fee. The investor receives the 8% hurdle rate before the manager receives any payment.

Most nontraditional asset class managers have held their clients to very high minimum investment requirements. It is not unusual for a hedge fund manager to require a minimum investment of $5 million. Even if an investor is worth $50 million and wanted to invest 20 percent, or $10 million of his or her assets, in nontraditional asset classes, investing in $5 million minimums does not allow sufficient diversification within those classes and within managers. Someone worth $5 million or less couldn't participate at all.

As a result, an entirely new investment management business has developed called *fund of funds*. This arrangement enables smaller investors to invest in the nontraditional asset classes by participating in a fund that itself invests in a number of different hedge funds, venture capital funds, or leveraged buyout funds. Fund of funds managers perform due diligence on the underlying managers and put together a complementary portfolio of investment styles and sectors; these managers charge a fee of 1 to 2 percent, and sometimes charge a carried interest of 2 to 5 percent with or without a hurdle rate. It becomes expensive for smaller investors to participate, but given the returns available in some of the nontraditional asset classes, it can be a price well worth paying.

Also, consider that banks, brokers, and RIAs all have proprietary investment products that they are likely to recommend (and they will demonstrate how these products stack up against the competition). As mentioned, most firms also offer nonproprietary products manufactured by competing investment management firms. Some firms will receive a portion of the fee from the underlying investment firm to distribute its product and service clients. Sometimes the underlying firms will not share fees, and the primary firm will simply charge extra for nonproprietary products. Generally speaking, the proprietary products will have a price advantage over the nonproprietary products, and that will have to be factored into your decision-making process. Transparency here is important, and you should look to work with firms whose process and fees you can understand.

Monitoring the Investment Management Process

After you choose advisors, you'll want to monitor the investment management process. Usually, the firm that guided you through your investment planning will be best positioned to help you do this. You will need to observe the performance of your investment managers for performance and changes in process or in their firms as a whole. You will also need to rebalance your asset allocation quarterly or semiannually, based on the investment results from different asset classes. Conventional wisdom used to be that investment planning had to be done every two to four years. But in our rapidly changing geopolitical and economic environment, you should regularly review and challenge the assumptions used in your investment planning process.

If you're consistently dissatisfied with your results, sometimes the difficult decision must be made to fire your advisor. The task can be very traumatic because you must sever a relationship. I have seen many intelligent investors retain their advisors and cope with a mediocre performance simply because they can't bear to fire them. Don't fire your advisor if you look at just one statement and think you've lost too much. It may be that others have lost more, or that your advisor has a plan that hasn't yet taken effect.

Still, there are times you should grit your teeth and take care of business. Perhaps your advisor has developed a bad track record over the last few years, or maybe he or she has not able to change with the investing environment. Unless your advisor can make convincing arguments that the market will come back his or her way, you have reason to be suspicious. For example, after the technology crash of 2000, many advisors continued to recommend their clients buy these stocks at what they called bargain basement prices; yet many of these stocks continued to drop another 50 percent or more, and a number of them went out of business.

Sometimes even successful advisors can give you reason to wonder. Their record is good, but they may in turn become susceptible to the challenges that accompany success. Perhaps the firm has grown too fast, and what was once a small boutique now requires a great deal of management. Remember, the number of good investment professionals who are also good managers is limited. You should certainly leave an advisor when it becomes clear to you that he or she no longer is using good common sense, or the performance will never recover.

As you can see, managing your wealth requires dedication, discipline, knowledge, and a trusted advisor to help you coordinate your wealth management needs. But the right advisor can provide you with immense peace of mind.

Coordinating Your Planning

Financial Planning

Financial planning requires the analysis of your current financial condition in order to develop a plan to meet your short- and long-term financial and related objectives. Virtually every firm in the personal planning business is involved in financial planning: Brokers, RIAs, and banks and trust companies are joined by accountants, lawyers, and insurance agents.

Financial planners need to be proficient in all areas of planning, and should also have extensive experience dealing with a wide variety of issues, from how to handle concentrated stock positions to dealing with the alternative minimum tax and the generation-skipping transfer tax. Firms that offer computer-generated financial plans generally don't have the experienced personnel to do customized financial planning for the truly affluent. Planners also should be in a position to help you implement their recommendations. For example, if your planner recommends a second-to-die insurance policy, he or she also should identify potential insurance agents and review the policy recommendations, carriers, and pricing. Even the best plan fails unless it is put into action, and the planner should stay engaged throughout. Fees can run from a few hundred dollars for a computer-generated plan to $25,000 or more for sophisticated planning by true professionals.

Estate Planning

Estate planning allows you to meet your objectives for the disposition of your assets during your lifetime and at and after your death. Estate planning has historically been handled by estate planning lawyers, bank trust departments, and life insurance agents. As with investment planning and financial planning, virtually all financial services firms have now positioned themselves to offer estate planning recommendations.

However, lawyers are the only professionals who can prepare wills and trusts, as well as the other documents that are required in an estate plan. To deal with estate planning properly, you need a team consisting of an estate planning lawyer, a financial planner, and perhaps an insurance agent. Estate planning lawyers charge by the hour; fees can run from $100 an hour to more than $500 an hour based on experience and location. In seeking out an estate planning attorney, relevant experience is a key consideration.

Retirement Planning

Retirement planning allows you to retire based on a predetermined life style at an age you choose, and it is a subset of the financial planning discipline. A retirement plan should be reviewed regularly as part of the financial planning cycle or whenever you contemplate a change in employment. If you have funded retirement plans such as a 401(k), they should be reviewed on the same cycle as your investments. It is vital to coordinate all your retirement options as retirement approaches. Retirement planning should be performed by your financial planner and the same guidelines apply.

Income Tax Planning

Income tax planning and preparation, which allow you to conduct your activities in a tax-efficient manner, is another continuous process. Reviewing income tax projections early in the year, in the fall, and in December makes sense, as does timing these reviews to estimated payments if you are self-employed. Income tax preparation is provided by CPAs and a few bank trust departments. The process is straightforward and is generally billed by the hour with rates running from $100 to $300. Make sure your provider can efficiently produce your tax projections. Many CPAs also can offer a light audit of your broker or custodian to make sure you have received all of the interest, dividends, and principal disbursements to which you are entitled. Your tax planner's input is essential in investment, financial, and retirement planning.

Insurance Planning

Insurance planning and implementation permit you to purchase the appropriate amounts of life, property, casualty, and liability insurance in an efficient manner. Property, casualty, and liability insurance should be reviewed every two to three years, or when there is a change in your circumstances, such as the purchase of major art, jewelry or a new residence. If life insurance or annuities are part of your investment management plan, they should be reviewed on the same cycle as your investments. You will need insurance agents to help you implement the recommendations of your financial planner. Your financial planner usually can help you find a good insurance agent; you may need both a life agent and a property and casualty agent. These agents receive a commission on the products they sell.

Private Banking

Private banking often is the best option for handling your personal banking requirements. Private banking is provided exclusively by banks. Turnover is the bane of personal service, so find a private bank with bankers who plan to stay there for years. In an era of impersonal business, this service allows you the pleasure of picking up a phone and obtaining a loan, stopping a check, or arranging whatever service is required with someone you have known and worked with for years.

U.S. Trust Survey of Affluent Americans Results

In 1996, the U.S. Trust survey asked affluent men and women various questions to compare their attitudes toward their finances and their advisors. When asked to rate how well women and men perform 14 different tasks related to taking care of a family's financial matters, many women and men felt both sexes were equally capable of doing these jobs. When they discerned a difference in how the sexes handle money, men and women tended to agree about their individual strengths. Both the women and the men surveyed felt men were better at minimizing the taxes they must pay, developing a financial plan for the future, selecting good investments, choosing a wise financial advisor, and researching major purchases. The men also thought they were better at these jobs. The women surveyed felt they were better than the men at finding bargains, keeping good records, paying bills on time, getting good value for the money they spend, and sticking to a budget. The men also agreed that women were better at these five tasks.

For the most part, those surveyed felt that the most important reasons to value money are that it allows you to live comfortably and that it provides you with security. Affluent women felt more strongly than men that money is also important because it enables you to give advantages to your children, allows you to enjoy life's luxuries, and permits you to leave an inheritance to people you care about. Both men and women felt that the least important reasons to value money were that money makes it possible for you not to work too hard, and it is a good measure of your success.

The financial goals of both men and women are similar: to have enough money to be financially secure, to be able to enjoy a comfortable retirement, to have enough money to lead your current lifestyle, to be able to live off the investment income, and to have enough money to travel. However, women place more importance on providing for their children's education, on saving, and on providing an inheritance to family members.

When it comes to professional advice, women (75 percent) rely on it more than the men (53 percent) to help them determine the best course of action with regard to financial matters. When asked to rate the importance of one (or more) professional and/or nonprofessional sources of financial advice, a large majority of women—65 percent— considered their husbands to be their most important source. Thirty-two percent said CPAs were also important, 30 percent liked certified financial planners, and 28 percent cited investment managers or attorneys. Far fewer men (26 percent) considered their wives an important source of financial advice. When asked who they considered their most important source, 24 percent cited CPAs, 19 percent said investment managers, 16 percent said certified financial planners, and 15 percent cited attorneys.

When choosing a financial planner, the following characteristics were deemed very important by women: trustworthiness, understanding their situation and concerns, and a good education. Only trustworthiness ranked as highly for the men. In fact, it was the only characteristic that more than 75 percent of the men surveyed thought was very important.

Affluent women tended to be more risk-averse than men. When offered a choice between an investment offering lower-than-average returns but considerable safety of principal, and an investment offering better-than-average returns but some risk of losing the principal, 54 percent of the women preferred the safer investment, compared to 45 percent of the men. Thirty-seven percent of the men preferred the riskier investment, compared to 20 percent of the women (the others preferred neither, or they had no opinion).

The aversion to risk among women was further illustrated when married respondents were asked to describe the difference between them and their spouses regarding investments. Compared to their wives, 58 percent of the men believed they were more willing to entertain risk, 28 percent believed they were equally willing, and 10 percent felt they were less willing. Compared to their husbands, 23 percent of the married women believed they were more willing to entertain risk, 37 percent felt they were equally willing, and 37 percent believed they were less willing.

Gender-Related Trends

Consider that not so long ago, women seldom talked about their investments and financial affairs. Even today, some women feel most comfortable delegating financial authority to their husband, especially when he is the sole breadwinner.

Historically, most of U.S. Trust's female clients have delegated investment authority to males. But the world is changing, and one of the areas where that's most obvious is in women's relationship with money. Today we find that when women are breadwinners (or equal partners in two-income families), they feel both a new sense of responsibility and a heightened interest in investment that derive from actually earning the money themselves. As a result, finances are becoming gender neutral.

Recently, we have witnessed a phenomenon in which some women have become not just interested but much more actively involved in financial decisions than the men in their lives. Often, this may happen because they're newer to the role. Coming from a background where women were not involved with handling money, they very much want to change the status quo, especially when it comes to being a role model for their daughters. In fact, during preliminary sessions, we have seen several instances that defied our expectations: It was the wife, not the husband, who took charge, having done the appropriate homework and knowing which questions to ask.

Based on U.S. Trust's client base, we've noticed some gender-related trends as well, such as women tending to be more conservative with their assets than men. When making investment decisions, they are more likely to prefer safer vehicles such as bonds or real estate. For the most part, the men want the opposite—they look for vehicles that will increase their net wealth more quickly. Their greater comfort with risk comes at the cost of increased volatility, however, as well as the potential for much greater loss.

A decade ago we met with a certain couple; he was the CEO of a major industrial company, and she was a significant player in the world of charity. They held separate accounts, but between them had approximately $30 million to invest. The husband wanted to put the entire sum into the stock market; the wife wanted it all to go into the bond market. Eventually, we reached a compromise: Instead of merging these accounts, which had been their original intention, the couple decided to keep them separate. With his monies, the husband bought only stocks; with hers, the wife bought only bonds.

In the late 1990s the husband died and the wife inherited all his money. Over the years his account had done much better than hers, but she still felt strongly about the bonds, and insisted that we sell everything in his account and buy bonds with it. We tried to talk her into a slightly more evenly distributed asset allocation, but she was resolute. As luck would have it, she did quite well selling stocks in early 2000. We still stand by our original recommendation, but if she had kept her late husband's portfolio, she might have lost a great deal, instead of making money as she did. She simply benefited from good timing.

I do remember one situation in which it was the wife who was the far more aggressive investor. Alice and Max had been clients for many years, and for many years they had battled over asset allocation. In this case, Alice felt strongly that equities were the best investment for the future, but Max, who was conservative in all things, wanted to keep their money in the safest possible vehicles. Each time Alice and Max came in, they fought about their portfolio. This battled raged for years, with Alice always trying to push more aggressive stocks, and Max wishing all their money could be placed in Treasury bills.

Eventually, one of our employees became friendly with the couple and began seeing them socially; in these situations she realized that the argument about finances pervaded their entire relationship. The couple brought their she-is-risk-prone, he-is-risk-averse dynamic to everything from vacations (she wanted to learn sky diving, he preferred sitting on a beach) to dining out (she loved exotic international cuisine, he opted for steak and potatoes). Often enough, a couple's financial inclinations are simply an extension of the pattern they establish long before they have any money to invest.

Conclusion

U.S. Trust Survey of
Affluent Americans Results

According to half of our survey's respondents, the best route to success
in the twenty-first century is starting your own business; they believe
entrepreneurism is the key to the future. Another fifth of respondents
recommended entering such venerable professions as law and medicine, whereas a smaller percentage thought the best path is to sign up
at a large corporation; a slightly smaller proportion recommend looking for a job, but with a small company.

The industries deemed to have the most potential to bring future financial success are technology (recommended by 89 percent), finance (67 percent), communications (51 percent), health care (39 percent), and leisure and entertainment (28 percent). Receiving the lowest recommendation were manufacturing and retailing.

These results above were in response to our 1999 survey. Because economic conditions have changed considerably since then, a new poll might reveal different answers. I believe a more constant theme can be found in our respondents' sense of what it takes to be successful. They felt that the most important traits to make it to the top are, in order of importance, ambition, the willingness to work hard, technological savvy, intelligence, an advanced degree, communication skills, an entrepreneurial spirit, flexibility, financial expertise, and management expertise. The least recommended trait: coming from a well-to-do family.

For would-be entrepreneurs or corporate executives with an international bent, respondents thought the major countries likely to have the strongest economies over the next 20 years will be the United States, China, Germany, and Japan. At the bottom of the list are Russia, France, and India. Seventy percent of respondents felt that the globalization of business will make it more difficult for the United States to control its own economy, and a little more than half said that the unification of Europe will diminish the global importance of the United States; exactly half thought that China, not the United States, will eventually dominate the world economy.

Given all the problems in the world today, 57 percent of the affluent thought that young people will have more difficulty achieving financial success in the twenty-first century. Only 31 percent thought the next generation will have an easier time than they did.

Your Financial Future

Your financial future isn't simply about how much money you earn. More important is how intelligently you handle that money after you've earned it. And although your investment choices are crucial, as we have seen, you cannot isolate one part of financial planning from any another. The art of good wealth management consists of marrying the various elements into a coherent whole.

The other day I met with a family who has worked with U.S. Trust for several generations. The patriarch had done an excellent job of increasing an already large inheritance through his own career and his careful investing philosophy. He believed, based on his first-hand knowledge of the 1970s bear market, that the stock market had become overvalued, and so through the 1980s and early 1990s he insisted that his family keep 70 percent of its money in bonds, and only 30 percent in equities. Despite the low return on these investments, the family's wealth continued to grow because they spent less than they earned, and compounded that return through the success of their bond portfolio.

When the patriarch died in late 1999, the next generation, all children of the 1990s, told us that they were not as conservative as their father; they wished to follow a different long-term strategy. As a result, we helped the family create a more aggressive plan that would eventually convert the family investments to a well-diversified portfolio, with 75 percent of it invested in equities (or assets that would produce equity-type results).

Unfortunately, our aggressive new strategy was launched just as the stock market began its steep decline. Even so, because we'd constructed a diversified portfolio across most asset classes that consisted of long equity managers, passive managers, liquid and illiquid hedge funds, and domestic and international managers, and because we averaged into our positions, we were able to keep the family's losses well under 10 percent over the last four years, which—compared to the market's performance—was an excellent result. The family was nevertheless disappointed with our performance because they now had less money than when they started their new investment plan.

Had they committed some kind of error? Were we doing a good job for them? Perhaps we hadn't made the risks of the family's new investment strategy clear or paid enough attention to their reaction.

As we examine the disciplines involved in wealth management, there's no question that investing takes center stage, because it appears to have the greatest impact on our day-to-day lives. And it's hard to ignore the seemingly nonstop financial reports broadcast all over the media like sports scores. Yet despite its almost unavoidable presence in our lives, investing remains very confusing, because there are no hard-and-fast rules—and whatever rules we think we understand seem to change regularly. However, certain truths about investing do seem to hold over time.

From a simple risk point of view, you can create two kinds of investment portfolios. One is called a *sleep-well* portfolio, the other an *eat-well* portfolio. In other words, one portfolio virtually guarantees that you can sleep at night because it is so safe—but it is not going to guarantee that you will make a great return. The other type of portfolio is designed to earn as much money as possible so that you can eat (and do whatever else you want)—but it's not going to help you sleep at night, because there will be swings in the market that show up in your net worth.

The role of wealth management is to help you navigate the course between sleeping well and eating well. Most people can't eat well unless they are prepared to take some degree of risk. If that risk prevents you from sleeping, you either need to reduce your expectations or learn to live with some worry. The key is to understand what your portfolio is designed to accomplish, and to make sure that the worst-case scenario is something you can live with.

Unfortunately, many people in the 1990s wanted to do well and feel safe, but they got carried away by the moment and the wonderful feeling of a booming stock market, as well as a bit of greed. Only when the music stopped did they realize they were at risk, and fear set in. Many people have made the somewhat cynical observation that indeed Wall Street is primarily motivated by two emotions: fear and greed. The 1990s were a greed cycle, when people wanted to make as much money as possible, and they acted on that desire. In 2000 we entered a fear cycle, as people suddenly realized that the markets were filled with risk, and they feared they would lose all their money if they were heavily invested.

Like the family mentioned at the beginning of this section, many clients came to us in the 1990s and insisted that they wanted 80 if not 100 percent of their assets in the stock market because they wanted those excellent returns their friends were getting, and they rejected our entreaties to be more diversified. Those prospects and clients are now angry and afraid.

We will see what happens when the current fear cycle ends and the next greed cycle begins. The French have an ages-old saying: "The more things change, the more they remain the same." Cycles present a good example of this. Every few years they change, yet at their heart, these cycles always seem to bring back the same patterns. But I wonder in the future if one particular aspect of these cycles may change. As the average age of the U.S. population lengthens, these cycles may lengthen as well, because people who have been through a dramatic cycle don't tend to forget it. Those who weathered the Great Depression never forgot what that felt like. It's not improbable that many people who lived through these last four years will not forget them either, particularly those people who lost 75 percent or more of their investment portfolio.

Risk is an abstract idea for most people, but they understand it best when by ignoring it, they learn a lesson about risk's dangers. The last few years were an excellent learning opportunity for many investors. Although it's impossible to predict how long each cycle of greed and fear will last, it's not hard to know that from each, smart investors will learn important lessons. Indeed, the move to alternative investments—particularly hedge fund management—is a growing trend, because it tries to bridge the gaps between eating well and sleeping well; between fear and greed. How this will play out over the next 10 to 20 years is yet to be determined.

Not long ago one of our clients presented us with a embroidered cushion that reads, "It's no longer a sin to be rich, it's a miracle." The quote applies quite well to current times, but the cushion was actually embroidered back in the late 1970s. That was a difficult decade; we had to deal with a variety of financial ogres, including inflation and stagflation, as well as a dearth of entrepreneurial activity and, of course, a flat stock market.

The great bull market of the 1980s and 1990s followed, and many people who hadn't been doing very well found themselves wealthy again. Those who were affluent in the 1990s were much wealthier than their 1970s counterparts, and there were more of them. Corporate CEOs became American icons and role models for everyone everywhere.

But after the decade of the 1990s ended, its excesses revealed an equal wealth of scandals. Several CEOs were discovered to have engaged in criminal behavior, and others still stand accused, although not yet convicted (not that there were no scandals during the boom years—few can forget those involving financiers Michael Milken and Ivan Boesky, who were convicted of manipulating the markets). In addition, a few trusted advisors eager to participate in the boom, such as accountants and financial services firms, bent rules that had served them well for decades—with disastrous results for clients and investors. These bad apples focused a great deal of attention on the dramatic rise in shareholder value, and just who actually was being enriched. Suddenly, becoming wealthy took on a potentially sinister connotation.

These cycles likely will continue as long as capitalism is the rule of the land. The only financial issue I can think of that remains constant is the debate over the rich. Is it good for the country to have an affluent class? Do the affluent help the rest of the country, or hurt it? Such questions are part of an ongoing argument that frames many of the political and social agendas of the day. For instance, how much of the income tax burden should the affluent shoulder? Should there be an estate tax? Should taxes be eliminated?

Personally, I'm of the camp that stands against any reform that allows the gap between the haves and the have-nots to widen. A nation shouldn't have increasing numbers of the affluent while increasing numbers of people go without health insurance. I don't want our country to lapse into the oligarchic fiefdoms that have historically marked the downfall of great societies. To me, taxes play a role in leveling the social geography. Using the income tax this way helps guard against a system that could someday lead to class warfare.

There's yet another old Wall Street maxim that goes: "Bulls win, bears win, but pigs always lose." If the affluent become too avaricious, they can end up losing more than a few political debates. Fortunately, most wealthy people don't become that greedy. Our surveys support the view that although a small percentage do live the lifestyle of the rich and famous, most of the affluent take the responsibility of their wealth very seriously. The vast majority are hard-working individuals and couples who certainly enjoy their share of luxuries but don't take anything for granted. If they're urbanites making a combined income of maybe $350,000 a year and putting children through private school, chances are they are living mainly off their salaries, and budgeting to pay all their expenses as well as to save for retirement.

Whatever the future holds, no society can continue to exist if the process of gaining affluence doesn't lift all the ships in the harbor. But if we can steer a smoother course, under which government remains stable (rather than one in which taxes are raised and lowered according to momentary political advantages), we will arrive at a sound strategy with a clear view of what's good for the country in the long run.

It's true, as our survey shows, that the affluent themselves do their share to minimize economic gaps through philanthropy. It is wonderful that so many give to their alma mater and cultural organizations, but we need more help in addressing the true social ills this country faces.

Beyond these problems, and the battles they engender, the great American dream will survive, because new tax laws, changes in government, dishonest CEOs, and shifts in economic cycles don't affect the fundamental American work ethic. A foundation remains in place, assuring that if you work hard, you, too, have a chance to become wealthy.

Because these opportunities always beckon, in the future we will see a portrait of the affluent different from what we knew just a few decades ago. The very face of wealth is changing. When I started my career, there were very few black or Hispanic millionaires in the United States—the face of affluence was truly monochromatic. Now many people of minorities count themselves in the top 1 percent of America's wealthy, and their numbers are growing. As well, many more women are wealthy in their own right, because there are many more female executives and entrepreneurs.

Our capitalist system and our democracy are both merit-driven. Over time, race, religion, and gender are not obstacles. Today, as I see the affluent become more representative of America in general, I can honestly say, "Anyone can become affluent," and thoroughly believe it.

Examples of
Financial Planning Schedules*

The following schedules are for a hypothetical couple, John and
Terry Sample. They include:

- Balance Sheet

- Stock Option Holdings

- Option Exercise Projection

- Savings Plan Projection

- Savings Investment Plans: IRA Rollover Projection

- Current Portfolio Asset Allocation

- Annual Lifestyle Analysis

- Estate Tax Calculation

- General Plan Assumptions

They are intended to provide you with an understanding of the
importance of customized financial planning.

---

*Financial planning schedules are discussed in Chapter 1.

Balance Sheet

John and Terry Sample

Present Assets		John	Terry	Joint	Total	Kids Accts.
Liquid Assets						
U.S. Trust Joint Checking Account		$0	$0	$45,239	$45,239	
U.S. Trust Savings Accounts		195,000	0	50,000	245,000	
U.S. Trust Fixed Income Account		0	0	2,700,000	2,700,000	
① ABC Inc. Stock:	*Shares*					
ABC in John's name	*122,000*	2,287,500	0	0	2,287,500	*gifts of ABC*
ABC in Trust	*20,000*	375,000	0	0	375,000	168,750
ABC in Terry's name	*60,000*	0	1,125,000	0	1,125,000	
② Non-Qualified Options *(After-Tax Spread)*		433,312	0	0	433,312	
U.S. Trust Capital Account *(All Equities)*		0	0	2,600,000	2,600,000	
Total Liquid Assets		$3,290,812	$1,125,000	$5,395,239	$9,811,051	168,750
Illiquid Assets						
Home - Bernardsville, NJ		$0	$0	$1,000,000	$1,000,000	
Vacation Residence - West Hampton, NY		0	0	875,000	875,000	
Austin, TX Property		525,000	0	0	525,000	
② Unexercisable NQ Options *(After-Tax Spread)*		226,103	0	0	226,103	
Tangibles & Automobiles		0	0	500,000	500,000	
Total Illiquid Assets		$751,103	$0	$2,375,000	$3,126,103	
Gross Present Assets		$4,041,915	$1,125,000	$7,770,239	$12,937,154	
Less : Liabilities						
Additional Tax Liability		$0	$0	$0	$0	
Mortgage *(Hampton Home)* - 5.5% ARM		0	0	679,000	679,000	
Total Liabilities		$0	$0	$679,000	$679,000	
Net Present Assets		$4,041,915	$1,125,000	$7,091,239	$12,258,154	
Deferred Assets ③ (as of 12/31/02)						
Traditional IRAs	*Shares*	$60,000	$57,000	$0	$117,000	
ABC Savings / 401(k) *(ABC)*	*29,500*	553,125	0	0	553,125	
ABC Savings / 401(k) *(Cash)*		202,000	0	0	202,000	
ABC, Inc. Deferred Comp Plan *(Fixed Income)*		224,926	0	0	224,926	
Total Deferred Assets		$1,040,051	$57,000	$0	$1,097,051	
Tax Liability on **All** Deferred Assets		(451,902)				
Total Assets		$4,630,064	$1,182,000	$7,091,239	$12,903,303	
Net Worth (Excludes Life Insurance)		$8,175,684	$4,727,620			
Assets at Death	*Beneficiary*					**Ins. Trust**
ABC Group Term - UL	*Terry*	$500,000	$0	$0	$500,000	0
Executive Life *($1,500,000)*	*1990 ILIT*	0	0	0	0	1,500,000
Total Assets at Death		$500,000	$0	$0	$500,000	1,500,000
						Outside Estate
Gross Estate		$8,675,684	$4,727,620		$13,403,303	$1,668,750

$18.750	*Note: Outright ABC share amounts are rounded estimates.*
$8.000	*Assumed average Cost Basis of ABC shares.*
43.45%	

Stock Option Holdings

John and Terry Sample

ABC, Co., *Non-Qualified*

Income Tax Rate 2002 (w/medicare) :	44.43%
Dividend :	$0.72
Current Stock Price :	$18.75
Est. Growth Rate :	6.00%

EXERCISABLE :

Grant Date	Vesting Date	Expiration Date	Number of Shares	Basis per Share	Total Basis	Market Value	Pre-Tax Spread	After-Tax Spread
12/5/97	*Vested*	12/5/07	23,000	8.250	189,750	431,250	241,500	134,203
6/25/98	*Vested*	6/24/08	33,000	11.250	371,250	618,750	247,500	137,537
12/4/98	*Vested*	12/3/08	46,000	14.875	684,250	862,500	178,250	99,055
12/3/99	*Vested*	12/3/09	100,000	25.875	2,587,500	1,875,000	0	0
12/2/00	*Vested*	12/3/10	100,000	17.625	1,762,500	1,875,000	112,500	62,517
Total NQs			**302,000**		**$5,595,250**	**$5,662,500**	**$779,750**	**$433,312**

NON-EXERCISABLE :

Grant Date	Vesting Date	Expiration Date	Number of Shares	Basis per Share	Total Basis	Market Value	Pre-Tax Spread	After-Tax Spread
12/2/00	*12/2/03*	12/2/10	120,000	17.625	2,115,000	2,250,000	135,000	75,020
12/4/01	*12/4/04*	12/4/11	120,000	19.750	2,370,000	2,250,000	0	0
12/1/02	*12/1/05*	12/1/12	145,000	16.875	2,446,875	2,718,750	271,875	151,083
Total NQs			**385,000**		**$6,931,875**	**$7,218,750**	**$406,875**	**$226,103**

Grant Date	Vesting Date	Expiration Date	Number of Shares	Basis per Share	Total Basis	Market Value	Pre-Tax Spread	After-Tax Spread
Vested and Unvested :			**687,000**		**$12,527,125**	**$12,881,250**	**$1,186,625**	**$659,415**

250

Option Exercise Projection

John and Terry Sample
ABC, Co., *Non-Qualified*

Current Stock Price :	$18.75
Est. Growth Rate :	6.00%

Grant Date	Vesting Date	Expiration Date	Number of Shares	Basis per Share	2003 $19.88	2004 $21.07	2005 $22.33	2006 $23.67	2007 $25.09	2008 $26.60	2009 $28.19	2010 $29.88	2011 $31.68	2012 $33.58
Vested														
12/5/97	Vested	12/5/07	23,000	$8.25	$267,375	$294,803	$323,876	$354,693	$387,360					
6/25/98	Vested	6/24/08	33,000	$11.25	284,625	323,378	365,691	409,908	456,777	$506,459				
12/4/98	Vested	12/3/08	46,000	$14.88	230,000	284,855	343,001	404,635	469,970	$539,223				
12/3/99	Vested	12/3/09	100,000	$25.88	-	-	-	-	-	72,223	$231,307			
12/2/00	Vested	12/3/10	100,000	$17.63	225,000	344,250	470,655	604,644	746,673	897,223	1,056,807	$1,225,965		
Total Vested Shares			*302,000*											
Unvested														
12/2/00	12/02/10	12/2/10	120,000	$17.63	270,000	413,100	564,786	725,573	896,008	1,076,668	1,268,168	$1,471,158		
12/4/01	12/04/11	12/4/11	120,000	$19.75	15,000	158,100	309,786	470,573	641,008	821,668	1,013,168	1,216,158	$1,431,328	
12/1/02	12/01/12	12/1/12	145,000	$16.88	435,000	607,913	791,200	985,484	1,191,426	1,409,724	1,641,120	1,886,399	2,146,396	$2,421,992
Total Unvested Shares			*385,000*											

		2003	2004	2005	2006	2007	2008	2009	2010	2011	2012
Annual Cash Flow of Shares Exercised:		$0	$0	$0	$0	$213,435	$621,234	$137,715	$1,602,347	$788,698	$1,334,579

251

Savings Plan Projection

John and Terry Sample

401(k) ABC, Co.

Pre-Tax Earnings Growth Rate:	5.50%
Assumed Retirement Date:	*12/31/07*

	2003	2004	2005	2006	2007
401(k) Plan					
Beginning Balance	$553,125	$590,666	$646,868	$707,215	$772,437
Pre-Tax Contributions to 401(k) Plan	12,000	13,000	14,000	15,000	15,000
Company match (5% of salary up to IRS limit)	10,000	10,000	10,000	10,500	10,500
Assumed Earnings Growth	15,541	33,202	36,348	39,722	43,309
Ending Balance	$590,666	$646,868	$707,215	$772,437	$841,246

Savings Investment Plans: IRA Rollover Projection

John and Terry Sample
Distributions to Begin at Age 70½

Year End	John's Age	Terry's Age	MDIB Divisor (IRS Regs)	Principal 5.50%	Required Minimum Distributions	After-Tax Distributions 43.45%
2007				$994,180		
2008	56	52		1,048,860	$0	$0
2009	57	53		1,106,547	0	0
2010	58	54		1,167,407	0	0
2011	59	55		1,231,615	0	0
2012	60	56		1,299,354	0	0
2013	61	57		1,370,818	0	0
2014	62	58		1,446,213	0	0
2015	63	59		1,525,755	0	0
2016	64	60		1,609,671	0	0
2017	65	61		1,698,203	0	0
2018	66	62		1,791,604	0	0
2019	67	63		1,890,143	0	0
2020	68	64		1,994,101	0	0
2021	69	65		2,103,776	0	0
2022	70	66		2,219,484	0	0
2023	71	67	26.20	2,252,183	84,713	47,905
2024	72	68	25.30	2,282,138	89,019	50,340
2025	73	69	24.40	2,308,981	93,530	52,891
2026	74	70	23.50	2,332,317	98,255	55,563
2027	75	71	22.70	2,352,198	102,745	58,102
2028	76	72	21.80	2,367,735	107,899	61,017
2029	77	73	20.90	2,378,441	113,289	64,065
2030	78	74	20.10	2,384,417	118,330	66,916
2031	79	75	19.20	2,384,541	124,188	70,229
2032	80	76	18.40	2,378,968	129,595	73,286
2033	81	77	17.60	2,367,209	135,169	76,438
2034	82	78	16.80	2,348,750	140,905	79,682
2035	83	79	16.00	2,323,061	146,797	83,014
2036	84	80	15.30	2,290,644	151,834	85,862
2037	85	81	14.50	2,249,965	157,975	89,335
2038	86	82	13.80	2,201,705	163,041	92,200
2039	87	83	13.10	2,145,486	168,069	95,043
2040	88	84	12.40	2,080,948	173,023	97,845
2041	89	85	11.80	2,009,350	176,352	99,727
2042	90	86	11.10	1,928,885	181,022	102,368

Total					$931,969	$527,028
Discounted at Rate of Inflation:					$201,884	$114,165

	Beginning balance consists of:		
	12/31/02		12/31/07
Traditional IRAs	*$117,000*	5.50%	*$152,934*
ABC Savings / 401(k) (ABC)	*553,125*		*841,246*
	$670,125		*$994,180*

Current Portfolio Asset Allocation
John and Terry Sample

Asset Allocation	$	%
CASH	492,239	5%
Fixed Income	2,924,926	28%
Large Cap Equities	2,080,000	20%
ABC concentration	5,000,040	47%
Small and Mid Cap Equities	57,000	1%
International	60,000	1%
Private Equity/Venture	0	0%
Absolute Return	0	0%
Total	**$10,614,206**	**100%**

Cash to Equity

Cash/Bonds
32%

Equities
68%

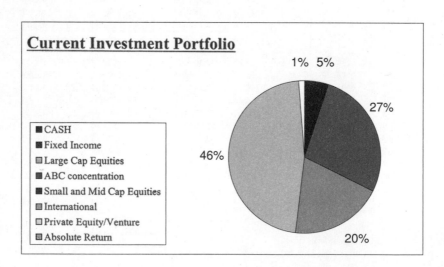

Current Investment Portfolio

- CASH
- Fixed Income
- Large Cap Equities
- ABC concentration
- Small and Mid Cap Equities
- International
- Private Equity/Venture
- Absolute Return

1% 5%

27%

46%

20%

Annual Lifestyle Analysis

John and Terry Sample

$500,000 After-Tax Retirement on December 31, 2007

Lifestyle (Yr. 2003 $'s):	$500,000
Inflation Rate:	4.00%
After-Tax Total Return:	4.93%
Income Tax Rate (Federal/NJ):	43.45%

Year End	JS's Age	TS's Age	Life Style 4.00%	Annual Dividends ABC stock	Annual Base & Bonus Comp. 8.00%	Social Security 2.00%	After-tax Stock Option Proceeds	Pension Annuity	IRA Distrib.	Income Taxes 43.45%	Additional Medicare Taxes 1.45%	Investment Income (After-tax) 1.27%	After-Tax Surplus/(Deficit)	Liquid Assets 3.66%	ABC shares 6.00%	Children's Assets 6.00%
					$1,540,000									$5,590,239	$3,787,500	$165,750
2003	51	47	(500,000)	145,440	870,370	0	0	0	0	(436,803)	(12,628)	71,980	138,859	5,831,308	4,014,750	174,921
2004	52	48	(520,000)	154,166	940,540	0	0	0	0	(465,372)	(13,638)	75,414	171,109	6,215,653	4,255,635	181,317
2005	53	49	(540,800)	163,416	1,015,783	0	0	0	0	(591,291)	(14,729)	79,865	202,244	6,645,186	4,510,973	187,947
2006	54	50	(562,432)	173,221	1,097,045	0	213,435	0	0	(528,112)	(15,907)	85,594	249,410	7,137,592	4,781,631	194,820
2007	55	51	(584,929)	183,615	1,184,809	0	621,234	0	0	(568,920)	(20,275)	93,411	501,145	7,899,740	5,068,529	201,944
2008	56	52	(608,326)	194,632	0	0	137,715	0	0	(76,180)	(9,008)	101,293	223,644	8,412,256	5,372,641	209,329
2009	57	53	(632,660)	206,309	0	0	1,602,347	0	0	(80,751)	(1,997)	104,673	(266,710)	8,453,160	5,695,000	216,983
2010	58	54	(657,966)	218,688	0	0	788,698	322,170	0	(211,695)	(23,234)	115,510	1,365,821	10,128,091	6,036,700	224,918
2011	59	55	(684,285)	231,809	0	0	1,334,579	322,170	0	(216,830)	(21,436)	131,604	561,730	11,060,177	6,398,902	233,142
2012	60	56	(711,656)	245,718	0	0	0	322,170	0	(222,274)	(11,436)	146,766	1,095,951	12,560,569	6,782,836	241,668
2013	61	57	(740,122)	260,461	0	0	0	322,170	0	(253,138)	(19,351)	157,205	(253,425)	12,766,451	7,189,806	250,505
2014	62	58	(769,727)	276,089	0	0	0	322,170	0	(259,928)	0	159,693	(271,704)	12,961,581	7,621,194	259,665
2015	63	59	(800,516)	292,654	0	0	0	322,170	0	(267,125)	0	163,039	(290,779)	13,144,772	8,078,466	269,161
2016	64	60	(832,537)	310,213	0	25,800	0	322,170	0	(274,755)	0	164,229	(310,679)	13,314,762	8,563,174	279,003
2017	65	61	(865,838)	328,826	0	26,310	0	322,170	0	(301,130)	0	166,351	(315,061)	13,486,587	9,076,964	289,205
2018	66	62	(900,472)	348,555	0	26,840	0	322,170	0	(310,412)	0	168,390	(336,176)	13,543,579	9,621,582	299,781
2019	67	63	(936,491)	369,469	0	27,380	0	322,170	0	(310,412)	0	170,236	(358,185)	13,784,300	10,198,877	310,743
2020	68	64	(973,950)	391,637	0	27,920	0	322,170	0	(320,243)	0	171,870	(381,136)	13,907,218	10,810,810	322,106
2021	69	65	(1,012,908)	415,135	0	28,490	0	322,170	0	(330,651)	0	173,273	(405,062)	14,010,700	11,459,458	333,885
2022	70	66	(1,053,425)	440,043	0	29,050	0	322,170	0	(341,680)	0	174,424	(429,983)	14,093,050	12,147,026	346,094
2023	71	67	(1,095,562)	466,446	0	29,630	0	322,170	84,713	(390,168)	0	175,605	(407,745)	14,200,650	12,875,847	358,750
2024	72	68	(1,139,384)	494,433	0	30,230	0	322,170	89,019	(404,412)	0	176,814	(431,711)	14,288,200	13,648,398	371,868
2025	73	69	(1,184,959)	524,098	0	30,830	0	322,170	93,530	(419,483)	0	177,763	(456,692)	14,354,031	14,467,302	385,466
2026	74	70	(1,232,358)	555,544	0	31,450	0	322,170	98,255	(435,420)	0	178,432	(482,565)	14,396,371	15,335,340	395,562
2027	75	71	(1,281,652)	588,877	0	32,080	0	322,170	102,745	(452,082)	0	178,796	(509,690)	14,413,113	16,255,460	414,173
2028	76	72	(1,332,918)	624,210	0	32,720	0	322,170	107,899	(469,905)	0	178,831	(537,633)	14,402,521	17,230,788	429,318
2029	77	73	(1,386,235)	661,662	0	33,370	0	322,170	113,289	(488,755)	0	178,514	(566,635)	14,362,653	18,264,635	445,017
2030	78	74	(1,441,684)	701,362	0	34,040	0	322,170	118,330	(459,523)	0	177,236	(688,747)	14,199,000	19,360,513	461,290
2031	79	75	(1,499,352)	743,444	0	34,720	0	151,085	124,188	(481,503)	0	174,954	(721,154)	13,997,077	20,522,144	478,158
2032	80	76	(1,559,326)	788,050	0	35,410	0	151,085	129,595	(504,723)	0	172,193	(755,184)	13,753,473	21,753,473	495,643
2033	81	77	(1,621,699)	835,333	0	36,120	0	151,085	135,169	(529,254)	0	168,895	(790,500)	13,466,134	23,058,681	513,767
2034	82	78	(1,686,567)	885,453	0	36,850	0	151,085	140,905	(555,165)	0	165,027	(827,230)	13,131,312	24,442,202	532,554
2035	83	79	(1,754,029)	938,581	0	37,580	0	151,085	146,797	(582,091)	0	161,553	(865,329)	12,746,177	25,908,734	552,028
2036	84	80	(1,824,191)	994,895	0	38,330	0	151,085	151,834	(610,972)	0	155,430	(905,457)	12,306,860	27,463,258	572,215
2037	85	81	(1,897,158)	1,054,589	0	39,100	0	151,085	157,975	(640,948)	0	149,615	(946,535)	11,810,299	29,111,054	593,139
2038	86	82	(1,973,044)	1,117,864	0	39,880	0	151,085	163,041	(672,562)	0	143,064	(989,838)	11,252,332	30,857,717	614,528
2039	87	83	(2,051,966)	1,184,936	0	40,680	0	151,085	168,069	(705,899)	0	135,725	(1,034,833)	10,628,964	32,709,180	637,311
2040	88	84	(2,134,045)	1,256,033	0	41,490	0	151,085	173,023	(740,387)	0	127,548	(1,081,576)	9,936,061	34,671,731	660,616
2041	89	85	(2,219,407)	1,331,394	0	42,320	0	151,085	176,352	(777,431)	0	118,475	(1,130,998)	9,168,398	36,752,035	684,773
2042	90	86	(2,308,183)	1,411,278	0	42,320	0	151,085	181,022	(777,431)	0	108,450	(1,181,453)	8,322,200	38,957,157	709,813
												Discounted at Rate of Inflation:	$3,690,988	56,320,250	$140,821

255

Estate Tax Calculation

John and Terry Sample

	Present Plan		Present Plan with Credit Shelter Trust	
Year of Death - 2003	John	Terry	John	Terry
Gross Estate	$13,403,303	$0	$13,403,303	$0
Inheritance From Spouse	---	13,135,237	---	12,135,237
Funeral and Admin. Expenses (2%)	(268,066)	(262,705)	(268,066)	(242,705)
Adjusted Gross Estate	13,135,237	12,872,533	13,135,237	11,892,533
Charitable Deduction	0	0	0	0
Marital Deduction	(13,135,237)	0	(12,135,237)	0
Taxable Estate	0	12,872,533	1,000,000	11,892,533
Post-1976 Taxable Gifts	0	0	0	0
Federal Estate	0	12,872,533	1,000,000	11,892,533
Federal Tax Per Schedule	0	(6,108,341)	(345,800)	(5,628,141)
After 1976 Gift Taxes	0	0	0	0
Unified Credit	0	345,800	345,800	345,800
Federal Tax + Max Credit	0	(5,762,541)	0	(5,282,341)
State Death Taxes--Max Credit	0	768,003	0	689,603
Total Federal Death Taxes	0	(4,994,538)	0	(4,592,738)
State Death Taxes Per Schedule	0	(768,003)	0	(689,603)
Net Income Tax on IRD	0	(203,356)	0	(203,356)
Total Death Taxes	0	(5,965,897)	0	(5,485,697)
Family Share	0	6,906,636	1,000,000	6,406,836
Family Share - Both Spouses	---	6,906,636	---	7,406,836
Irrevocable Insurance Trust	---	0	---	0
Total Family Share		**$6,906,636**		**$7,406,836**

General Plan Assumptions

John and Terry Sample

General:

	Ordinary (w/MC)	Ordinary	Capital Gain
Federal Marginal Tax Rate (Post-2010)	39.60%	39.60%	20.00%
New Jersey State Marginal Tax Rate	6.37%	6.37%	6.37%
Combined Income Tax Rate	44.90%	43.45%	25.10%
Inflation	4.0%		
Estimated Growth Rate on ABC stock	6.0%		
Estimated Portfolio Turnover Rate	20.0%		

Investment Conservative Return Assumptions:

	Equities	Taxable Bonds
Appreciation Factor	5.50%	0.00%
Income Factor	1.50%	4.00%
	7.00%	4.00%

Portfolio Asset Allocation :

	Equities	Fixed Income	Total	After-Tax
Asset Allocation	70.00%	30.00%	100.00%	
Appreciation	5.50%	0.00%	3.85%	3.66%
Income	1.50%	4.00%	2.25%	1.27%
Total Return	4.90%	1.20%	6.10%	4.93%

Qualified Plans :

	Equities	Fixed Income	Total
Asset Allocation	50.00%	50.00%	100.00%
Appreciation	5.50%	0.00%	2.75%
Income	1.50%	4.00%	2.75%
Total Return	3.50%	2.00%	5.50%

Please note: This analysis reflects the changes to marginal Federal income tax rates mandated by the Economic Growth and Tax Relief Reconciliation Act of 2001.

Index

A

Adjusted gross income (AGI),
 116
Affluent Americans
 few attained wealth through
  inheritance, 4–5
 financial worries of, 12*t*
 jobs as source of wealth, 5, 6*t*
 more mainstream than one
  would expect, 3–4
 overview, 6*t*
 sacrifices by, 6–7
 survey of. *See* U.S. Trust Survey
  of Affluent Americans
Affluenza, 209
Age, financial planning and,
 10–11
AGI (adjusted gross income), 116
Allen, Fred, 139
Allen, Woody, 187
Alternative investment asset
 classes, 9
Alternative minimum tax
 (AMT), 25, 121–123

Annual renewable term
 insurance, 144
Annuitant, 174
Annuities, 148–149, 174
Asset classes
 alternative, 9
 correlations between, 58*t*
 leadership of, 59*t*
 10-year forecasted risks and
  returns, 61*t*
Assets, safety of, 40–41
Automobile insurance, 154

B

Back-end fund, 90
Banks as financial advisors,
 226–227
Bernstein, Peter, 9
Bierce, Ambrose, 139
Blue chip stocks, 82
Boesky, Ivan, 244
Bonds
 coupon, 86

Bonds *(continued)*
  credit risk, 84, 86
  interest rate risk, 84
  market risk, 86
  overview, 84
  role in a portfolio, 85*f*
  total return, 86
  types, 87–89
    corporate, 88
    mortgage-backed securities,
      87–88
    municipal, 88
    taxable, 88
    tax-exempt, 88
    treasuries, 87
    zero-coupon, 89
Brokerage firms, 224–225
Buffett, Warren, 54
Business owners, investments for
      advice, 94–95
  U.S. Trust Survey of Affluent
      Americans, 92–94
Buying on margin, 83

C

Cap (capitalization), 57
Capital gains, 116–121
  long-term *versus* short-term,
      117–118
  mutual funds, 118–121
Capone, Al, 111
Carnegie, Andrew, 187
Certified Financial Planner, 34
Certified life underwriter (CLU),
      144

Certified public accountants
      (CPAs), 109
Charitable giving, 123–126
  charitable gift annuity,
      134–135
  charitable lead trust, 125, 203*t*,
      206
  charitable remainder trust
      (CRT), 124–125,
      134–135, 186, 203*t*, 206
  charitable remainder unitrust
      (CRUT), 101–102
  donor-advised funds, 125,
      135
  foundations. *See* Foundations
      and philanthropy
  tax planning, 123–126
Charitable lead trust, 125, 203*t*,
      206
Charitable remainder trust
      (CRT), 124–125,
      134–135, 186, 203*t*, 206
Charitable remainder unitrust
      (CRUT), 101–102
Children's trust, 203*t*
Churchill, Winston, 217
Cisco, 73
Closed-end fund, 90
CLU (certified life underwriter),
      144
College, saving for, 9–10
Concentrated stock positions
  diversifying
    charitable remainder unitrust
      (CRUT), 101–102
    outright sale, 97

sale of covered call options,
97–98
tax-efficient diversification
through indexing and loss
harvesting, 101
varying forward contract,
99–100
zero-premium equity collars,
98–99
overview, 95–97
Convertible term insurance, 145
Corporate bonds, 88
Cost of living, increases in, 15*t*
CPAs (certified public
accountants), 109
CRT (charitable remainder
trust), 124–125, 134–135,
186, 203*t*, 206
Crummey trusts, 147
CRUT (charitable remainder
unitrust), 101–102
Custody accounts, 38–41

D

Defensive stocks, 83
Deferred annuity, 149
Defined-benefit plans, 173,
183–184
Defined-contribution plans, 183
Depository Trust Company, 40
Directors insurance, 157
Disability insurance, 149–150
Dividends, 81
Doctors, retirement planning,
167

Donor-advised fund, 125–126,
135
Durable power of attorney, 199

E

Eat-well portfolio, 242
Economics and Portfolio Strategy, 9
Economy, history of, 13–17,
14*t*–15*t*, 17*f*
Efficient frontier of portfolio
investing, 57
Efficient portfolios, 57
Eifuku Master Fund, 92
Equities, 81
blue chip stocks, 82
buying on margin, 83
defensive stocks, 83
dividends, 81
growth companies, 82, 82*f*
large-capitalization stocks,
81–82
preferred stock, 83
price/earnings (P/E) ratio, 81
range of returns for different
holding periods
(1933–2001), 64*f*
real estate investment trusts
(REITs), 83–84
return, 81
selling short, 83
small-capitalization stocks,
81–82
stock options, 126–127
incentive stock options
(ISOs), 127

Equities *(continued)*
    nonqualified stock options
      (NQSOs), 126–127
    tax planning, 126–127
  stock splits, 81
  superior performance of, 77*f*
  value companies, 82, 82*f*
Estate planning, 28, 232
  children
    money and, 210–216
    overview, 208–209
    U.S. Trust Survey of Affluent
      Americans, 209–210
  executor, choosing, 195–196
  importance of, 190–195
  options
    charitable lead trust, 206
    charitable remainder trust
      (CRT), 206
    estate tax credit, 202–203
    generation-skipping transfer
      tax, 206–207
    grantor retained annuity
      trust (GRAT), 204
    keeping up to date, 207–208
    life insurance trust, 204, 205*t*
    marital deduction and QTIP
      trust, 203–204
    overview, 202
    personal residence trust, 204,
      206
    tuition and medical
      exclusion, 204
    valuation discounts, 206
  overview, 187
  power of attorney, 199–201
  scenarios, 189–190
  tax laws and, 201–202
  trusts, 197–199, 203*t*
  U.S. Trust Survey of Affluent
    Americans, 188–189
Estate tax, 104
  life insurance trust and, 148
Executor, choosing, 195–196

F

Family limited partnership
  (FLP), 206
Fannie Mae (Federal National
  Mortgage Association),
  87
Federal Reserve, 40
Financial advisor, choosing
  coordinating planning
    estate planning, 232
    financial planning,
      231–232
    income tax planning, 233
    insurance planning,
      233–234
    private banking, 234
    retirement planning,
      232–233
  overview, 217–218
  prerequisites, 219–224
  selecting and working with
    fees, 228–230
    monitoring investment
      management process,
      230–231
    overview, 227–228

types of financial advisors
  banks and trust companies,
    226–227
  brokerage firms, 224–225
  registered investment
    advisors, 225–226
  U.S. Trust Survey of Affluent
    Americans, 234–238
  gender-related trends,
    236–238
Financial planning, 231–232
  custody accounts, 38–41
  data
    analyzing, 31
    gathering, 29–30
  description of, 24–26
  goals and objectives, 30–31
  implementing, 32
  importance of, 7–13
  private banking, 35–38
  questions to ask a potential
    financial planner, 34
  record keeping, 40–41
  scenarios, 19–22
  setting up financial plan
    estate planning, 28
    insurance planning, 27
    investment planing, 26
    retirement planning, 27
    tax planning, 26–27
  steps after plan is in place, 33,
    35
  strategies, potential, 31–32
  team, creating, 28–29
  trading, 39–40
  why people don't plan, 22–24

FLP (family limited partnership),
  206
Forbes 400, changes in net worth
  (1982–2000), 17f
Foundations and philanthropy
  foundations
    setting up, 130–134
  giving, 134–136
  taxes and, 125–126
  U.S. Trust Survey of Affluent
    Americans, 128–130
401(k) plan, 25, 29, 166, 173
  solo plan for small business
    owners, 181
Freddie Mac (Federal Home
  Loan Mortgage
  Corporation), 87
Front-end load fund, 90
Fund of funds, 91, 229

G

Galbraith, John Kenneth, 43,
  161
General Electric, 57
Generation-skipping transfer tax,
  206–207
Generation-skipping trust, 203t
Gift tax, life insurance trust and,
  148
Ginnie Mae (Government
  National Mortgage
  Association), 87
Giving. See Charitable giving;
  Foundations and
  philanthropy

Grantor retained annuity trust
  (GRAT), 203*t*, 204
"Great compression" of wages and
  incomes, 13
Great Depression, 13
Growth companies, 82, 82*f*

H

Health care proxy, 200
Health insurance, 150–152
Hedge funds
  insurance as "wrapper," 185
  management, 9
Helmsley, Leona, 103
Henry, Patrick, 103
Holmes, Oliver Wendell, 217
Hurdle rate, 228

I

Immediate annuity, 148–149
Incentive stock options (ISOs),
  127
Income tax. *See* Tax, income
Individual Retirement Accounts
  (IRAs)
  beneficiary designations,
    178–180
  description, 168–169
  nondeductible Roth IRAs,
    169–172
  nondeductible traditional
    IRAs, 169
  nonemployed spousal IRAs,
    169

  rollover to a Roth IRA, 172
  traditional *versus* Roth IRAs,
    171
Insurance
  annuities, 148–149
  automobile, 154
  broker, finding, 158–160
  directors insurance, 157
  disability, 149–150
  health, 150–152
  kidnap insurance, 156–157
  liability, 154–156
  life insurance, 142–148
  long-term care, 151–152
  overview, 139–142
  planning, 27, 233–234
  property and casualty,
    152–154
  rules, 157–158
Inter vivos trust, 197
Investments
  advisors
    active *versus* passive
      managers, 79–80
    balance, 78–79
    number needed, 77–78
  for business owners
    advice for, 94–95
    U.S. Trust Survey of
      Affluent Americans,
      92–94
  concentrated stock positions.
    See Concentrated stock
    positions
  creating and preserving wealth,
    50–53

diversification, 56–57, 62
  risk, 53–54, 56
  time, 62–65
planning, 26, 54, 56*f,* 240–246
scenario, 47–49
taxes and, 76–77, 77*f*
truisms about, 65–76
  be patient, 74–76
  be willing to let go, 69–71
  know yourself, 66–69
  think contrarian, 71–74
types and terminology
  bonds, 84–89
  equities, 81–84
  mutual funds, 89–90
  nontraditional asset classes,
    90–91
U.S. Trust Survey of Affluent
  Americans, 43–47
IRAs. *See* Individual Retirement
  Accounts
Irrevocable trusts, 177
ISOs (incentive stock options),
  127

K
Keoghs, 182
Kidnap insurance, 156–157

L
Large-capitalization stocks,
  81–82
Level load, 90
Level term insurance, 144–145

Liability insurance. *See* Personal
  liability insurance
Life insurance
  overview, 142
  planning, 142–144
  policy, 147–148
  trust, 148, 203*t,* 204, 205*t*
  types of
    permanent, cash-value,
      145–147
    term insurance, 144–145
Life-only annuity, 149
Limited liability company (LLC),
  206
Living will, 200
Load funds, 90
Long-only managers, 91
Long Term Capital
  Management, 92
Long-term care insurance,
  151–152

M
Margin, buying on, 83
Market timing, 63
  hazards of, 75*f*
Maugham, W. Somerset, 19
Microsoft, 57, 74
Milken, Michael, 244
Money purchase pension plan
  (MPPP), 183
Mortgage-backed securities, 87–88
Municipal bonds, 25, 88
Mutual funds
  load, 90

Mutual funds *(continued)*
   open-end, 90
   overview, 89
   taxation, 118–121
      average cost method, 121
      first in, first out (FIFO)
         method, 119
      specific identification of
         shares, 119

N

Needs analysis, 142
Net worth
   Forbes 400, 17*f*
   U.S. households, 16*t*, 17*f*
New York City tax, 10, 105
New York State tax, 10
Nifty 50, 50, 51*t*–52*t*
No-load fund, 90
Nondeductible Roth IRAs,
   169–172
Nondeductible traditional IRAs,
   169
Nonemployed spousal IRAs,
   169
Nonqualified plans, 176–177
Nonqualified stock options
   (NQSOs), 126–127

O

1-and-20, 228
Open architecture, 77–78
Open-end fund, 90
Optimization, 58

P

P/E (price/earnings) ratio,
   81
Personal liability insurance,
   154–156
   excess personal liability
      insurance, 156
   professional liability insurance,
      156
   worker's compensation,
      156
Personal residence trust, 203*t*,
   204, 206
Philanthropy. *See* Foundations
   and philanthropy
Planned gift, 134
Pooled income fund, 134
Portfolio. *See also* Investments
   apportioning assets in
      survey results, 45, 46*f*, 47*t*
   management, 9
Power of attorney, 199–201
Preferred stock, 83
Price/earnings (P/E) ratio,
   81
Private banking, 35–38, 234
Private placement variable
   universal life, 146–147
Professional liability insurance,
   156
Profit-sharing plan (PSP), 175,
   183
Property and casualty insurance,
   152–154
   replacement-cost insurance,
      153

Q

Qualified personal residence trust
(QPRT), 203*t*
Qualified retirement plans
annuities, 174
beneficiary designations,
178–180
defined benefit plans, 173
lump-sum distributions from,
178
profit-sharing plans, 175
401(k)s, 173
savings incentive match plan for
employees (SIMPLE),
175
Qualified terminable interest
property (QTIP) trust,
203, 203*t*, 204

R

Rabbi trusts, 177
Radcliffe, Daniel, 170
Range of returns for different
holding periods
(1933–2001), 64*f*
Real estate investment trusts
(REITs), 83–84
Real estate taxes, 25
Registered investment advisors
(RIAs), 225–226
Required minimum distributions
(RMDs), 179
Retirement
charitable remainder trusts
(CRTs), 186

Individual Retirement
Accounts (IRAs). *See*
Individual Retirement
Accounts (IRAs)
insurance, 185
nonqualified plans, 176–177
overview, 161–162
planning, 27, 165–168,
232–233
qualified plans
annuities, 174
beneficiary designations,
178–180
defined benefit plans, 173
lump-sum distributions
from, 178
profit-sharing plans, 175
401(k)s, 173
savings incentive match plan
for employees (SIMPLE),
175
scenarios, 164–165
self-employed people
defined-benefit plans,
183–184
defined-contribution plans,
183
overview, 181–183
savings incentive match plan
for employees (SIMPLE),
184–185
simplified employee pension
(SEP), 184
small business owners, 181
tax law, new, 175
tax savings, 167

Retirement *(continued)*
U.S. Trust Survey of Affluent
Americans, 162–164
Return, 81
Revocable trust, 203*t*
RIAs (registered investment
advisors), 225–226
RMDs (required minimum
distributions), 179
Roth IRAs, 169–172

S

Savings incentive match plan for
employees (SIMPLE),
175, 184–185
Self-employed people
defined-benefit plans, 183–184
defined-contribution plans, 183
overview, 181–183
savings incentive match plan
for employees (SIMPLE),
184–185
simplified employee pension
(SEP), 184
Selling short, 83
Seth Sprague Educational and
Charitable Foundation,
133
Shaw, George Bernard, 19
Shorting the stock, 91
Simplified employee pension
(SEP), 184
Sleep-well portfolio, 242
Small business owners, retirement
planning for, 181

Small-capitalization stocks,
81–82
Split gift, 134
Springing power of attorney, 199
Stocks. *See* Equities
Survey of affluent Americans. *See*
U.S. Trust Survey of
Affluent Americans

T

Taxable bonds, 88
Tax-exempt bonds, 88
Tax, income
adjustments, 113
checklist, 114
alternative minimum tax
(AMT), 25, 121–123
avoiding mistakes, 136–137
capital gains, 116–121
long-term *versus* short-term,
118
mutual funds, 118–121
deductions, 113–116
charitable giving, 123–126
checklist, 115
deferrals, 113
estimated tax payments, 127–128
foundations
setting up, 130–134
U.S. Trust Survey of
Affluent Americans,
128–130
giving, 134–136
gross income, 111–113
checklist, 112

life insurance trust and, 148
overview, 103–104
planning, 26–27, 233
stock options, 126–127
tax planning, 105–109
tax preparation, 109–110
U.S. Trust Survey of Affluent
    Americans, 104–105
Taylor, Fred, 52
Term certain option, 174
Term insurance, 144–145
Testamentary trust, 197
TMT group (technology, media,
    telecommunications), 52,
    72–73, 80
Trading, 39–40
Traiman, Susan, 43
Treasuries, 87–89
Trust companies as financial
    advisors, 226–227
Trusts
    benefits of, 203*t*
    estate planning, 197–199
    inter vivos trust, 197
    testamentary trust, 197

U

Unified credit trust, 203*t*
Universal life insurance, 145–146
U.S. Trust Survey of Affluent
    Americans, 2–7, 12*t*,
    239–240

business owners, 92–94
children, 209–210
estate planning, 188–189
financial advisors,
    234–238
foundations and philanthropy,
    128–130
income tax, 104–105
investments, 43–47
retirement, 162–164

V

Valuation discounts, 206
Value companies, 82, 82*f*
Variable life insurance, 185
    variable universal life (VUL),
    146

W

Wealth-transfer objectives,
    179
Wealthy Americans. *See* Affluent
    Americans
Whole life insurance, 145
Williams, Tennessee, 161
Worker's compensation, 156

Z

Zero-cost collar, 98
Zero-coupon bonds, 89